# India's Second Liberation

PRAN CHOPRA

# India's Second Liberation

THE MIT PRESS
Cambridge, Massachusetts

Copyright © Pran Chopra, 1974
Published by Vikas Publishing House Pvt Ltd, 1974
First MIT Press edition, 1974

ISBN: 0-262-03048-9
Library of Congress catalog card number: 73-10928

PRINTED IN INDIA

# Preface

In the writing of this book I have benefited greatly from sitting with the men and women who planned and carried out India's political, diplomatic and military strategy for the war which liberated Bangladesh.

However, for the time being they must remain anonymous: some because they gave me their confidence on this condition; others because to name only some would distort the picture. The only exceptions to this constraint are named in the text.

I am aware of what the book loses by my not naming my sources. But loss is qualified by two compensations: first, much of the information contained in these pages would not have been available on any other basis. Second, this is not intended to be a book of disclosures but of such analysis and appraisal as the passage of time has made possible for me. Whatever the romance, named or unnamed, and however lofty by designation, has been accepted as fact unless corroborated by the contemporary context or subsequent events or by thorough cross-checking with other available sources. What was important for me, and I hope will be for the reader, was not who said to me what but how credible the information was.

There is another limitation. The book is only concerned with the consequences of Bangladesh, the politics and diplomacy, the strategic causes and consequences of this event, its importance for India and South Asia and beyond for the global forces. I have not discussed other relevant factors, such as India's remaining economic and rapidly growing administrative weakness. These may decide between them whether India's second liberation will be incomplete as the first, attained 25 years ago, would be have been without the second.

Thanks are due, and are gratefully rendered, to all those, named and unnamed, who generously spared their valuable time to share their information and thoughts with me; to the Indian Council of Social Science Research, New Delhi, for a financial grant which gave me the leisure to write this book; to the Institute of Defence Studies and Analyses, New Delhi, which allowed me affiliation for this period and in many other ways gave assistance and guidance; to my wife and many others who helped me in writing the book and preparing it for the press.

PRAN CHOPRA

# I The Argument

In a very real sense, the liberation of Bangladesh has been a second liberation for India. It carries a stage further the independence she won 25 years ago.

During this quarter century India's independence was never less real than when she herself and others believed her to be weak, a plaything of circumstances controlled by others, harassed by smaller countries and dominated by the big. Imagined weaknesses multiplied the real and made her feel more insecure and helpless than was warranted by her objective condition.

But, as the next 25 years of her freedom begin, India stands higher in her own eyes and the eyes of other countries than she has ever done; self-confidence now enlarges her objective capability to look after her security.

The emergence of Bangladesh as an independent nation, even if brought about by the willing consent of West Pakistan, would have made a difference for the better in the objective universe of Indian security. But its emergence in a war of liberation, and the quality even more than the quantity of India's contribution towards it—that is, not only the winning of the war but the way it was won—has made a difference for the better in the subjective universe as well. Perhaps this difference will prove more important in the long run.

One of India's greatest security assets has been the strategic significance of her enormous size and geographic location. But it has been of value to her only in the measure that it has been perceived to be of value by her and others. In phases of low perception her friends and enemies and she herself have regarded her size only as a flabby and unmanageable cumbersomeness, tempting enemies to nibble away at her bulk, discouraging friends from investing in her security.

But high perception has also been dangerous for her when unaccompanied by matching capability. In such phases her importance has aroused envy and her weakness made the envious bold. India discovered this to her very great cost in 1962. Whenever she has lacked the confidence to use its importance herself, her strategic significance has always whetted the appetite of other countries to use it for their own ends.

Now at last perception and capability are rising together. The liberation of Bangladesh, the result of three wars, not one, is making this valuable contribution to the liberation of India.

But the new universe of Indian security will be more full of hazards, at least for some time, than the old one was. In entering it, India enters the zone of maximum danger. Many countries have praised her for the capability which she has demonstrated. But in others the desire to forestall her emergence into a status corresponding to her size and significance has become sharper still. They will test her forbearance and capabilities yet.

By winning the war in the way she did, India has made herself more secure than she ever was in any single and non-nuclear combat, banishing the fears she inherited from the 1962 debacle. But she has yet to ensure that by her own unaided capability, or a combination of capabilities which are more favourable to her than those against, she is secure in a combat which may not remain either single or non-nuclear.

The trials through which Bangladesh emerged were a serious enough challenge for India as well; what follows will put a further strain upon her. It will call for the maximum use of her highest resources in defence, diplomacy, and political resolution. India's own security and the power balance in Asia will be shaped by the measure in which these resources are—and are seen to be—mustered by her.

# II  The Background

# Balance Gained and Lost

Geography has conferred upon India one of the main determinants of her foreign and defence policies, shaping her attitude towards other countries and her own towards them. Jawaharlal Nehru had a keen appreciation of this, and he made India's weight, size, and geographic location the main resource of his policies. He used them to meet the core requirement that while India developed her defence capability she should prevent by political means the building up of any combination against her which would be stronger than the best available combination in favour.

Nehru calculated, and rightly, that attack could come only from Pakistan to begin with, and against Pakistan, unless it was aided by another power, India would be able to defend herself unaided. This was proved at the very dawn of India's independence. When Pakistan attacked Kashmir in the autumn of 1947 with a very large para military force, India met the challenge unaided. Indian leadership showed tremendous forbearance by confining its retaliation against Pakistan to Kashmir despite India's very great logistical disadvantages there. Instead of retaliating on grounds of her own choosing, for example, opposite Lahore, where Pakistan was known to have withdrawn its defensive screen in order to reinforce the expected assault on Srinagar by its irregulars, India put together an amazing air supply link with Srinagar which surprised Mountbatten by its swiftness and efficiency, as Allan Campbell-Johnson records in his *Mission with Mountbatten*. With this air-bridging effort India began a counter-attack which stopped only where the cease-fire line later came to be, and even there stopped only because Nehru insisted, probably on Mountbatten's advice, that if Indian forces went further afield a bigger war with Pakistan would become unavoidable. The story has been extremely well told by Lieutenant-General L. P. Sen in *Slender was the Thread* and need not be repeated. The point here is only that unaided Pakistan's measure was satisfactorily taken by India, unaided.

But this only activated a chain of events which threatened to bring together a stronger combination against India. Nehru had to prevent or counter-balance the combination. This gave him the chance to use India's mass and location as a bargaining advantage, and the immediate result was that a security component was added to what soon became famous as Nehru's nonalignment.

At the outset of the first Kashmir war between them, India and Pakistan were unassociated with either of the two main protagonists in the developing cold war—the Soviet Union and the USA. But they could not remain so for long. An area of such importance as the subcontinental land mass of India and Pakistan could not have indefinitely stayed unaffected by such a global phenomenon as the Super Power cold war. But Pakistan made a wide opening for the strong winds of this war by its eager alliance with the USA. Pakistan made the alliance to acquire a military edge over India; the USA used it for bigger purposes. Superficially, it was open to India to forestall the event. She could have outbid Pakistan in seeking American support. Alternatively she could have obtained an opposite and proportionate alliance with the Soviet Union. Russian mistrust of India, though very unpleasant while it lasted, did not last very long, and from fairly early on in the 1950s the question was not how close the Soviet Union would allow India to be to it but how close India would allow herself to be to Russia. But neither an alliance with the USA nor with the Soviet Union would have served Indian interests better than nonalignment could, and nonalignment could do it only because of India's geo-strategic significance.

An Indian alliance with the USA would have ended Pakistan's, but Pakistan would have sought—and obtained—the support of the communist land mass against India. This would have been a bad bargain for India. Whatever the lead of American power over communist power in global terms those days, its lead in Asian terms was very small even then, particularly in relation to India. Physical proximity and political receptivity would have made India vulnerable to communist power; her strategic attractiveness would have made the effort to subjugate her worth making. Not only India's external security would have been impaired; the peaceful evolution of her domestic polity would have been endangered. On the other hand, an outright alliance with the Soviet Union would have severely reduced India's economic options. Without a compensating increase in Soviet aid, at that time very low to all non-communist countries, American assistance would have disappeared once India put herself beyond the reach of America's competitive counter-bidding. India therefore chose the strategy of a graduated instead of an outright diplomatic response to the menacing overtones of the US-Pakistani military alliance. She shifted her position on the Washington-Moscow scale of antagonism in just such measure as was needed to counter-balance the overt threat of the opposing combination and she was able to shift it because she was not tied down to one end of the scale or the other.

This gave the security rationale to nonalignment, which was in no way less important than its moral value aspect. By dint of his own very convinced advocacy of the importance of India, Nehru assisted both sides in the cold war to appreciate that India was too important a country to be driven by either side into the arms of the other. Placed in alliance with the USA, she would expose the belly of the communist power to constant trouble, much more than allied Pakistan could. Placed in alliance with the communist block, she would give its reach an enormous extension into southern Asia, much more than any ally of communism in South-East or West Asia could. At the same time by his non-alignment Nehru held India up as something which, desired by both sides, had been lost by neither to the other. Both the Super Powers therefore found India's nonalignment worth paying for, and the worth went up as nonalignment won an increasing number of adherents in the newly free Asian and African countries.

Being engaged in a cold war, the two sides were competing as much for political as for military ascendency, and in this the attitude of the nonaligned countries was more important for them than the military contribution to their prowess which most of their outright allies could make. As the first preacher of the gospel, India received her share of attention from both the power blocs; but her greater achievement was that, with prestige added to size as a security resource, India, for 15 years of upheaval in the Asian land mass, forestalled the emergence of any direct threat to her security which would exceed her own ability to meet it. Pakistan alone she could meet unaided; Pakistan's ally she sought to deter by the risk of provoking an Indo-Soviet alliance or a Soviet retaliation with or without such an alliance.

By and large she succeeded in maintaining these opposites in balance.

But success imposed its own penalties. Among all countries belonging to or interested in southern Asia the thought was activated that the emergence of a new power of the size of India, as a strong and independent centre of authority, would change the established system of power in this region. Such changes are usually resisted by all established powers, as Russia, Germany, Japan and China discovered successively during different phases of the twentieth century and many others earlier. It would have been too much to hope that India would escape this law of resistance. From the early 1950s onwards, India encountered resistance successively from the USA, China and the Soviet Union, each using the instrument most readily available, Pakistan, and to some extent Nepal and Ceylon, both being willing to help when they felt free to do so—that is, when they saw India as a stricken giant.

The cold war added a more immediate penalty. While it enhanced the importance of India in the eyes of both the Super Powers, it also enhanced the value of Pakistan to the USA as a committed ally and a link in the American chain for the containment of Russia. This multiplied India's difficulties with the USA and added to the relentlessness with which the USA used its position in the UN against India on Kashmir. US policies towards the subcontinent gave practical shape to what was implied in the writings of Sir Olaf Caroe, one of the founders of the policy which later developed into the Baghdad Pact. In 1949 he wrote in the *Round Table* that if India wished to be included as a factor of defence in an area (West Asia) "where Pakistan stands in the first line, it will be for India to adjust her differences with the sister state in such a way as to strengthen and not weaken their mutual defences. Failing a new approach in this matter the pattern will assume a different shape and the Indo-Pakistan frontier will become a permanent limit between the two systems." The difference began to take shape as the USA, prompted by concern over possible Russian pressure against West Asia, adopted Pakistan as an ally that would be the eastern anchor of the so-called "northern tier" against this pressure. Once the shape hardened into the Baghdad Pact it became virtually indestructible; certainly it was proof against the ample

*The Background*                                    11

evidence which Pakistan gave that it was more interested in
using American aid against India than against any communist
power.

Long after Pakistan put it beyond doubt that its apparent opposition to the communist power bloc was only a pretext for acquiring teeth against India, and long after satellite technology proved
that the spy base Pakistan had allowed the Americans to build
at Peshawar in return for aid was quite dispensable, American
military aid to Pakistan continued. Gratitude to an ally who
was useful once might have been one reason for it. But in the
second half of the 1950s the developing Indian position in international affairs became the more important reason; in the closing
years of the decade it became the greatest single reason. As India
saw it, her position was only a graduated response to the growing
alliance between the USA and Pakistan. But in American eyes
it was a much bigger move and, being regarded as part of the
Soviet-American equation, called for accelerated counter-
measures. Any shift India made on the Washington-Moscow
scale was therefore treated as important enough to call for a
counter-balancing shift against her by using Pakistan, and using
it for American reasons.

During the height of the cold war a broad affinity developed
between Indian and Soviet foreign policies, and not only on
issues of specific Indian interest such as Kashmir and Goa but
also wider world issues. As the architect of nonalignment India
opposed the network of alliances in which the United States saw
its security and Russia a menace; as a strident opponent of coloni-
alism India opposed countries which the Soviet Union considered
to be its enemies and the USA its allies; as a newly emerging
nation India wanted a shake up in the world's pattern of power
in which the western world had a higher stake than the communist
bloc. This indicated a parallelism between the growth of
Indian influence in southern Asia and of Russian in the world,
and American antagonism towards Russia began to envelop
India as well, using Pakistan as the instrument of its policies in
the subcontinent.

Increasingly, the USA now began to suspect that Indian influence in southern Asia would only be Russian influence by proxy.
This marks the beginnings of American thinking that India is a
proxy power of Russia, a thought which was to play havoc with

Indo-US relations in 1971.  In the later 1950s it justified the use of Pakistan as a counter-weight against India, or at least justified it in American eyes.  It also justified in American eyes US reluctance to do anything which Pakistan saw as a serious addition to Indian capabilities.  This is not contradicted either by the assurance Eisenhower gave Nehru, that the United States would not allow the use of American arms against India, or by the supply of American arms to India following the Chinese attack in 1962.  The United States did not implement Eisenhower's assurance in any of the numerous clashes between India and Pakistan.  The supply of American arms to India against China was very small in quantity, was confined only to such items as could be defensively used in mountain warfare against China, and was soon cut off.  And while it lasted it was far more strictly monitored to ensure that it was used against China only than the arms supplied to Pakistan ever were.

A specific instance of this general approach was the US refusal to give India the assistance she wanted for improving her air capability against China.  A former Chief of the Indian Air Force, Air Marshal Arjun Singh, confirmed in 1969 that when the Chinese attacked "we in the air force were not aware of the complications of operating at high altitudes, and I think that was a big drawback," which he attributed to difficulties "in operating at those altitudes."  To remove these, India sought American supersonic aircraft which were superior to anything the Chinese had.  The United States refused.  Later, when India acquired equivalent aircraft from the Soviet Union, the United States intervened with its theory of counter-balancing India and replaced Pakistan's subsonic aircraft with an unspecified number of supersonics, a decision which in any strategic calculation could only be related to India's strength, not China's or Russia's, because China had already begun to woo Pakistan instead of threatening it, and a few squadrons of supersonics in the hands of Pakistan were no answer to a threat from the Soviet Union.

Fred Greene later wrote in *US Policy and the Security of Asia* (Council of Foreign Relations, New York):  "Even when we did give military help to India, Pakistan's opposition played a crucial role in our refusal to offer modern fighter aircraft that India sought in order to overcome the danger of Chinese air power."  Chester Bowles confirmed more specifically in

*Foreign Affairs* of July 1971, that when, after the Chinese attack, India asked for military assistance of the value of $500 million over five years "the old Dullesian argument began to be raised" that this would "upset our loyal ally, Pakistan," and the aid programme petered out. Nixon helped in this at a critical time. As US Vice-President in the middle 1950s, he was an ardent advocate of the policy of building up Pakistan against India. According to his biographer, Ralph Toledano, Nixon urged the 1954 US security pact with Pakistan "not for the purported defence value against Soviet aggression but for the very reason Pakistan had sought the aid, as a counterforce to the confirmed neutralism of Jawaharlal Nehru's India." Nixon himself is not on record as saying as much in so many words. But he implicates himself by his own formulation. In a remark, probably about Russian aid to North Viet Nam, he said on 6 May 1972: "Those who give arms are responsible for their uses." When he was Vice-President or President, Nixon never had any reason to doubt to what uses Pakistan was putting American military aid. His advocacy of the aid as Vice-President and his own decision to extend it when he became the President attract responsibility for the use of American weapons by Pakistan against India.

Other observers and practitioners of American policy have been more explicit on this subject. In July 1959, the Foreign Affairs Committee of the US House of Representatives warned the Administration: "Our military assistance has in many places disrupted delicate regional balances of power between the recipient nation and its non-communist neighbours." Lyndon B. Johnson, as Vice-President, recommended in 1961 in a personal memorandum to the President, according to his biographer William S. White, that while improving relations with India the USA should continue to back up Pakistan. When he became the President his views on aid to India continued to be influenced by this attitude. More recently, Fred Greene wrote that the whole US policy in the subcontinent continued to be "the balance of power doctrine against a state that means no harm to us, merely to maintain a balance abroad." More explicitly Galbraith, US Ambassador in India, both during the presidency of Kennedy and for a time Johnson's, explained in an interview on National Education Television on 8 December 1972, that something like the "North American formula"—where there is one big power, the United States, and a number of smaller ones are arranged around it—"can maintain an equilibrium on the Indian subcontinent." He added: "If you think of this in terms of the subcontinent, you have India, and the most mischievous thing that was ever done and the most mischievous action in the history of American foreign policy was that we kept this equilibrium from developing. We provided the arms under Dulles, we provided the arms for building Pakistan up as a competitor. It was a poor competitor of India. But it was just enough of a competitor so that it encouraged all the wrong attitudes in India."

India could not see the justification, then or later, of trying to equate Pakistan with her. Those who separated from India in 1947 to form Pakistan voluntarily opted for what was bound to be a smaller entity by far. Therefore, it did not make sense to India that an attempt should be made to inject an artificial parity from outside into a situation of natural disparity. India protested against this and has continued to do so ever since. At the very dawn of this policy, when the United States signed a mutual security pact with Pakistan in 1954, Nehru said that it tended to "encircle us in two or three directions." Mrs Gandhi, far more explicitly and sharply, said at a press conference in London on 1 November 1971, when this policy was about to fall apart: "Nothing will work if people continue to equate India and Pakistan. We are tired of this equation which the western world is always making . . . . We are *not* equal and we are not going to stand for this kind of treatment."

On the other hand, throughout this period Pakistan made it clear by the implications of its actions and more explicitly through policy statements that it saw American military aid only as a weapon for use against India and that it expected Washington to go along with it. About the time that the pro-Pakistan lobby was busy in Washington hastening the security pact, the *New York Times* reported from Karachi that hopes were being expressed there that "strong voices in Washington will favour a firmer course with India's Prime Minister, Mr Nehru." As India's relations with the United States improved a little in the second half of the 1950s, partly on account of the warmth of Nehru's meeting with Eisenhower and partly on account of growing Indian apprehensions about China, Pakistan's relations with the United States grew cooler. To underscore the implication, the Prime Minister of Pakistan, Feroze Khan Noon, said in Parliament in 1958: "I hear rumblings that from 1959 they [the Americans] probably want to stop our military aid. I am sure if they do that, it will be under pressure from India. I can tell the world that if our people find their freedom threatened by India they will break all pacts to save freedom and will shake hands with those whom we had made our enemies for the sake of others."

He need not have worried. In 1959 the USA signed a new agreement with Pakistan which gave Pakistan even greater satisfaction than the one before. After the agreement the Pakistan Foreign Secretary declared that now aid would be available against "any aggression," not only communist aggression as under the previous treaties, and "there was no reason to believe that the USA would put an interpretation other than Pakistan's upon the word aggression." This confidence, which was to have an interesting sequel in 1965, was shared at the highest level in Pakistan. In a BBC interview on 18 February 1972, Z. A. Bhutto referred to "a balance of power . . . not a genuine balance of power but nevertheless some kind of a balance of power" which Pakistan was able to maintain against India— thanks obviously to US arms aid policies though Bhutto did not specifically name them as the balancing mechanism—until it was destroyed in the late 1960s.

But to go back to the 1950s, Moscow and Peking saw the situation in the same light as Nehru, Noon and Nixon. Noting that the 1959 bilateral security agreement signed by the USA with Iran, Turkey and Pakistan omitted the specific limitation in the CENTO agreement that US aid could be invoked only in the event of aggression by a country "under the control of international communism," the Chinese Communist Party newspaper, *Jen Minh Ji Pao*, said: "The United States and its followers have also put forward a new idea, that resistance to any direct or indirect aggression includes non-communist aggression. This clearly shows that these new pacts are directed not only against the socialist countries but are, in the first place, also a threat to such nationally independent countries as India, Iraq and Afghanistan." The Soviet Union went further. Making the same allegation as the Chinese, only at greater length and more strongly, an official Soviet statement said: "The foreign press reports that the American-Indian and American-Pakistani agreements have secret supplements defining specific commitments by the parties and the methods of implementing the agreements in practise. These reports have virtually not been refuted....The deliberately indefinite character of some of the formulations in the agreements opens up broad possibilities for the United States ruling circles to interpret them as they please."

But in spite of the penalties exacted by the success with which Nehru used India's strategic significance as a security resource, deploying the interest taken in her position by one side as a deterrent against any hostile intention by the other side, the overall benefits of this success were, on balance, greater. Nehru balanced the competition for India between the rival power blocs against the reactions of envy or antagonism generated by the competition. By and large the problem was well managed and the requirements of security were satisfactorily met. India had sufficient unaided capacity to meet the only threat she faced in this period—from Pakistan—and by political means she ensured that she did not have to face a hostile combination which would be too strong for her. So long as US assistance to Pakistan was limited to free supply of military hardware, India was able to cope with it, unaided or with such aid as she could get. More than that she did not have to face because of the safeguard she built with her policy of nonalignment. What India could not physically or directly face she could balance off.

But in 1962 this balance was shattered when China, not the USA, exacted the heaviest price and inflicted the maximum penalty for India's success during the 1950s in becoming the most important country of the Indian Ocean region and potentially able to dominate it. Nehru's pronouncements and actions during the first half of the 1950s would have suggested that a Sino-Indian clash was impossible. India became not only the most ardent campaigner for the admission of China into the United Nations, next only to the Soviet Union, but for China's sake Nehru declined a veiled offer of a permanent seat for India in the Security Council. In reply to the offer, he wrote to the Indian representative at the UN: "We must stand by the People's Government of

China coming into the Security Council....India, because of many factors, is certainly entitled to a permanent seat. But we are not going in at the expense of China." In further correspondence with India's representative, he said : "I am sure that it is of great importance to Asia and to the world that India and China should be friendly. How far we shall succeed I cannot say [but] I have a strong feeling that the future of Asia is rather tied up with the relations between India and China."

However, there is deep irony in the contrast between what Nehru believed about China and what he had to face at the hands of China. He believed, and in the early 1950s wrote in so many words, that in the first place "it is a complete misunderstanding of the China situation to imagine that they function like a satellite state of Russia"; and, in the second place, "I see that both the USA and the UK on the one hand, and the USSR on the other, for entirely different reasons, are not anxious that India and China should be friendly towards each other. This itself is a significant fact which has to be borne in mind."

These views, however, are only the visible tip of Nehru's belief, which is not difficult to surmise from his actions though he did not voice it in public : that a strong and independent China, not only independent of the western powers but also, and perhaps more importantly for India, of the Soviet Union, would be a security asset for India.

It is true, as confirmed by B. R. Mullik, who was for many years Nehru's chief of intelligence, that Nehru's trust in China was far less unquestioning than is popularly imagined. In his book, *My Years With Nehru*, Mullik says that as far back as 1950, Nehru allowed him to spread his intelligence cover across the Sino-India frontier because Nehru accepted that India should keep a watch on China's intentions. But Nehru believed that so long as China was strong, India need not fear a threat of predominance by Russia, in whom Nehru had far less faith than in China. In other words, he thought of the simultaneous presence of Russian and Chinese power across India's frontiers a possibly useful factor for India's security, just as the simultaneous presence of communist and anti-communist power was on the larger stage. He proved right, but in converse. Russia became a support for India against the risk of a threat of Chinese predominance, and not the other way round, as Nehru had thought during his earlier years.

But beneath the surface of Sino-Indian relations and Nehru's convictions, as well as the cordiality of his views about China through the 1950s, four causes of the coming Sino-Indian war were steadily building up. Each was a compliment to the importance of India's size and location but their combined effect was to shake up India's own self-confidence severely and also the confidence of other countries in her.

The first was the development of India's role across the frontier with Nepal and Bhutan. A dispute with India over Tibet, when China first began to subjugate Tibet in 1951-52, had already made China sensitive to the possibility of such a role. In the midst of the dispute India concluded treaties with Nepal and Bhutan, which under the customary title of "treaty of friendship," had the customary security aspects. It was agreed under confidential letters exchanged along with the treaties that "neither country shall tolerate any threat to the security of the other by a foreign aggressor. To deal with such a threat the two governments shall consult with each other and devise effective counter measures." In the context the aggressor referred to could only be China.

Nehru amplified the meaning of these letters when, with the incipient dispute between India and China now public knowledge, he said in October 1959 : "From times immemorial the Himalayas have provided us with a magnificent frontier . . . we cannot allow that barrier to be penetrated, for it is also the principal barrier to India. Much as we stand for the independence of Nepal, we cannot allow anything to go wrong in Nepal or permit that barrier to be crossed or weakened because that would be a risk to our security." Nehru toured Nepal and Bhutan a month later and on his return declared that any aggression against either country would be considered aggression against India.

China took the same view of these developments that India would have in its place. Like any nation which constitutes a strategic land mass, China had the desire to ensure, as India also had, that no country on its border should be hostile to it, especially if it constituted a buffer between itself and another strategic land mass on the other side. So long as relations between India and China were cordial, Indo-Nepalese relations did not worry China; they began to as the Sino-Indian border dispute intensified.

The worry was about the effect on Tibet if India got away with taking neighbouring Himalayan states under her security umbrella. Apart from the acrimonious background of the early 1950s, there was also the more recent irritant of the Dalai Lama's flight to India and the demand it had generated in India for efforts to secure at least autonomy if not independence for Tibet as a buffer between India and China.

The demand no longer had the standing which Sardar Patel, then India's Deputy Prime Minister and Congress party boss with a "strong man" image, had lent to it in 1950. But it furnished a background which aggravated the Chinese reaction when the Dalai Lama fled to India in 1959. Patel had an acute awareness of the importance of Tibet for India's security, which was partly inculcated in him by his close personal relations with the Chinese Ambassador in New Delhi, who at that time represented the Kuomintang. Under Patel's authority and at a request directly conveyed to him from the Dalai Lama, the Indian Air Force carried out a close reconnaissance, of which the Chinese could not have been unaware, to see whether the Dalai Lama could be abducted out to safety in India if the need arose.

The second stream of causes of the Sino-Indian war was India's role in spreading the gospel of nonalignment and its benefits. So long as Sino-Soviet relations were close, nonalignment by itself was not an irritant in Sino-Indian relations; only the importance India acquired from it was. The Soviet Union welcomed nonalignment as a doctrine because it fitted in with the Soviet objective of checking the growing power of America's military alliances, and China had no particular objection to it. But once the Sino-Soviet split arose on the issue, among others, of peaceful coexistence versus the inevitability of war, the peace mongering of the nonaligned became anathema to China. Especially the preaching of nonalignment by India.

Only a country of the size and strategic significance of India could become the exemplar of nonalignment because of the reluctance of either of the alignment blocs to push her too far. It was this example which converted many countries to non-alignment, to the further enhancement of India's position, by proving to them that nonalignment was a painless way of ensuring security. If it could be shown that India had not been able to ensure her own security with it, a heavy blow would be struck at both the doctrine and the preacher, China reasoned.

The third stream of causation was Sino-Soviet relations. Whether China was concerned or not over Russia's ideological heresies, it could not but be concerned over Russia's developing relations with India. India and the Soviet Union, close enough to each other to coordinate their moves, are the only two sizeable neighbours of China and both neighbour upon areas which are far removed from the true centre of Han power, which have rebellious elements within them still, and which have sufficient ethnic and cultural links with elements across the frontier to become credible problems of irredenticism. Therefore, as the Indo-Soviet relations improved, Sino-Indian relations deteriorated in parallel stages. China could see the danger of a coordinated threat to Sinkiang and Tibet.

The easier way to break the bond between Russia and India, in China's view, would be to knock India out. If it were done soon, Russia would not dare to physically support India against China; the Sino-Soviet break was not ripe enough yet to justify, in the eyes of the communist world, Russian support for nonaligned India against communist China.

Enveloping and enlarging all these particular causes of the Sino-Indian conflict was the more pervasive one : that in their diplomatic rhetoric many countries, especially the USA, began to propel forward a virtually unwilling India as a democratic alternative to China's communist and authoritarian model. The verbal effort increased as the growing tension between India and China became public knowledge. John F. Kennedy was particularly eloquent when, without meaning to embroil China with India but contributing towards it, he said in November 1959 : "No struggle in the world deserves more time and attention from this administration—and from the next [which was to be his own] than the battle between India and China...for the economic and political leadership of the East...for the opportunity to demonstrate whose way of life is the better....We want India to win that race with Red China."

China was justified in taking the view that whether India saw herself as China's rival or not other countries saw her as such, and that was almost as bad as China saw it. But she also saw that the rivalry between the two models, whoever may have generated it and for whatever reason, made it an even more profitable exercise to inflict upon India a sufficiently convincing, demonstrative and humiliating defeat.

Each bit of these calculations was to be vindicated by events in the first half of the 1960s, and the fact that for unleashing these events China chose the Aksai-Chin area of Ladakh, which links Tibet and Sinkiang, adds to their meaning.

China responded to all these causes, making an ironical start with an opening it discovered at the Bandung conference. It was there that it saw the possibility of exploiting India's differences with her neighbours and their fears or suspicions of her power. Ceylon and Pakistan gave conspicuous evidence of it and Professor Rushbrook Williams in his book, *The State of Pakistan*, says: "I have been assured on unimpeachable authority that soon after the Bandung conference Karachi received a private message from Peking. The Chinese People's Government assured the Government of Pakistan that there was no conceivable clash of interest between the two countries which could disturb their friendly relations; but that this position did not apply to Indo-Chinese relations, in which a definite conflict of interests could be expected in the near future. Pakistan reciprocated by making it clear to China that it had joined the western military alliance only as a safeguard against India, not against communism or China."

The last sentence in what Rushbrook Williams says shows that even as early as 1955 China's attempts to improve bilateral relations with other countries had a salient which was aimed at India; the salient grew with remarkable speed from 1962.

The same thing happened in relation with Ceylon. Almost ever since the two countries became independent, relations between India and Ceylon had been clouded by two dominant facts of geography: that if a power hostile to India were to get a foothold in Ceylon the whole of the south Indian peninsula would be exposed to a threat, especially naval, and that important elements in Ceylon, over-impressed by India's physical mass and proximity, have always suspected India of trying to control if not absorb Ceylon in order to forestall such a threat. This gave the Chinese reasonably fertile soil, with consequences which are deeply engraved in the history of Ceylon's relations with China and India from the mid-1950s onwards.

Nepal is an even better example of the success of China's diplomatic bridge-building at India's expense. In 1956 Chou En-lai went to Nepal after visiting New Delhi and emphasized in his conversations that a country's sovereignty was not complete so long as it depended upon another for its security. In the course of 1959 Chou En-lai threw the whole of Nehru's concept of the Himalayan frontiers of Indian security, which was the rationale of the special position of Nepal in India's security framework as conceived by Nehru, into the melting pot of the Sino-Indian border dispute. While Nehru insisted that India alone was competent to discuss the Sino-Bhutan frontier with China, Chou En-lai insisted that this frontier could not form part of a Sino-Indian discussion. Nepal caught the meaning. If in China's view India was not competent to discuss the frontiers of Bhutan, which had a special treaty relationship with India, she must be much less competent to have a say in Nepal's relations with China. It was rightly concluded in Kathmandu that this position would be popular in Peking.

In November 1959, the Prime Minister of Nepal declared that "In the event of any aggression on Nepal it will be Nepal who will decide whether there has been any aggression" (thus ruling out an automatic right of intervention by India such as Nehru had claimed only a little earlier) and in 1960 came the payoff for Nepal, a boundary agreement and treaty of friendship with China. Two years later, and two weeks before China attacked India, the Chinese Defence Minister, Chen Yi, underlined the meaning of the new relations between Nepal and China. He declared that China would stand by the people of Nepal "should any foreign power dare to attack Nepal." The good people of Kathmandu showed their appreciation by stoning the office of the Indian Commercial Attache the day China attacked India.

But China's most telling response was on the field of battle. Notwithstanding Neville Maxwell's impassioned advocacy on China's behalf in *India's China War*, the cause of the war was not India's refusal to negotiate a border settlement with China. Such dispute as there was about the border was not the cause of the war but an excuse for it. Like every country which achieved independence from foreign rule, India began life with the frontiers inherited by her at birth. She could not have said she did not know where her frontiers were. But, being aware that some of these frontiers were set by the previous rulers in a phase of imperialist expansionism, India recognized her duty to be open to their revision by peaceful negotiations with those who might have rival claims upon them, especially with countries like China which had themselves been heavily encroached upon by imperialist powers. India's position hardened only at a later stage because, while assuring India that it would make no unilateral changes on the border pending negotiations for an agreed border demarcation, China occupied 30,000 square kilometres of territory—Aksai-Chin—which it knew was shown on Indian maps as Indian territory. But even then India did not refuse negotiations. India only took the position that negotiations should take place without the duress of prior occupation by unilateral action. That she was not rigid in her claims on Aksai-Chin was clearly demonstrated by Nehru.

Despite the persuasive distortions in which his book abounds, Maxwell admits two facts: that India only inherited the frontier which China disputed later and that long before China waged war upon India on the pretext of a border dispute, India had consistently offered peaceful negotiations. India very specifically said that she had an open mind on the piece of territory about which China was most concerned, namely Aksai-Chin, which the inherited frontier, the Johnson Aradagh line, had clearly placed within India. Nehru made at least three solemn statements on Aksai-Chin, all of them in Parliament, offering unrestricted negotiations. On 12 August 1959, Nehru said : "It is a matter for argument as to what part of it [Aksai-Chin] belongs to us and what part to somebody else. It is not at all a dead clear matter. I have to be frank to the House. It is not clear." On 31 August 1959, he said : "The Ladakh border... is clearly one for consideration and debate." On 4 September 1959, he said : "There are two viewpoints .... It is not in our reach...in places like this decisions can only be made by conference, by agreement."

Even about the McMahon Line, or the eastern sector, which the Chinese themselves had accepted in 1951 as Maxwell concedes, Nehru said if there were any doubts about the exact alignment "I am prepared to discuss any interpretation...any kind of a conciliatory or mediatory process ..arbitration of any authority agreed to by both parties." Some of these statements are quoted by Maxwell but ignored by him when he exclusively blames India for the Sino-Indian war of 1962. From the title onwards his book betrays his bias, offsetting its great virtue as a vivid and skilful narration of the war and of India's total incompetence in waging it.

India had lost the battle politically before it was joined militarily. What China was after was not Aksai-Chin but a demonstrative victory which would serve its larger political purposes. The causes of the war lay in these purposes, not in a border dispute, and they could only be met by a victory which would impress everyone. India, however, did not realize this and neither prepared herself to prove her claims in war nor forestalled a war by quietly giving up her claims.

Even until a year before the war broke out, Nehru could have sold it to India that for the sake of peace with a friendly neighbour he had given up a remote and barren area on which India's claims were in any case doubtful. But he allowed himself to be overruled by two of his cabinet colleagues, Morarji Desai and Pandit Pant, when the Defence Minister, Krishna Menon, tried to work out a private arrangement with his Chinese counterpart, Chen Yi, under which China would recognize, or so Menon thought, the McMahon Line in exchange for Aksai-Chin. Thereafter Desai and Pant gradually brought Nehru to their own position that while India should go into negotiations with an open mind, the extent of her openness having been indicated by Nehru already, she should not go in under duress, which meant that China must withdraw from areas claimed by India and occupied by China (in return, as Nehru publicly said, India would withdraw from areas claimed by China) so that negotiations could take place without duress. But China shot down this idea in an exchange of angry notes. Thereafter, a small but clamorous opposition in Parliament further narrowed down Nehru's options, which were narrow already, giving the Chinese a clear opening for a war which proved disastrous for India.

A successful strategy for India could have only been to avoid battle on these remote and high altitude frontiers against troops which were fully acclimatized already and close to their base concentrations in Tibet. In his book, *My Years With Nehru*, Mullik discloses that the curious reasoning prevailed in top government circles, with his own very influential backing, that territory which was indisputably Indian could not be given up without a fight   It seems to have been forgotten that a legitimate and by no means dishonourable distinction can be made, and would have been to the profit of India's interests and honour, between delaying action right up at the border, in which Indian forces would have had the authority to fight as strong a rearguard operation as they could but nevertheless a rearguard operation, followed by serious defence on ground of India's choosing where the chances of inflicting a heavy defeat upon the enemy would have been greater.

India should have withdrawn to a favourable line of defence, held the Chinese there until the winter snows on the Tibetan passes threatened to cut them off, and then rolled them back or decimated them. The corps commander who was facing this front sent three appreciations between 11 and 29 September, with well argued supporting papers by his general staff, that India should not accept battle in these forward areas. He was stripped of his command of this front. The pressure of an artificially worked up domestic opinion forced Nehru not to give ground even for tactical gain, though the primary responsibility is with the generals who, playing politics, said they would hold it. Lacking the resources to do anything better, India tried to hold a thinly stretched out line on the ultimate front where Indian troops were outnumbered 20 to one according to Maxwell. This was done in the mistaken belief that China would never attack India in strength. When this illusion was shattered by a massive Chinese onslaught down Thagla Ridge, India responded by putting together an under-strength and hastily assembled division, grandiloquently called a task force and falsely described as a corps formation to impress the Chinese, which was not given time to become a fighting formation before it was pushed out to the front where it could only put five battalions against six Chinese brigades.

The only thing worse than the state of this force was the chain of command consisting of generals who, apart from being in-experienced and incompetent, were either powerless against political games or engaged in them. Even with the inadequate forces at their command, they could have offered much better resistance if they had not, in panic, abandoned their good defensive positions at Se La; moving out in a hurry without a plan of retreat they walked into a Chinese trap and were simply shot to bits.

The Chinese understood the situation extremely well. They knew they could defeat such a force at any point whatever but instead of opening the attack in Aksai-Chin, the main area which was in dispute, they struck first and more massively in NEFA, across the McMahon Line, in order to maximize the political significance of their victory. Given their purpose this was a brilliant choice. India's only transgression here, according to the Chinese themselves, was that a few months earlier an Indian police picket of ten to 12 men had set up a post allegedly across the McMahon Line commanding an area of 64 square kilometres below Thagla Ridge. In the west, by contrast, the Chinese had occupied an area of 30,000 square kilometres which Indian maps had shown to be Indian since 1947. Explaining why China made the switch Maxwell says : "The real provocation for China lay in the west; but politically as well as militarily the opportunity for a demonstrative and destructive retaliation lay only in the east" because of the tremendous logistical advantages which China had over India in this far off sector. Chinese troops which poured down Thagla Ridge were only three hours away from the nearest terminus of their extensive new network of roads in southern Tibet which were capable of carrying seven-ton trucks. The hastily assembled Indian formations opposing them were six days march from the nearest Indian roadhead at Towang. "The Indians' actions below Thagla Ridge thus served China's needs admirably, that they provoked retaliation where that had to be deployed if it were to be effective."

What stands out most from India's experience of the war is not how unfair the combat was but how great was the disparity between the size of the battle and its political consequences. China defeated a small Indian force in a most unequal battle and then, with a magnanimous but tactically necessary gesture, withdrew its forces unilaterally before snow on the Tibetan passes could cut them off. But with this it won the "race" for Asia and Africa which Kennedy had spoken of, and at least for the time being demolished India's image in every field of her operations. Among the Afro-Asian countries the impression grew that the importance India had in their eyes during the preceding decade was only an optical illusion created by Nehru's personal glamour; the United States, after an initial spurt of interest, began to write India off; the Soviet Union began to mix increased interest in India with increased interest in Pakistan as well; the stability of India's domestic politics was reduced to ruins; and Pakistan was encouraged to sharpen its knives for its second war with India.

There were several causes of this dire constellation of circumstances for India. But the main cause was that as a result of the "demonstrative and destructive retaliation" by China, the perception of India sank in her own eyes first and then in the eyes of other countries too. The smaller countries of Asia decided the time was ripe for them to contribute their own little bit to the hauling down of the Indian flag. Indonesia not only moved away from India but set itself up as a rival focus, symbolizing the change by renaming the Indian Ocean as the Indonesian Ocean. With less drama and greater shrewdness, Ayub made timely calls on Ceylon and Nepal in 1963 and there began from then onwards a diplomatic concert which could not but displease the Indian ear. All of them found great reassurance in the humbling of India by another Asian entity which loomed even larger. Any thought that this too was something to worry about was not present yet. In 1967 Iran transferred an unspecified but suspectedly fair number of US supplied F86 aircraft to Pakistan in violation of undertakings given to the USA.

A study mission of the US Senate Foreign Relations Committee which toured South-East Asia soon after the war said it found the whole region deeply impressed with what "many observers" believed to be a Chinese design "to discredit Indian leadership and to demonstrate to the nations of South-East Asia that the new China could be ruthless and magnanimous but, either way, it was the power to be reckoned with in Asia"; the mission said that the war "points clearly to the possibility of deeper projection of Chinese power into Southeast Asia," a possibility because of which the whole region began to propitiate China.

The USA proved to be no less responsive to the new situation than China's neighbours. If they began to avoid India's company, as India found to her cost in every diplomatic initiative she took in this region right up to Mrs Gandhi's proposals in 1968 for collective security, the USA also began to disinvest in her. The immediate American reaction, stoked as it was by Kennedy's personal interest, was a generous seeming commitment to India's defence against China. But it soon tapered off, first because the USA would not run the risk of an objection by Pakistan, and next because of a general decline in American interest in the area from 1963 when US troops began to be involved in Viet Nam. When military aid was suspended to both India and Pakistan in 1965, India had received only $83 million worth of arms and equipment out of the $500 million promised in 1963, while Pakistan had received aid variously estimated at between $672 million (US Defence Department information released on 20 April 1972), $730 million (Defence Department testimony in Senate in March-June 1967), and $2,000 million (Senator Saxbe in the Senate on 12 October 1970).

From 1964 onwards, preoccupation with Viet Nam and a general disenchantment with the rest of the Asian mainland persuaded the USA to shrug the Indian subcontinent from its own back to the Soviet Union's, a change welcomed by Russia because of the importance of the subcontinental land mass in the Sino-Soviet conflict. The Soviet Union eased itself in as rapidly as the USA eased itself out. In 1965 the USA gave two interesting examples of its withdrawal, one during the 1965 Indo-Pakistan war, the other immediately afterwards.

During the crisis in Indo-US relations in 1971, the American Embassy in New Delhi assured the Government of India that when the US-Pakistan military pact was signed in 1959 Pakistan was clearly told that the pact could be invoked only in the event of aggression from a communist country. Hence, it was said, the reference in the pact to CENTO and other documents which specifically contained this limitation. The embassy maintained that Pakistan had accepted this view. But the position in 1965 was different. The day Indian forces crossed into Pakistan on 6 September, the American Ambassador in Islamabad was summoned to an hour-long meeting by President Ayub and told that Pakistan expected the USA to implement the assurance it had been given. Pakistan told a US Congress mission which visited India and Pakistan soon after the war, "The United States should have come to [Pakistan's] aid in accordance with [its] commitments." Bhutto, who was Foreign Minister in 1965, confirms in *The Myth of Independence* that according to Pakistan such commitments existed.

In response to Ayub's demand on 6 September, the USA

promised implementation of the agreement, but by that it only meant, as it later explained to Pakistan in self-justification, joint work through UN to bring about a cease-fire, not assistance, as the agreement says "to suppress and vacate the aggression." Joint work of the kind the USA undertook is not debarred under the treaty, and there is no inescapable legal compulsion to give aid with teeth. The US response can range from the minimum necessary to the maximum possible. But if the US sense of involvement in the subcontinent had been deeper, then, in the given state of relations with India, the US response would have been much more satisfactory from Pakistan's point of view. Kissinger showed in 1971 what kind of an interpretation could be put upon the treaty if the USA desired. As it was, the USA did everything it could to deflate the commitment.

Immediately after the war, the USA gave another example of its retreat from the subcontinent. In the summer of 1965, that is, just before the war, Shastri and Ayub were scheduled to visit Washington on Johnson's invitation. In India there was high expectation that the visit would give a turn for the better to Indo-US relations; Shastri, far more eager than Nehru for good relations with the USA, would not jar on Johnson's nerves as Nehru might have. But Johnson abruptly cancelled both invitations when India and Pakistan went to war, and instead both statesmen found themselves in Tashkent the following winter. Johnson may have had the hope that the Soviet Union, closer to the subcontinent and able to exercise heavier leverage in it, would be better able to combine India and Pakistan against China than Dulles had been able to combine them against Russia. If so, he and the Russians were to be equally disappointed. But the American hope in the mid-1960s enlarged Russian entry into the area, which Russia consolidated at the Tashkent conference.

Russian interest did not compensate India for the decline in American interest, and the Tashkent conference became, probably literally, a heart-breaking proof of that for Lal Bahadur Shastri. Russian commitment to India's defence against China did not falter on account of India's defeat at the hands of China. Russia carried out its promise of supplying MiGs and helping in a project to manufacture them here. But confidence in India's ability to resist Chinese pressure on the subcontinent, which constitutes

Russia's southern flank in the geopolitics of its confrontation with China, faltered very badly. This became the root cause of the Russian attempt throughout the second half of the 1960s to carry Pakistan too, instead of supporting India against Pakistan. At Tashkent, Russia strictly equated Pakistan with India. In fact, Pakistan got a little more out of it because India had to surrender the fruits of her victory in the 1965 war.

Both for personal and national reasons, Shastri had the gravest misgivings about the Tashkent Summit before he left New Delhi. Shortly before his departure he called in three editors, the present author included, to make a searching assessment of how the Indian public would receive it if he had to give up the areas across the cease-fire line in Kashmir which India had won. He was assured that if this put an end to the 20-year old Kashmir dispute the public would accept it. His closest adviser in the government and Principal Secretary, L. K. Jha, had earlier persuaded him to go to Tashkent on the specific assurance that if India withdrew from these territories, agreement could be reached on dividing Kashmir along the cease-fire line, and this would become a permanent international frontier. But all that Shastri got in exchange for the territories, which he agreed to give up under relentless Russian persuasion, was the Tashkent Declaration of peace which not only did not end the Kashmir dispute but was no better from India's point of view than the Nehru-Ayub communique of 1960 which Nehru had obtained without any cost to India. Shastri did not return alive from Tashkent; he died of a heart attack.

For the next four or five years the effect of Russian policy towards India and Pakistan, as of American policy earlier, began to be that Pakistan became a counter-weight against India although the motive, to build up a subcontinental counter-weight to China, was much more acceptable to India than the American motive had been. The Soviet Union would not subordinate India's interests to Pakistan's because, with China as its major concern, India with her size, location and resentment against China was obviously more valuable than Pakistan, which still had to be wooed out of its fascination for China. But the wooing made India wonder as to what would happen if Pakistan threatened Indian security with covert Chinese support. Would Russia still practise parity, treating the threat as a bilateral matter, or would it give due weight to the Chinese inspiration behind Pakistan?

On this India received a succession of shocks in 1968. There were hints that Russian support for India on Kashmir might be less constant in future. The Russian position did not in any way become overtly anti-Indian. But Russia indicated that it would no longer be always available to stand up and be counted on the Indian side. Next, reports appeared in Pakistan that the Russians would shortly give it a large supply of offensive arms and Marshal Grechko would be visiting it. Both things happened. There was turmoil in Pakistan, Ayub's fall was impending, and the Russians saw rather more clearly and quickly than others did that the ruling force would still be the army, not politicians, and Yahya Khan would be the army's next man in. They decided to make a timely investment in both the man and the force—and in the usual way, by promising arms, the standard currency of diplomacy in such equations. But in doing so they went back on the assurance Kosygin had given Mrs Gandhi that only non-lethal weapons, if any, would be given to Pakistan. Now it turned out that the "inducement" to Yahya Khan would include 200 tanks. India's protest, as might have been expected, was as strong as India's anxiety was great. But it not only proved unavailing; through unending reiteration it became counter-productive. Russian opinion about India tended to become as irritable and unflattering during this phase as American opinion used to be.

But, learning little and by now thrown off balance by an anxiety neurosis, India tried to retaliate, again ineffectually, with two gestures marked by petulance. First, India tried to improve her relations with the USA, by mid-1969 going so far as to take the opportunity of Nixon's—even Nixon's—visit to New Delhi to discuss the security of Asian countries in a context different from and wider than the Russian interest in the security of the subcontinent. (Russia itself was to widen the context a little later but had not done so yet.) The second response was a complicated manoeuvre to convey to China an impression of Indian neutrality in the Sino-Soviet clashes on the Ussuri.

Contrary to the advice of professional foreign policy experts, important political leaders in the Government of India pointedly let two opportunities for supporting Moscow slip, one in Parliament and one at a meeting of the Congress Parliamentary Party on foreign affairs. On the latter occasion (a private meeting in any case, where anything said in support of Russia would have been no substitute for a public stand) the Foreign Minister went so far as to say "everyone knows where India's sympathy lies" but he declined to go beyond that because "India wanted a peaceful settlement of all border disputes," thus repeating the stand Moscow took during the Sino-Indian border war in 1962. On the former occasion the Defence Minister confined himself to criticizing some Naxalite communists for sending a telegram of congratulations to Mao Tse-tung. His brief included expressions of Indian support for Moscow but he declined to voice them because, as another Cabinet Minister explained in private: "No one asked him to, and sometimes it is best to let a diplomatic situation remain a little vague and let people come to any conclusions they may on the basis of impressions."

The Russians noticed India's silence and conveyed their disappointment to the Indian Embassy in Moscow. But they were far from scared. There were some obvious limitations upon the Indian gestures which India should not have forgotten and Russia did not forgive. India's relations being bad both with China and America, she had little room for manoeuvre left in her relations with the Soviet Union. Pakistan was much better placed in this respect. Secondly, Russia could always outmanoeuvre India in the game of pressures by stepping up arms transfers to Pakistan. Thirdly, just about this time, Pakistan had Russia hooked on the possible cancellation by Pakistan of the American ground lease in Peshawar for the US electronic spy base. Pakistan gave the USA formal notice of its intention in May 1969 and refused to be bought off by an American kite that Italy would be allowed to sell 100 M47 tanks to Pakistan. And in July 1969 the base was shut down—an objective Russian diplomacy had been aiming at for a few years at least.

Driven to the ultimate choice, the Soviet Union would have been forced to choose India, not Pakistan, as it ultimately did because of India's superior geo-strategic location with regard to China. But in order to take advantage of this, India would have had to play a much tougher diplomatic game than she was capable of doing with the psychological resources she had at that time. The Soviet Union, on the other hand, had the resources as well as the need to be resolute in pursuing what had become the

highest aim of her policy in the subcontinent: to prevent China
from enlarging its salient here and to eliminate the salient it had
established already by using Pakistan's anxieties about India or
exploiting Pakistan's ambitions about Kashmir.

The most adverse effect of India's defeat was, of course,
upon India herself. In the western sector in Ladakh, Indian
troops fought well and grimly held on to their positions wherever
they could. But China's three-year old occupation of Aksai-
Chin was further consolidated. In the eastern sector, China's
victory shook the entire Indian structure from Bihar eastwards
to the borders of Burma. The damage it directly did was not
much but it inspired a state of unrest which hollowed out the state
structure from inside. The insurgency which rocked West Bengal
in the second half of the 1960s was partly due to the impact
of the Chinese victory. The older insurgency in Nagaland
received a new lease of life as Chinese aid became available
through East Pakistan and northern Burma.

Regional dissidence, encouraged by the helplessness of the
central leadership in coping with the turmoil in eastern India,
sprouted in other parts of the country too, such as Punjab and
Tamil Nadu. Kashmir's disaffections took a violent turn and the
state experienced its worst bout of rebellion in more than a decade,
Sheikh Abdullah's later contact with Chou En-lai adding to the
resulting complexities.

Much worse than these specific events was the spirit of gloom
which enveloped India and refused to let her extract an ounce
of self-assurance from some solid achievements which adorned
this period, such as the smooth management of the succession of
Shastri to Nehru in 1964 and of Mrs Gandhi to Shastri in 1966,
the good performance of the Indian armed forces in the war with
Pakistan in 1965 despite a simultaneous Chinese threat, and the
nasty rebuff given to China in 1967 during a clash on the Sikkim
border. The assumption everywhere was that a general and total
collapse was imminent and the few signs of political or military
health were only the last flicker; this nearly became a self-fulfilling
prophecy when the ruling Congress split in 1969 under the
weight of the fractiousness which had infected the whole polity.

The denigration of Nehru's ideas of defence was a special feature
of these dark seven years from 1962 to 1969. He was to be
harried till his death, and his name beyond that, for rejecting a

proposal by President Ayub for a joint Indo-Pakistan defence partnership. In the hands of his enemies, Nehru's remark "defence against whom?" became a satirical epitaph. Nehru had as good a reason for rejecting Ayub's idea in 1960 as both Nehru and Liaquat Ali had for rejecting a similar proposal by Mountbatten in December 1947. Mountbatten had gone no further than to suggest that India and Pakistan should coordinate their plans for meeting their defence problems, and as Hudson records in *The Great Divide*, quoting Mountbatten's papers, both Nehru and Liaquat Ali Khan "took the line that it would be valueless to pursue the question of joint defence until their governments were more in line politically. They pointed out that defence policy could not stand on its own but was intimately connected with foreign policy; the necessary preliminary to detailed discussion of the former was some degree of coordination of the latter."

It was even more difficult to coordinate the foreign policies of India and Pakistan at the end of the 1950s than at the end of the 1940s. For the entire intervening decade they had followed, as they have continued to follow since, diametrically opposite foreign policies. To leave Nehru in no doubt regarding what "joint defence" would mean Ayub had pointed out, practically on the eve of making his proposal in October 1959, that it would be directed against China, the Soviet Union and Afghanistan. In March 1962, in an interview with Louis Dupree, an American scholar then working in Pakistan, Ayub said, as quoted by Dupree in *First Reflections on the Second Kashmir War* : "Pressure from the Soviet Union and Red China will continue to mount during the next decade and it is absolutely essential that we get our (India's and Pakistan's) armies pointed in the right direction." The parentheses are by Dupree.

No one could have expected Nehru to accept such a foreign policy frame for his defence policy and yet, because he would not, it began to be alleged after the Chinese attack that his whole strategic concept of defence had fallen to the ground since India had not been able to defend herself single-handed and no one had come forward to assist her while the battle was on. Pakistan fully shared this perception of India's security predicament during the mid-1960s and it decided to seize its chance before India could recover her domestic balance or repair this weakness in her security to become strong again.

## The Double Danger

The northern threat to India's security was serious enough in its unidimensional aspect—China's bilateral hostility to India. But it was more serious in its multi-dimensional aspect where it joined up with two parallel problems, the old one of the Indo-Pakistan conflict and the new one of the growing Sino-Soviet antagonism. This gave an enormous strategic significance to two areas: in the north-west Gilgit and in the north-east the Siliguri corridor. They became the new hinges of Indian security, and both were weak.

The importance of Gilgit would not have worried India, at one level. As a diplomatic and logistical causeway for China, leading into Pakistan and beyond that into the countries of the Arabian Sea, it was an asset for China without being a liability for India. But at another level it was an area of danger for India. The influence China had been gaining here ever since the Sino-Pakistan border agreement in 1962, which itself became one of the baleful influences on the Kashmir negotiations that Britain and the United States forced India to start after her defeat by China, was a simultaneous threat to the western flank of the Indian positions in Ladakh and the southern flank of the Soviet frontage on Sinkiang. At the same time, as a barrier between India and the Soviet Union, it was a more hostile wedge than the finger of Afghan territory jutting in here would have been or, left to itself, even Pakistan would have been without China's instigation.

At the opposite end, the 30-kilometre wide Siliguri corridor, India's only link with its 25 million square kilometre eastern region of Assam and the surrounding territories, was now exposed to a double threat, from the north by China and from the south by East Pakistan. Either could have threatened it in the past but now the two together could pinch it out at will. With the amity developing between China and Pakistan the vulnerability of this corridor became China's safeguard against any Indian threat to Tibet from NEFA, and Pakistan's safeguard against the vulnerability of East Pakistan which is surrounded on three sides by India and on the fourth by the sea and separated by 1,600 kilometres of Indian territory from the main base of Pakistan's military strength, the western wing. Obversely, China and Pakistan could now expose India to a one, two or three front war and neither India's own strength nor any visible support from others had the answer to this danger.

This offered Pakistan the tempting possibility that if China cooperated a large enough section of the Indian Army could be tied down to the northern and eastern fronts by China making threatening movements in Tibet and Pakistan in the eastern wing, while the bulk of the Pakistan Army, leaving the defence of the eastern region to a Chinese umbrella, would get the chance of making a breakthrough in the west with the enormous punch its armed forces had, thanks to ground and air weapons given to it by the USA. China was willing to support such an ambition because it suited its larger purposes. For five years it had been trying to break down the world's bi-polarity under which India could expect support from one side if the other made an attack upon her in strength. Now a fluid triangle was beginning to emerge and would be hastened if, under Chinese auspices, Pakistan got away with a slice of India while the Super Powers proved unable or unwilling to do anything about it. If the slice happened to be Kashmir, the Gilgit causeway would become much bigger and many times more useful for China.

Since the Chinese attack, India had started developing independent army formations which would be adequate for a long enough holding operation to give time to other developments to intervene. But progress was slow on account of American hesitations after Kennedy's death in giving the equipment assistance which had been promised by Kennedy. Johnson as President implemented the policy of "backing up" Pakistan which as Vice-President he had urged upon Kennedy. Sino-Soviet hostility had not yet developed enough for the Soviet Union to back India sufficiently and openly. As Kosygin later told Mrs Gandhi, Russia was at that time still hoping for normal relations with China and was discouraging approaches by Mao's domestic enemies. In this mood Russia was not likely to do very much to pull the chestnuts out of the fire for India.

India placed her hopes, such as they were, in a complicated calculation which worked only because of India's ability to summon up hidden resources of will of which no one suspected her, including herself. She calculated that China would physically intervene only in such strength as would ensure another startling success; by making a half-hearted and possibly unsuccessful intervention it would not jeopardize the prestige it had gained on the cheap in 1962. At the same time, with American power still confronting it in the east and beginning to confront it increasingly in the south as well, and with Russia unpredictable on the western front, China would find it difficult to spare a large enough force for the Sino-Indian front, and if India made an easy victory impossible for it, China would not risk a serious engagement. Anything which looked like an attempt would be a bluff which India could call.

By 1965 this had become conventional wisdom in the Ministry of External Affairs. Its counterpart in Defence was that, first, a large enough force should be kept in the north for effective passive defence; second, a strong enough force should be assembled in the west to quickly carry out offensive defence if Pakistan attacked, which it would only do in the west, and third, there should be no retaliation against the softer eastern wing of Pakistan so that China may not be needlessly provoked into action, and certain incipient tendencies which were visible in East Pakistan already may be further promoted. But this was at best a calculation. How mistaken one could be in calculations about China had become shatteringly clear in 1962 and the memory of that, still raw in the Indian mind, grated harshly upon it when in April 1965, the Pakistan Army laid a trap for India in Kutch after high level political consultations with China.

Within this overall picture the local picture was also brighter for Pakistan, at least as Pakistan saw it. Pakistan was superior to India in military hardware as well as in that intangible, the fighting spirit, while its perception of India was that she was, as Bhutto put it later in *The Myth of Independence*, a "feeble, flippant and decadent society." Louis Dupree in his *First Reflections on the Second Kashmir War* wrote : "Almost all observers are agreed that the Pakistani forces are superior to the Indians in morale and fighting spirit." They had reason to be, as they looked at the arms balance between India and Pakistan. The Indian Army was superior in numbers but inferior in every department of equipment, especially as a strike force. Since the Chinese attack, India had increased its infantry, the only arm which can be quickly expanded in India, from 500,000 men to 825,000. But an accompanying five-year plan for armament expansion was drawn up only in 1964 and its implementation had barely started by 1965. Infantry expansion therefore had all the weaknesses of a severe imbalance. The only troops which had new arms were seven mountain divisions, as yet under-strength and only partly equipped; in any case they were fully committed on the northern front.

In armour on the other hand, which is what Pakistan was counting on, India was inferior in the power and number of operative formations while in overall numbers it had only a slight edge. According to Dupree, Pakistan had a full armoured division consisting of 600 combat-ready tanks, including 200 Pattons, the equivalent of another armoured division consisting of one independent armoured group and two independent armoured brigades, and a few other unattached elements. India had one armoured division, one armoured brigade, and four light tank regiments, or about 360 tanks in all, the majority of them old Centurions. In artillery, Pakistan's superiority was much greater. It had a full regiment of medium artillery with each of its ten infantry divisions, plus three extra regiments of medium artillery and one regiment of heavy artillery. India had only three regiments of medium artillery and none of heavy artillery at all.

India's air fleet of fighters and fighter-bombers was larger by a ratio of two to one, but apart from having to look after the long northern front as well, it consisted only of subsonic aircraft, mostly old Hunters, Vampires, Mysteres and Gnats (of which, however, Gnats in the hands of good pilots achieved tactical superiority over better planes). The majority of Pakistan's fleet consisted of F-86 Sabre jets, supersonic F-104 Starfighters, both armed with missiles, and supersonic Lockheed Shootingstars. India had parity with Pakistan only in deep strike capacity, with 80 Canberra bombers on either side. India had superiority at sea, though partly offset by an Indonesian loan of missile boats to Pakistan, of the same kind as India acquired later from Russia and used very successfully against Karachi in 1971.

Pakistan at this point had a push and pull incentive to try its luck on the battlefield because of its present superiority over India and the danger of loosing it later as India's defence plan got under way. It began with a pilot project in April 1965. In a manner reminiscent of what China had done in Aksai-Chin, Pakistan built a track across a disputed part of Kutch, an area difficult of access from India, like Aksai-Chin. And soon after the Chinese Prime Minister and Foreign Minister, Chou En-lai and Chen Yi, had visited him, President Ayub launched an attack in brigade strength, heavily supported by tanks and artillery. For his timing he chose the third week of April when this low lying marshy area, close to the coast, is only a few weeks away from heavy inundation by sea tides. He exposed India to the difficult choice, and this of course was the calculation, either to accept helplessness and all the protest this would raise at home or to commit forces to an indefensible area where they would shortly be immobilized and trapped.

India wisely chose to back down, but this only confirmed Pakistan in the mood of self-confidence which was sweeping through it. Dupree later wrote : "The jubilant Pakistanis saw the Indian withdrawal as a sign of the continued erosion of Indian morale and unwillingness to fight. Possibly the whole of the Rann of Kutch episode was simply a Pakistani test of Indian strength and stamina." Pakistan therefore ignored Shastri's warning that if Pakistan persisted, India would attack at a time and place of its own choosing.

Pakistan now felt strong enough to try its hand in Kashmir, and once again caught India at a serious tactical disadvantage. Under the terms of a truce which Britain had brought about following the fighting in Kutch, both sides had to withdraw their forces, pulled up to the border by both in May and June, back to their peace-time stations. This is always a disposition of advantage to Pakistan because its peace-time stations are close to the border—in some cases only a few hours of deployment time away from forward launching positions. India's stations are much farther in the rear. But in the autumn of 1965 there was a further disadvantage for India : the normal summer time turnover of forces, held up by the tension over Kutch since the beginning of April, was now in full swing, especially from Kashmir. When Pakistan struck at this well-chosen time, slipping about 5,000 well-trained guerrillas into Kashmir down mountain trails in the first week of August to break out across the cease-fire line at a given signal, quite a few Indian formations had to be turned back while

in transit to other stations. They had to take to operations straight
after disembarkation while others had to go directly to battle
positions from their peace-time cantonments.

Having already formed a poor opinion of India's will to fight,
Pakistan decided that India's will to hold Kashmir was also
weak because just before his death Nehru had offered to bring
India and Pakistan together in a confederal relationship with
Kashmir and earlier, in the 1962-63 talks with Pakistan, had
offered to divide Kashmir along the cease-fire line. Therefore
Pakistan launched a plan with a three-layered intention. At
the minimum its plan was that while the Indian Army was held
back by the fear of a dual Sino-Pakistan threat, a guerrilla force
should raise a strong enough rebellion in Kashmir to prize the
state out of India's grip. The hope was founded on the very
encouraging fact that in the winter of 1963 Kashmir had been
rocked by the worst wave of unrest in 15 years.

The next higher intention was to assist the expected uprising,
and also to trap the Indian forces already in Kashmir, by cutting
off the state's only surface link with the rest of India with an attack
on Jammu through the Chhamb-Akhnoor corridor, an area very
difficult to defend and a death valley for any forces India might
commit there. Pakistan did not believe that India would retaliate with an attack on Pakistan itself; such an attack would
mean crossing an international frontier, and that, Pakistan
thought, India would not do because in spite of his threats
Shastri would not do what Nehru had not done in 1948 in the
face of a graver provocation although Lahore lay completely
defenceless before India then. But against the chance that
Shastri might, Pakistan had its third and highest intention: an
attack with a massive armoured fist in the plains of southern
Punjab, outflanking from the south the area in which India would
retaliate, if at all she did.

Much of Pakistan's central Punjab front was even then heavily
defended—by 1971 it had been reinforced still further—by a
north-south system of static defences built around the Ichhogil
canal, which is in fact a tank trap. Pakistan's very intelligent
anticipation was that if India retaliated in order to relieve
the pressure on Jammu, she would do so north of the Ichhogil
line; an attack south of it would be too far off to influence the
battle in the north. That would so heavily commit India to an

area well north of the horizontal Lahore-Amritsar axis that it
would leave Pakistan free to stage the southern assault, well
below this axis, in which it would have two important advantages : Pakistan's armoured punch was far heavier and more
mobile than India's then, ideally suited to a wide-swinging
attack in open country, which is what Pakistan intended; and
with much better north-south communications and much closer
to the front than India had, Pakistan could move reinforcements
at will from the north to the south of the static defences.

Confidently superior in logistics and armour, and not only
audacious but brilliant in planning, Pakistan intended, as proved
by documents captured after the war, to break into India on the
Kasur-Khem Karan axis with its main strike element, the 1st
Armoured Division; split the attack force into two prongs thereafter; send each prong up along the country by pushing it up
both banks of two canals which flow down from the north-east;
and then wheel north to cut the Grand Trunk Road at two points
between Amritsar and Jullundur, one at a vital bridge on the
Beas, close to Jullundur, and the other at Jandiala Guru, halfway
between the bridge and Amritsar. This would be the Akhnoor
strategy on a grander scale. It would not only cut off the forces
in Kashmir but almost the whole of Western Command west of
the Beas and north of the Lahore-Amritsar axis. Any bargain
could be struck with India in negotiations from such a commanding position.

India's calculation on the other hand was that for military as
well as political reasons she must take the battle outside Kashmir.
Political unrest in the state would grow if Pakistan was seen battl-
ing India inside Kashmir; besides, under a limiting agreement
with the United Nations, India was unable to move into Kashmir
a sufficient force level for effective defence in the hills, which
simply swallow up troops. Outside, India would have certain
advantages—not over Pakistan but over her own position in
Kashmir. During May and June, when India, like Pakistan,
had pulled up her main forces to the West Pakistan border her
forces had perfected their plans for a future attack. In a phase
of divergence between political and military projections, Shastri
ordering rapid total disengagement and deep withdrawals, his
commanders anticipating trouble in the near future, the Chief
of the Army Staff, General Chaudhuri, and the General Officer

Commanding the western army, General Harbaksh Singh, had decided between them that come the day again and they must carry the war into Pakistan. In anticipation of that, Western Command had given the troops full dress rehearsals in probable and alternative launch formations, complete with lines of attack and every attendant detail. They could hope to offset Pakistan's advantage in armour with their own advantage in surprise if the political leadership gave them the clearance promptly enough upon the need arising.

Larger political factors also favoured such a course. India could hardly hope to carry anyone with her if she lost Kashmir to Pakistan in fighting limited to the state; half the world had doubts as to who should have Kashmir, Pakistan or India. But any other Indian territory Pakistan took would not be allowed to remain with her for long. If India took slices of Pakistan, there would be the danger, admittedly, of a Chinese intervention. (Pakistan began the war in autumn, late enough for the end of the rains on the upper slopes in NEFA and early enough for an invading Chinese force to go back before snowfall on  the Tibetan passes.) But politically that would work more against Pakistan than India. If siding with Pakistan also meant siding with China, the West would still side with India instead and the Soviet Union would probably make the choice, if a choice became necessary, which she had to make five years later.

Thus, India as well as Pakistan tailored their military strategy to a clearly perceived objective and a political frame. This has not been understood by some who have commented on the war, for example Leo Heiman. Writing in the February 1966 issue of the *Military Review*, the professional journal of the US Army, he said both countries "lacked a clear-cut war strategy and commanders in the field were uncertain about their mission. Was it to be an all-out general war, a limited war for certain clearly defined objectives, a prestige campaign for vaguely defined psychological advantages and political influence factors, a campaign of attrition to weaken the enemy's striking forces or a war of  conquest to annex new territories and sources of raw materials?"

The answers to these questions are very clear. Pakistan had a single and definite objective—to wrest Kashmir from Indian control and it used for the purpose a tool which in its perception of India at that time was adequate, namely a limited external attack which would enable Kashmiris to rise in revolt. But Pakistan also had supporting alternative plans to meet the maximum Indian retaliation which Pakistan thought it could expect. Similarly, India had a clear objective—to inflict the maximum damage on the enemy war machine—and it had clear political reasons for not aiming at annexation of territory. Furthermore, India and Pakistan placed their battle strategies within a definite view of the overall global political environment; both took readings of the likely reactions on the part of China and the two Super Powers. Heiman should have had no difficulty in discovering these very simple truths. Pakistan did not succeed in its aims, nor did India in full. But wars do not always end in decisive victories even if they are planned with sufficient sophistication to impress Heiman.

Pakistan's first plan did not ignite. For no reason anyone can give even today, Kashmiris refused to take Pakistan's bait and the state was quieter throughout August and September than at most other times. Nor was there any Muslim unrest elsewhere in India, which was Pakistan's subsidiary hope. This became a probable additional reason for the Chinese not making any moves in support of Pakistan. Their main reason was that Pakistan, confident of its unaided power, did not ask for Chinese help or even coordinate with it. But the state of Indian public morale was also not very encouraging for China. It shifted a division towards the border with Ladakh after India had moved away its only brigade in this sector to the south-west for dealing with the infiltrators. But they did not move up thereafter as far as could be seen.

Unencumbered by domestic unrest, India retaliated and sealed off the infiltration routes by crossing the cease-fire line and capturing Haji Pir and other passes; the guerrilla force was trapped just when it was ready to move on Srinagar in a beautifully coordinated plan to tie down the entire Indian force inside Kashmir, including reserves. But their plan was foiled by Kashmiri apathy.

Pakistan's second plan began as thunder, Yahya Khan attacking in division strength down the Chhamb-Akhnoor corridor with a strike force of 90 Pattons. India tried to hold the tanks with air attacks but although they took a heavy toll of the tanks they could not stop the advance. India simulated reinforcing movements across the bridges at Akhnoor and Jammu but that did not deter the advancing Pakistanis. Then India reacted as Pakistan had half expected. Chaudhuri went through the offensive strategy with Shastri on 3 September morning, obtained his clearance in the afternoon and passed it on to Harbaksh Singh the same evening. Harbaksh Singh ordered complete suspension of all heavy movement west of the Beas from the last light of 5 September to build maximum surprise behind an attack he planned for the 6th morning.

Just before dawn on the 6th Indian troops were launched from well rehearsed positions, and because of the surprise they achieved they were able to cross the Ichhogil at several points within a few hours. But they set up only light bridgeheads since this was only a feint; even a raid on Lahore, much less its capture, was never a part of the Indian plan. Here political and military judgment coincided. India realized that any territory captured by either side would have to be disgorged. Therefore capturing it would be wasted effort and holding it, especially a big city like Lahore, would consume an enormous force level. It would be much better to damage the enemy's war machine as much as possible in the process of relieving the pressure on Kashmir. After keeping Pakistan guessing for a day, Harbaksh Singh launched India's main armoured assault towards Sialkot. It was here, in open, fast country south-east of the Jammu-Sialkot axis and resting from the north on the Shakargarh bulge, which was to become famous in 1971, that the heaviest tank battles anywhere since World War II were fought and extensive damage was inflicted on Pakistani armour.

But in the meantime, south of the Ichhogil system, Pakistan launched its third and most ambitious plan. A discussion on later pages will show that this operation had a substantial impact upon the strategy which the two sides were to follow in 1971. It cast a spell on Yahya Khan's imagination and to India's strategic thinking *vis-a-vis* Pakistan it added a fateful twist. But in the context of 1965 it is interesting that the operation was launched at all. Captured documents show that this was a carefully worked out plan which was based upon a standing contingency plan but was updated and reissued first by verbal orders and then in writing. The written orders are dated

8 September, that is a week after Pakistan had opened its second plan with the tank attack led by Yahya Khan, and three days after India had retaliated by crossing the international frontier between the two countries. According to the sequence of thinking in Pakistan's GHQ as reconstructed above, the third plan was to be launched only if the first and the second further up north failed in their objectives. Therefore by 8 September Pakistan's General Staff must have concluded that neither the raiders across the cease-fire line nor Yahya Khan in the Chhamb corridor had succeeded in isolating the Indian force in Kashmir. Yet such was Pakistan's confidence in its superiority in armoured thrusts that, as succeeding paragraphs will show, the updated third plan was launched without making any reassessment of the Indian response and capability.

The plan assumed possession of certain crossing points and launching positions. The assessment by Pakistan would appear to have been that there would be no difficulty at all in attaining these preliminary and qualifying objectives. The position on the ground was in fact very different, but Pakistan did not think it necessary to reassess it before playing its ace, its mailed fist— the 1st Armoured Division.

Advance elements of this division plus the supporting forces on its left flank pushed back the few light bridgeheads Indian forces had thrown across the Ichhogil canal. For India this was a planned withdrawal from what was only a tactical move to probe the enemy, to keep him guessing and, per chance, to move forward if opportunity offered. Pakistan on the other hand took it to be a major reverse, a substantial retreat forced upon the main enemy force. Therefore it decided to roll forward to plan.

But before any part of the 1st Armoured reached Khem Karan, the starting point of its intended double drive to the Grand Trunk Road, it began to pay the price for living on a borrowed doctrine. Along with Pattons Pakistan had imported implicit faith in the invincibility of superior firepower and massed armour. Therefore it made itself weaker in the one element on which India was counting the most, trained manpower and its superior use of the ground. The Indian war machine here was weaker and smaller. But it was thoroughly integrated with ground conditions—the crops, the canals and the lie of the land.

Pakistan could have known everything about the ground that

it needed to know. Within 24 hours of the Indian crossing of the frontier up in the north, Pakistan had rolled the 1st Armoured Division from its forward concentration area in the Changa Manga forest to its launching positions around Kasur. Therefore it had two full days for taking close bearings. But Pakistani generals, probably out of sheer over-confidence, invested very little in coordination with infantry and even less in ground survey and reconnaissance in depth. The divisional headquarters sent in only one "recce" party, on the morning of 8 September, and therefore knew little of Indian defence, of which the key elements were put together only after the "recce." It had no knowledge of the ground and therefore allowed successive regiments of Pattons to be lured into country thickly covered with tall sugarcane and overrun with clever defensive flooding, the one blinding the gun sights, the other bogging down the tracks. When it began to sink in the battle it had no infantry to come to its aid. It had no knowledge that less powerful Indian tanks placed in strongly defensive positions were waiting to chew up the immobilized Pattons.

Pakistan's plan was excellent in concept. When Indian Army Headquarters realized its implications they had to wheel to the south the left flank of the corps-sized Indian attack further north. One of the officers engaged in higher conduct of the war later commented that one day we were speculating whether we should go forward to Lahore, the next day we were wondering whether we could hold Amritsar. But Pakistan lost the day through bad execution, India saved it by close attention to detail. Thoroughness of tactics defeated brilliance of strategy. Pakistan lost the war in Sialkot as well, as it had earlier lost it on the cease-fire line. But it was the battle in the Khem Karan area which rubbed the defeat in; fighting six engagements spread over two days, Pakistan lost more than 90 tanks and the Commander of the 1st Armoured.

The Khem Karan and Sialkot battles took a heavy toll of the enemy war machine. Being kept on an ammunition ration by its main supplier, the USA, his capacity to keep up even a defensive battle was running low, and Indian commanders in many sectors reported a 50 to 60 per cent decline in his firing rate. Therefore it is a sad comment on President Bhutto's military knowledge (or regard for truth) that in an interview with the BBC on

18 February 1972 he should have said that if the war had continued a few days longer in 1965, Pakistan would have made significant gains. The fact is that if the war had continued beyond the 22 days it lasted, India would have multiplied and enlarged her thrusts. Indian commanders were strongly urging that war should be allowed to continue till the end of the month. But realizing his predicament Ayub accepted a UN cease-fire call which a few days earlier, India, much to the army's disappointment, had accepted and Pakistan had not.

India's political leadership gave evidence of shrewd judgment and stamina in handling China's threats. On 4 September, with Yahya Khan's attack on Akhnoor still making headway, the Chinese Foreign Minister arrived in Pakistan, increasing India's anxiety about a two-front war. But this made for no second thoughts in New Delhi about the clearance given to the army the previous day to retaliate outside Kashmir. In discussions conducted by the Prime Minister and at a lower level the same day by the Prime Minister's Secretariat, the same conclusions were reaffirmed as had emerged in previous discussions. The conclusions were that there was no great likelihood of a Chinese attack. Areas across the northern front had been kept under close observation and no indications were found of any sizeable build up though at a few places there were some misleading movements. Therefore, the war should proceed as though it would remain on a single front, but no risk should be taken with China needlessly. There should be the minimum withdrawals for the west from the northern front and every possible care should be taken to avoid causing any provocation in the north.

From this several things followed in the course of the war. First, the only brigade withdrawn from the north was deployed so close to the Ladakh frontier of China that it could be quickly turned the other way if the need arose, a manoeuvre which became a scale model for an important element in the third war. Second, when China delivered a ludicrous ultimatum on 17 September, asking India to withdraw some non-existent intrusions into China and to return some imaginary sheep and yaks "within three days" or else face "grave consequences," India calmly called the bluff and China had to forget about it after extending the ultimatum by three days for no reasons given. Third, the language of the Indian reply to the ultimatum was kept at the

correct, firm but very polite level.   In fact, a somewhat truculent
draft put up by the Foreign Office was thoroughly overhauled
at the suggestion of the Prime Minister's Secretariat.   Fourth,
the Pakistani provocation of making air raids on Calcutta from
East Pakistan was completely ignored and no retaliation was
mounted in the east.   Shastri and Chaudhuri, in close consultation throughout the war, firmly declined repeated requests from
India's eastern army for permission to march into East Pakistan.

The   course   and   outcome   of   the war   had   a   three-fold
importance : militarily because of the defeat inflicted upon an
enemy who was superior in weapons, politically because of the
qualities shown by India's leadership and the solidarity shown by
the population, and psychologically because of success in calling
the Chinese bluff.   But neither India nor the world was ready
yet to take note of it.   If India had been, she would not have
descended into the severe political downturn which followed
Shastri's death and was mostly generated by a lack of self-confidence in the Indian polity; if the world had been then at least
from 1965 onwards India would have had a smoother passage in
international relations.   As things were, however, the major
powers continued to mark her down and the smaller either to
ignore her or take advantage of her difficulties for their own
benefit.   The military, political and to some extent economic
recovery which had begun soon after Shastri settled down as
Prime   Minister   remained   an   interlude   in   India's   darkest
phase.

It was only after India's domestic political institutions asserted
themselves, and so well that the turbulence they went through
could be seen in retrospect as a regenerative upturning, and after
Mrs Gandhi had reasserted the pre-eminence of a single leader,
that India could resume her search for a place in the world.   So
long as the suspicion persisted, as it did almost right up to the end
of the 1960s, that India was about to disintegrate, her principal
defence and diplomatic asset till then, her size and mass and the
potential importance of her geographic location, could not
deliver its full value.   But it did as soon as the suspicion vanished
with Mrs Gandhi's electoral triumph in March 1970, which put
an end to domestic political instability.

The change this made in the perception of India is sharply
etched out in the contrast between two American assessments

which are only a few months apart in point of time but poles apart in what they say. A year before the election, a report by the US Library of Congress said: "India stands at the threshold of the 1970s with little idea of the international role it will play in the years to come." It found "Asia's largest non-communist country" without "any meaningful influence in that strategic area adjacent to its eastern frontier, Southeast Asia." But a month after the election a study mission sent by the US House of Representatives found India "seeking a broader international role."

Neither statement was wholly correct. Even after 1970 there were many misgivings which beset such an Indian role—the state of the domestic economy for one—and even in 1969 the Prime Minister, the Deputy Prime Minister, the Foreign Minister and the Foreign Secretary had said during their tours in South-East Asia and the Far East that India was more than willing to promote and participate in regional institutions, which was a milder way of saying that India expected to occupy its place in the regional sun. But the *demonstration* of political stability, quite apart from its attainment (which ante-dated the election) made a difference to the way India looked upon herself and others looked upon her. That paved the way for her re-emergence into the world's perception. And immediately upon re-emerging India encountered the advantages and responsibilities which must accompany her geo-strategic situation.

India was important in the context of the old cold war: whether she remained independent of both the Super Powers or sided with one or the other made a difference to the power balance between the Soviet Union and the USA. That was the secret of her security in the 1950s. But in the new cold war, between the Soviet Union and China, which had replaced the old during India's absence from the world, her weight could make an even bigger difference: not her weight as the leader of the nonaligned group, which was at best an advantage for which she was dependent upon other countries, but as the biggest land mass contiguous to the two sides in the new cold war. This was a factor she could use to the best of her own judgment and capacity without having to carry a few score of other countries with her. And because the new cold war was the mainspring of the triangular diplomacy which now ruled the world, India's disposition was going to matter more than it had done before.

None of the conflict areas which have emerged since the Second
World War—Korea, eastern Europe, the Middle East and South-
East Asia—matters as much in this triangular diplomacy as the
Indian subcontinent. Eastern Europe matters tremendously
in Russo-American rivalries but China has not been much involved in it in any strategic sense; its interest has been limited to
using some opportunities to embarrass the Soviet Union. China
has taken more interest in the West Asian conflict but, lacking
contiguity, China and West Asia cannot make much difference to
each other's fortunes. Nor can West Asia really swing the
balance between the Soviet Union and the United States although
its own future depends upon what they do to it. It has an
immensely important commodity to sell, but it is doubtful whether
it can boycott, or be made to boycott, one market or the other for
very long. Viet Nam has contiguity with China but neither with
the Soviet Union nor the United States; they fight here from a safe
distance and their essential security interests would be even less
affected by the outcome here than in the Middle East. But the
subcontinent matters in the Sino-Soviet conflict as no other area,
and for this reason matters to the USA as well; like Japan and
Europe it has become a key factor in the balance of the global
triangle. That is why each diplomatic side of this triangle began
to impinge upon India as soon as she emerged from seven years
of an internal crisis.

Sino-Soviet antagonism was so intense now and such a marked
feature of the global landscape that India's immediate environment had again become virtually bi-polar. This led India to
believe that within limits she could practise once more the old
diplomacy of seeking a safe anchorage with one side while trying
not to antagonize the other. Hence, the traffic of gestures
exchanged with China in 1970, with the difference this time that
no attempt was made to take a side-swipe at the Russians as when
India used silence as a signal during the Sino-Soviet clashes on
the Ussuri.

India's Ambassador in Moscow, D. P. Dhar, had a series of
meetings in Moscow and with clear Russian foreknowledge,
with the Chinese Ambassador, the highest ranking Chinese outside China. At this as well as in other private contacts India
conveyed to Peking her willingness to discuss the old long-standing
border dispute without insisting—for the first time India agreed to

drop this ten-year old condition—that China must first accept the proposals put forward by the Colombo Powers in 1963 for a peace settlement. In August 1970, India's Foreign Minister gave public confirmation of this important change. India also conveyed her willingness to be the first to send her ambassador back to Peking provided China agreed in advance that it too would do so. To this India added the usual frills, like trade and cultural exchanges, etc.

But China made no response whatever, and this was an indication to India that the ground rules of the new cold war were much stiffer than those of the old; they would not allow the kind of bi-alignment she was able to practise in the old cold war, and a clearer choice would have to be made between China and Russia than she made between Russia and the USA. The expected result was a further widening of the Indian anchorage in Indo-Soviet relations.

Further impetus was added to this by the change in the direction of Sino-Soviet relations. Although Kissinger did not visit Peking until July 1971, there were indications much earlier that Nixon was putting himself in a position to exploit the Sino-Soviet rift in the interests of America's global strategy, in which the main drive still was competition with and containment of Soviet power. If necessary he would let China have a freer hand on its Asian periphery in the interests of containing Russia jointly with China. Nixon's tactics were fully understandable from the American point of view. America had erected its Asian commitments only as a subsidiary front for the containment of Russian power because China was then seen as part of a single monolith extending from the Danube to the Sea of Japan. Now China was available as a bulwark against Soviet power, a better bulwark than any Dulles had been able to build. It made eminent good sense to use it so. Asian commitments would be sacrificed in the process but only for the very purpose for which they were constructed in the first place.

The meaning of this for India was to be further spelt out a little later in the difference between what the USA communicated to India before and after Kissinger's visit to Peking. But three things were clear enough even before Kissinger left Washington. In the global triangle, much the shorter side would now be the one between Washington and Peking, and as this became shorter the sides joining Moscow with Peking and Washington would grow proportionately longer. Whether at any given time Moscow would be further apart from Washington or from Peking would depend upon variable circumstances, but Peking would be nearer Washington than Moscow. This was inherent in the logic of the continuing Soviet challenge to the USA's position as the world's number one power; the more the Soviet Union threatened to close the gap the more America would wish to see China operate as a constraint upon Russia. To let China's influence grow in Asia would not be a heavy price to pay for this because, with America disengaging, China would grow in Asia more at Russia's expense than America's. Russian influence in India would not be hurt but its expansion further east would be.

From this the second thing followed: that relations between India and Pakistan, and the relations of each with the Soviet Union and China, would be powerfully influenced by the Sino-Soviet antagonism. The subcontinent would weigh heavily in Soviet and Chinese calculations. But the Chinese, with very little at stake in their equation with India, would enlarge their anchorage in Pakistan, realizing that India's relations with Russia were now too close to be counter-balanced by any kind of "normalization" of Sino-Indian relations, whereas Pakistan's relations with Russia could become appreciably closer if China faltered in its hostility towards India. On the other hand, the Soviet Union would step up its investment in India as China stepped up its own in Pakistan, and if circumstances forced a choice upon it, as they probably would sooner or later, it would opt for India. The Bangladesh crisis and the role China decided to play only hastened the choice, but one of these days it would have been made in any case as India gave evidence of a stronger recovery and China used Pakistan as a constraint upon India.

In fact, so clearly would these lines be drawn one day that India and Pakistan would come to be regarded as the respective proxy powers of the Soviet Union and China. This development too was hastened by the Bangladesh crisis, leading to Nixon's deplorable adventure during the war in December 1971. But even without the crisis it would have come to the surface as the Indo-Soviet and Sino-Pak relationships developed into what the world would see as two rival axes in Asia. This was to be, as it became, the third consequence of the changed direction of Nixon's China policy.

It was in token anticipation of later developments that, in a soft parallel with the change in his policy towards China, Nixon personally decided to make the so-called "one-time" exception in 1970 to the five-year old ban on the sale of arms to Pakistan (and India). "So-called" because, as the best placed Americans in New Delhi admitted at the time, there could be no guarantee that the exception would not be repeated if the same circumstances (which they would not specify) were to recur; as it was, some of the arguments being given in 1970 were the same as were used once before, in 1967, to make another exception for giving Pakistan spares for the lethal equipment supplied to it earlier.

Justifying the exception in the vocabulary of the old balance of power formulations, the US Embassy in New Delhi conveyed it to the Government of India: "The US government believes that on account of the very large supply of Soviet arms to India and the establishment of arms manufacturing capability with Soviet assistance, the balance of armaments between India and Pakistan is no longer today what it was in 1965. . . . We do not envisage a weapon to weapon balance between India and Pakistan and we recognize that India's needs both of available arms and armament industry are much greater than Pakistan's because of the enormous confrontation imposed by China. But we do envisage and desire some sense of arms balance between the two countries."

The embassy and other American channels also emphasized that unlike the Soviet Union the USA had not agreed to give tanks to Pakistan though Pakistan was strongly pressing for them, and that it was surprising that there was louder protest against the smaller release of US supplies to Pakistan than against the much larger Soviet release.

In the first place, this is not exactly correct. As the controversy developed, official reports came in from Washington that the Administration had considered allowing Turkey to release 100 US tanks to Pakistan. Secondly, even if the USA had got its arithmetic right it hadn't its politics. Indian protest was disproportionate in terms of quantities of arms released but not in terms of the overall policies behind the releases : Chinese and American policies towards Pakistan were antagonistic towards India; the Russian were not in so far as they were not meant to enlarge Pakistan as a counter-weight against India. India took a view of these arms supplies which corresponded less to the quantities than to the policies behind them.

However, what no one, including India, was able to see at this point was that Pakistan was soon going to be unavailable as a counter-weight against anyone; it would be too preoccupied for that with trying to maintain its own internal balance.   In retrospect it was to stand out as an astonishing failure of Indian perspicacity that she had not noticed the consequences of what she had herself begun, once unwittingly and once with clear premeditation, though the consequences were going to rid India of her toughest single difficulty in discovering what her due place in the world could be.   In consequence of India's uncompromising stand that Kashmir was not negotiable property, a tendency towards militarism developed in Pakistan which alienated the eastern wing on account of the nature of inter-wing politics. India accentuated the alienation  by her  very careful  and calculated decision not to carry the second war into the eastern wing.  She took a singularly correct reading of the mood in East Pakistan and of its future possibilities.  But in later years she paid little attention to them and now she was to discover in them the gravest challenge to her survival—as well as her finest opportunity.

# III  The Trial

# A Lost Chance of Recovery

Whatever the regret in India over the partition of the country in 1947, or the disappointment in Pakistan over not getting Kashmir, war between the two countries was not inevitable. Nor was the break-up of Pakistan. There was great antagonism between the two countries and between the two wings of Pakistan, but neither of the two gulfs was unbridgeable. There was nothing like the Arab-Israeli syndrome here: Pakistan was no pump-house of a powerful alien culture which the Arab countries, consumed by a sense of inferiority, believe Israel to be; nor was Pakistan (nor is it now, though cut to half) so insignificant geographically that it should have lived in perpetual fear of being swallowed up by India. The more populous half of Pakistan, the eastern wing, had no great hatred of India either at the individual or collective level, and even in the less populous half the collective hatred, largely engendered by state policy, was not great enough to extinguish the warm personal empathy which exists even today. The gulf between the two wings of Pakistan was admittedly great, but even until the eleventh hour there was no widespread desire in East Pakistan to break away and form an independent state.

The conflict between India and Pakistan could have come to an end; the two wings of Pakistan could have stayed together in a viable even if a loose federation. The only requirement was the normalization of the internal politics of Pakistan. Normalization of relations with India would have automatically followed; the internal balance in Pakistan was such. India's economic self-interest would have helped a little, that of West Pakistan would have helped a little more, and most of all that of East Pakistan.

The drives which shaped East Pakistan's attitude to India were always very different from West Pakistan's. David E. Bell, supervisor of an advisory group attached to the Pakistan Planning Board for four years, said to the US House of Representatives Foreign Affairs Committee in 1956: "For many West

Pakistanis the proof of loyalty is the violence of a man's antagonism to India and her leaders. East Pakistan, on the other hand, preoccupied with her own backwardness, is apt to speculate on the advantage of closer ties with Calcutta and the Indian economy. There is a real difference in view towards the order of importance of various issues of foreign policy."

East Pakistan was physically far from Kashmir and culturally and ethnically even more so. Its emotions were not so overwrought by Kashmir as West Pakistan's were. Its economic links with India were far closer than the west's; their severance, imposed upon it by the policy makers whose roots were in the west, hurt it more. If Pakistan had been a democratic country, the logic of democratic politics would have brought domestic issues to the forefront; more important than that, the eastern wing with its bigger population would have been preponderant in the national government and the latter's relations with India would have been dictated by the needs and aspirations of the eastern wing, not the passions of the west. Allowed its due say in national affairs, East Pakistan would not have become a backward part of Pakistan, exploited like a colony by the western wing. The pressure of resentments in the eastern wing which finally broke Pakistan would not have built up.

This is not a post-facto theoretical speculation; from its very inception the short history of Pakistan bears testimony to it. Because Pakistan consisted of two separate wings, because the two were so very distinct in everything bar religion which may distinguish one nation from another, and because Pakistan finally broke along this cleavage, Indians and all others have been led to believe that this was Pakistan's operational cleavage. From this followed the myth which in India at least was widespread that the rulers of Pakistan kept a popular resentment against India stoked up in order to hold the two wings together. The observation and inference are equally wrong.

The more important cleavage, and one which finally broke Pakistan, was not between east and west but between the top and the bottom. Above this horizontal cleavage were those, mostly drawn from West Pakistan's feudal and aristocratic elite, whether bureaucratic, military or purely political, who were anti-democratic in their outlook, and in their policies bitterly anti-Indian. They stoked and exploited the popular resentment over Kashmir, but not for keeping the country together; they did it to keep themselves in power. They were the beneficiaries of military and authoritarian rule, of heavy expenditure upon the armed forces and of a close alliance with the United States. The sanction and justification for all this was the confrontation with India. They carried as an appendage a small minority from East Pakistan who were congenially feudalistic in their outlook.

Below the cleavage stood the great majority of East Bengalis, with probably the majority of West Pakistanis, who would have preferred a democratic system, would have benefited from it more than they did from the oligarchic rule of a military-bureau-cratic junta, and because of the predominance of the Bengalis among them would have tilted Pakistan away from a confrontation with India. Because the oligarchs were mostly from West Pakistan, another myth grew up: that it was the west as such which was denying democracy to the east as such—and mainly out of cultural antagonism. But culturally the two wings were not more antagonistic than north and south India. What separated them more was the absence of a political framework of state in which the two could have an equal sensation of shared power, and the oligarchy was denying this share as much to the people at large in the western as in the eastern wing though the western wing as a whole is more homogeneous culturally than India is. That is why until 1970 no elections were held in West Pakistan, not even in 1954 when they were held in East Pakistan. The shortlived and unstable rule of politicians was replaced in 1955 by a succession of military rulers and before that by a civilian martial law administrator who had no electoral or other popular sanction behind them.

In spite of the antagonism towards India over Kashmir which the oligarchy fanned for its own benefit, the democratic forces might have succeeded in asserting themselves, thus paving the way for normal relations with India, if the United States had not exploited the antagonism for its own global reasons (of doubtful soundness even from its own point of view). For American reasons American policies tilted the balance in favour of military forces as against the democratic, which incidentally meant tilting it in favour of West Pakistan against East Pakistan and which, at least after the middle 1950s, meant intentionally tilting it in favour of Pakistan against India. As militarism prospered in

Pakistan at the expense of democracy, the western wing prospered at the expense of the eastern and the antagonism against India grew, feeding on itself. The USA's disregard of its own democratic traditions in encouraging this was not incidental; in the given circumstances democracy would have been less congenial to US purposes than a military oligarchy, and both sides knew this.

In most countries which have a backlog of economic discontents to clear, genuine democracy, not of the fake variety which flourished in Pakistan up to the middle 1950s under the wing of feudalistic politicians, throws up strong politics of the left and the government is obliged to follow left of centre policies at home or abroad and sometimes both. That is why so often in the case of the developing countries US foreign policy throws its weight behind authoritarian regimes, often through the use of military aid policies, seeking to rationalize this choice with the suggestion, advanced among others by William Bundy, former Assistant Secretary of State for Near Eastern and Pacific Affairs, that in traditional societies authoritarian regimes can be more effective; some eminent US scholars have also adorned this theory with their names. With his experience on the White House staff, Bill Moyers said on National Education Television on 8 December in Washington: "In my opinion, about the only thing constant in our performance is that the favours we have bestowed on General Yahya Khan are consistent with our fondness for strong armed military rulers in South Viet Nam, Cambodia, Thailand, South Korea—and all the other countries we have been fighting to make safe for democracy."

Against this background an Indo-Pakistan settlement specifically over Kashmir became extremely unlikely after the early 1950s. So long as Liaquat Ali Khan was the Prime Minister of Pakistan, the only democratic Prime Minister Pakistan ever had, the rulers of Pakistan did not have a self-interest in perpetuating the dispute with India over Kashmir. But at that time an agreement could not have taken place even on the basis of Indian consent to a plebiscite in the state because, with Sheikh Abdullah still very popular in Kashmir and still opposed to the state's accession to Pakistan (in those days the Pakistan press used to denounce him bitterly as a traitor to Kashmir; Liaquat Ali Khan called him "a Congress Quisling"), there was every chance that Pakistan would lose and it refused to implement the conditions for a plebiscite laid down by the United Nations, such as the prior withdrawal of Pakistani forces. After that India had similar doubts, but the successive Presidents of Pakistan also enjoyed a domestic leverage out of the dispute which they were loath to forego.

This was the fatal basic flaw in the initiative Nehru took in 1964 in sending Sheikh Abdullah to Pakistan in the genuine hope that a settlement would be possible on the basis of some kind of a loose confederation between India, Kashmir and the two wings of Pakistan. Eighteen months before that, when in the aid negotiations following the Chinese attack, Duncan Sandys and Averell Harriman, representing respectively Britain and the United States, insisted on Indo-Pakistan negotiations, Nehru went along with them insincerely. He was convinced, and privately explained to Harriman (he did not think Sandys would even understand the point, let alone agree with it) that any settlement over Kashmir which India could be seen to have been forced to accept because of the pressures generated by the Chinese attack would give China even greater leverage in the subcontinent than India's defeat had given it already. Harriman did not reject the objection and Nehru was encouraged to adopt the tactics he did—to play for time, not a settlement. He instructed Swaran Singh, his Foreign Minister and chief representative in the monthly rounds of negotiations which had been set up under the two-power intervention, to prolong the talks as much as he could : Each round was worth a division to him, he said. Nehru expected three rounds at most before Pakistan became desperate once more. But Swaran Singh, a tireless weaver of words which always seem to be on the point of saying something, took his counterpart, Bhutto, to six rounds of talks; in a recent bit of private raillery he said he contributed half of the 12 divisions with which India fought the 1965 war with Pakistan.

But in 1964 Nehru was in dead earnest. In encouraging Abdullah to go to Pakistan and sound President Ayub on the possibilities of a triangular confederation he overruled his closest political colleague and successor, Lal Bahadur Shastri, who had grave misgivings about the confederal idea. Shastri was, if anything, even more keen on a reasonable settlement of the Kashmir dispute and for this reason too, apart from others, it is tragic that Sheikh Abdullah's highly indiscreet interview with Chou En-lai soon after Shastri became Prime Minister so inflamed Indian public opinion that it forced Shastri to drop Abdullah as the channel for working a way out of the impasse between popular sentiment in Kashmir and official Indian policy. But he was against any larger arrangements which might disturb the entire Indian polity. He never gave in to the fear which Morarji Desai and to some extent the Home Minister, Pandit Pant, had that if one bit of India were allowed to slip out of the Indian Union others would follow it out as well. His personal convictions were not against the risks of a plebiscite even. But he was convinced out of his far deeper knowledge of the politics of states than Nehru had that India would not be justified in taking the risks of a confederation with Pakistan.

Shastri was certain that West Pakistan would accept only the loosest kind of relationship with the confederal centre, and further, that once such a relationship was allowed into the confederation the existing, much closer bonds between the Centre and the states in the Union of India would be weakened by the force of this example. But Nehru overruled Shastri with the argument that he must make this attempt to put India's relations with Pakistan on a different course before life ran out on him, which it did only a few days later.

However, Shastri need not have had any anxiety on this score : Ayub turned down Nehru's idea for precisely the same reasons as Shastri's, that it would undo Pakistan. In the *New Republic* of 19 June 1971, Harrison quotes Abdullah as saying in "a recent interview" with him that "when Ayub was told of Nehru's proposal he said Nehru had put it forward 'only to split Pakistan' since Nehru knew very well that even exploratory talks on this would fan the fires of Bengali separatism and lead to demands for separate and equal status with West Pakistan, India and Kashmir." But nemesis was to overtake the leaders of Pakistan very soon because that very confrontation with India over Kashmir which they had intensified to sustain themselves in power was accentuating the causes of the separation of East Pakistan and the downfall of military rule in West Pakistan.

In this sense the Kashmir war between India and Pakistan in 1947-48 became the first war for the independence of Bangladesh; by incidental and casual connections it gave a slant to the domestic and external policies of Pakistan which almost inevitably led to the second war in 1965 and finally to the third in 1971 which delivered freedom to Bangladesh. The process, which had been more fully discussed in *The Challenge of Bangla Desh*, edited and co-authored by the present writer, began before Pakistan began.

At a conference in 1940 where the founding resolution of Pakistan was adopted, the delegation from Bengal expressed its grave anxiety whether the predominantly western Muslim League, the movement-like party which created Pakistan, would look after the interests of Bengali Muslims. It was in deference to this anxiety that Pakistan's founding resolution said that upon the partition of India the areas in which the Muslims are in a majority, as in the north-western and eastern zones of India, should be grouped to constitute independent states in which the constituent units shall be autonomous and sovereign.

Despite terminological confusion about states being simultaneously autonomous and sovereign, the political meaning was clear, that East Pakistan would have very substantial autonomy. But the first and virtually the only decision which the first national assembly of Pakistan took, in 1949, was that Pakistan would be a federation in which, it was obvious even then, power would mostly reside in the western wing on account of the nature of the power structure which was developing. The ruling heirarchy in the Muslim League was largely drawn from West Pakistan. Therefore, so long as the League was the ruling party, power resided in the western wing. Then, when the bureaucratic and military oligarchy took over in the name of the liberation of Kashmir, the eastern wing's share of power dwindled even further because it had no representation in the armed forces and very little in the senior ranks of the bureaucracy.

Popular leaders of East Bengal began to be denied the share in power (even in East Pakistan) which they were entitled to on account of their popularity as shown in elections; some were also charged with treason for urging better relations with India or more democratic institutions at least in East Pakistan. It was on such charges that H. S. Suhrawardy, Chief Minister of undivided Bengal at the time of the partition in 1947 and for a time Prime Minister of Pakistan later on, was arrested in 1948. It was also on this charge that another former Chief Minister of undivided Bengal, Fazlul Haq, was dismissed as the Chief Minister of East

Pakistan in 1954 after he and Suhrawardy had heavily defeated the Muslim League in the only elections held in East Pakistan until then and since then up to 1970. A joint front formed by Suhrawardy and Fazlul Haq had won an overwhelming mandate but it was replaced by martial law administered by General Iskandar Mirza who was sent down from Peshawar under orders of the Governor-General. In 1969, Sheikh Mujibur Rahman, more popular than either Suhrawardy or Fazlul Haq and in 1971 Prime Minister of Bangladesh, was arrested on charges of making a treasonable conspiracy with India.

It is probably not a coincidence that the more popular an East Pakistani leader happened to be the more likely he was to be accused of such a conspiracy and the more harshly he and his supporters were likely to be treated. The brutal suppression of the Awami League in 1971 after it had won 167 out of 169 seats in the East Bengal Assembly and the sentence of death on Mujib were only extreme but characteristic examples of the West Pakistan elite's intolerance of any assertion of their rights by the people of East Pakistan; the stronger the assertion the more total was the west's intolerance of it and the more brutal the suppression. Alleged treason by popularly elected politicians was the only excuse that could be given for this because popular politics could not be suppressed in East Pakistan in the name of confrontation with India as they could be in West Pakistan.

The economic exploitation of East Bengal was as marked as the suppression of democratic urges in it. The story has been pithily told in a joint paper by J. Lee Auspitz, President, Ripon Society, USA; Stephen A. Marglin, Professor of Economics, Harvard University; and Gustav P. Papanek, Lecturer in Economics and former Director, Development Advisory Services, Harvard University :

> The Central Government's instruments of tariffs, import controls, industrial licensing, foreign aid budgeting and investment allocation have been used to direct investment and imports to develop high-cost industries in West Pakistan whose profitability is guaranteed by an East Pakistan market held captive behind tariff walls and import quotas. Though 60 per cent of all Pakistanis live in the East, its share of Central Government development expenditure had fluctuated

between a low of 20 per cent during 1950-51 and 1954-55 and a high of 36 per cent in the period 1965-66 and 1969-70. East Pakistan's share of private investment has averaged less than 25 per cent. Historically, 50 per cent to 70 per cent of Pakistan's export earnings have been earned by East Pakistan's products, mainly jute, hides and skins. Yet its share of foreign imports (which are financed by export earnings and foreign aid) had remained between 25 per cent and 30 per cent. Basically, the east's balance of payments surplus has been used to help finance the west's deficit on foreign account, leading to a net transfer of resources, estimated by an official report to be approximately $2·6 billion over the period 1948-49 to 1968-69.

The political movement in East Pakistan was thus exposed simultaneously to two contrasting experiences: its nearly total sway over mass support in East Pakistan, and its total inability to influence the policies of the Central Government towards a fair deal for the eastern wing. This began to turn its thoughts from autonomy towards independence. If the movement for autonomy had gathered less support, its leaders might have resigned themselves to their fate; if their rights had been at least partly conceded they might have settled for some compromise. As it happened, however, since everything was denied them the demand for everything began to look like the only alternative.

While Suhrawardy and Mujib were still committed only to autonomy, a strong faction of the Awami League, led by the radical peasant Maulana Bhashani, broke away from the League on this issue, formed a separate party, the National Awami Party, and became the first to ask for total independence. Bhashani accused Suhrawardy in particular of betraying the autonomy programme of the Awami League during his brief spell as Prime Minister. But there was very little Suhrawardy could have done. The constitutional law of Pakistan allowed him few powers; political realities allowed him fewer still. The President (never a man from East Bengal) could dismiss the Prime Minister even if he had a majority in the legislature, as Khawaja Nazimuddin was. He could dismiss the constituent assembly, as it was dismissed while it had a resolution before it seeking to limit his powers. Few in West Pakistan would wish to protest against this, fewer still in East Pakistan could afford to do so. The dice was heavily loaded against them.

The course of the 1965 war convinced both the Awami League and the NAP that it was both necessary and possible to secure East Pakistan's interests against West Pakistan's; the only difference between them was whether China's help would be more useful or India's. The National Awami Party, viewing the event in one way and influenced by Maulana Bhashani's popularity in Peking, thought more of China; the Awami League, taking another view and more akin to the moderate politics of Mujib, thought more of India.

The NAP thought that India did not attack the east in 1965 because of fear of a counter-intervention by China. The Awami League thought India was acknowledging in this way that she expected and desired friendly relations with East Bengal when it came into its own, as India expected it would one day. India's reasons were a mixture of both. The pros and cons were seriously considered. The Indian Army Commander in the east, General Manekshaw, who as Chief of the Army Staff in 1971 conducted the victorious strategy of the third war, was strongly in favour of going into East Bengal in 1965 and repeatedly asked permission; the Chief of the Army Staff then, General Chaudhuri, himself a Bengali, was more sensitive to the political advantages of making the gesture which the Awami League correctly read.

Prime Minister Shastri with whom Chaudhuri's relations were particularly good, as Manekshaw's with Mrs Gandhi, decided in Chaudhuri's favour. He understood Chaudhuri's political reasoning as clearly as, to the surprise of everyone around her, Mrs Gandhi understood Manekshaw's military reasoning in 1971.

The option India took in 1965 gave the Awami League a double-barrelled propaganda weapon which proved two things: one, that the Pakistan Army had left East Pakistan completely undefended, which it had, and concentrated everything in the west, which proved that in any future Indo-Pak confrontation West Pakistan would be powerless in the east and Bangladesh would be free to liberate itself; and two, that since India had not attacked in the east in spite of the open opportunity, she could not be the ogre that West Pakistan had always presented her to be. At the same time China was shown up as a country which, for all its protestations of solidarity with Pakistan, had done little more to help it than to issue an empty ultimatum to

India. This enhanced the Awami League's position at the expense of the NAP's and India's at the expense of China's; the Awami League could now openly advocate, without fear of losing ground to the NAP, that Pakistan should switch from confrontation with India to friendly relations, especially economic and more especially between the eastern wing and eastern India.

The ascendancy of the Awami League at the expense of the NAP could have been equally good for India and Pakistan if West Pakistan had seen and taken the chance. For India it meant the ascendancy of a popular political force which would not allow, as Ayub had and NAP would have, the use of East Bengal as a base of support for eastern India's endemic insurgencies by Chinese influence or any other which might be hostile to India. For Pakistan it meant the decline of a party which was demanding complete independence for the eastern wing, not autonomy.

Sheikh Mujibur Rahman had announced his Six-Point Programme of autonomy for the eastern wing within a couple of months of the end of the war in 1965; thus he underscored the encouragement he had read into India's decision not to attack in the east. But he did not read into it an encouragement for independence. Pointedly and significantly Mujib dissociated himself from any demand for independence at a round table conference called by President Ayub in March 1969. He began and ended his speech with a fervent appeal for the unity of Pakistan and for autonomy as a means of ensuring this unity.

But unfortunately for Pakistan, parties in the west which were to show only a little later how popular the demand for autonomy was in Baluchistan, NWFP and to some extent Sind were not free to do so yet. Free political activity was still a little distance away. Mujib went back to Dacca with the conviction that it was impossible to have an all-Pakistan basis for the issues dearest to him, and he drifted a little further apart from the western wing.

This could only mean two things: either East Bengal would win autonomy with the consent of the government in Islamabad and within the framework of Pakistan; or Islamabad would again try to crush the Awami League, which would lead to turmoil and possibly to a complete break between the two wings. India could welcome the former possibility; the latter had in it seeds of acute instability which could spill over the frontier into eastern India. But a democratic upsurge in Pakistan created a more helpful third possibility. Ayub was overthrown by a tremendous wave of democratic protest which swept through East and West Pakistan thus promising fulfilment of the first and most important condition for Pakistan to have good relations with India—replacement of the oligarchy with a democratic system. The first successor to Ayub was another dictator, Yahya Khan, but recognizing the strength of the demand for democratic politics, he held the country's first ever free and nationwide elections, and a democratic constitution appeared to be on the way. In the elections in the eastern wing, the Awami League showed such maturity, moderation and overwhelming solidarity that it raised hopes of a peaceful and stable transition to democratic politics.

The international environment was also improving. Pakistan gave no sign as yet that from the 1965 war it had learnt what it should have, that Kashmir could not be loosened out of India by force. But it could no longer expect Russian support for its ambitions. When Kosygin came to New Delhi in January 1968, he still advised Mrs Gandhi, as Tito did too when he came two days earlier, that a settlement would be easier in Ayub's lifetime (a mirror image of the Soviet advice to Pakistan when Nehru was alive) because he was willing to settle other disputes first. Tito said Ayub would agree to the partition of Kashmir. Mrs Gandhi did not feel strong enough to take such an initiative. In fact she feared that if she did Morarji Desai would promptly take advantage and attack her for this; therefore she preferred that the initiative should come from other Cabinet colleagues. But it would have been embarrassing for her to ward off Kosygin's advice with a plea which was an admission of weakness. But Ayub himself ended the embarrassment for her: even while Kosygin was still in Delhi the Pakistan High Commission gave him a message from Ayub that nothing could be discussed without a Kashmir settlement; perhaps Ayub too did not feel strong enough now to make a concession. Thereafter Kosygin did not revert to the subject with Mrs Gandhi except in general terms. Before the end of his visit he became the first Russian leader to endorse the Indian assessment, which had by then become a settled policy aim—that partition along the cease-fire line was the only safe solution for the long-standing Kashmir problem.

Moscow's initial anxiety to woo Yahya Khan worried India for a time. But Yahya Khan soon blotted his book with the Russians. It was with his prior consent that Kosygin floated a proposal for a trade and transit agreement between India, Pakistan, Iran and Afghanistan. The proposal aimed simultaneously at all three Russian objectives in southern Asia: to cement it against Chinese penetration (hence the Indian interest in it), to expand Russian influence in this region, and to bring an age-old Russian dream a little nearer—a passage to the southern waters. But after Kosygin had obtained the consent of the three other countries, Yahya Khan went back on his word without any stated reason. The resulting embarrassment for Kosygin was so acute that he never forgave Yahya Khan for it.

Russia was still to press, and for a time it pressed very hard indeed, that India should keep out of Pakistan's internal crisis, but pressure for any kind of a Kashmir settlement which would not be acceptable to India was by then a thing of the past. American interest in this problem also continued to recede (though not yet in wooing Pakistan by means of arms). China's interest in it was still very great, on its own as well Pakistan's behalf, but correspondingly, Russia was becoming a very definite restraint upon any Chinese adventure.

Therefore, early in 1971, with the Awami League resplendent in its victory and Mrs Gandhi, now thumpingly re-elected in March 1971, and strong enough to say and do what she wanted without having to worry about Morarji Desai or any other cabinet colleague, it really began to look that a 25-year old drag upon India's position in the world was about to come to an end. But this was not to be. Or not this way.

## The Refugee Flood

Just as two factors combined to bring down Ayub, the eastern wing's demand for autonomy and the western's for democracy which Bhutto converted into his torrential election campaign, two others combined with Bhutto as the catalyst for this combination too to enable Yahya Khan to gather all power in his hands once more—the reluctance of the established power structure to let democracy in and the western wing's reluctance to loosen its hold on the eastern wing. Yahya Khan's anticipation had been that the elections would throw up a fragmented national assembly; party structures and combinations would be so weak in it that he would hold real power as the President. Bhutto confirms in *The Great Tragedy* that his is what Yahya Khan hoped for and expected. Bhutto's own anticipation was that his would at least be the biggest single party and although he would have to share power with Mujib and the eastern wing, the lion's share would be his. Both of them panicked when the Awami League acquired total control of the East Pakistan Assembly and, even without a single seat from the west, majority control of the national assembly.

Bhutto realized that even though he had swept the elections in the west he would be a second fiddle to Mujib in the national assembly and quite possibly powerless if Mujib mobilized other West Pakistani parties against him. This made him a willing agent of all those who wanted to destroy Mujib, the Awami League and East Bengal, his expectation being that as West Pakistan's most popular leader he would thereafter inherit the earth. Bhutto's support, and Bhutto's threat of creating chaos in the west if Yahya Khan did not thwart Mujib's demands in the east, gave Yahya Khan the fig leaf he needed for subverting elections which had been held under his own auspices. Throughout March he kept up the pretence of negotiations with Mujib, but he was using the time only to build up his army in East Pakistan. David Loshak, South Asia correspondent of the *Daily Telegraph* at the time, has given detailed evidence in *Pakistan Crisis* of how behind a facade of serious negotiations Yahya Khan was secretly using the time to fly reinforcements to the east. The intricate manoeuvring in these negotiations has been analyzed at length by Mohammed Ayoob and K. Subramaniam in *The Liberation War*.

Convincing evidence has yet to come on the one question which is relevant here and on which there has been much puzzled speculation: Did Mujib place, and if so why, his demand for autonomy for East Bengal above the chance he had of ruling the whole of Pakistan? One surmise has been that Mujib had always aimed at full independence and would have used autonomy as a stepping stone towards it. Mujib alone can say if this is so, and even if it is, he cannot say it until the war crimes trials on which he is insisting are either over or given up. Until they are, he cannot say that his aim was full independence; if he did, the Pakistani soldiers whom he wants to put on trial would have an argument to justify if not the brutality then at least the severity of their crackdown on the Awami League movement. But there is both negative and positive evidence to show that under a fully democratic constitution Mujib would have preferred to rule a united Pakistan even though now, as Prime Minister of an independent Bangladesh, he may find it not politic to admit that he would have settled for less than independence.

In an interview with the *Statesman* in March 1972, Mohammad Ayub, former President of Pakistan, said that if he had been in the place of his successor in March 1971, he would have simply told the political leaders of East Pakistan that they were free to secede if they did not wish to stay within Pakistan. But his actions belie him. In March 1969, after an abortive round table conference with East and West Pakistan political leaders, Ayub offered the Prime Ministership to Mujib but only under the existing constitution and political dispensation which gave the President the enormous power to dismiss the Prime Minister and Parliament. Mujib asked him if he was prepared to ensure that the Prime Minister would have real power so long as he had the confidence of the assembly. Mujib knew that without suitable changes in the constitution, he would not have the power, once he assumed the office under the present dispensation, to dismiss the oligarchical structure, based almost entirely in West Pakistan, which had a grip hand  on the reins of economic, political, and military power and which could not only make the Prime Minister a puppet in the hands of the President but the President himself a puppet in its own hands. Mujib told Ayub that the principal changes he wanted were fully democratic elections and a Cabinet responsible to Parliament alone. Ayub refused and Mujib declined the office.

Because of this background, which Mujib disclosed in an interview he gave me in Dacca in May 1972, it is difficult to see on what basis Yahya Khan announced in January 1971, after talks with Mujib in the preceding December, that Mujib would be the next Prime Minister. Mujib told me that Yahya Khan made the announcement without authorization and there  was  no justification for it in the talks between them. With the Legal Framework Order proclaimed by Yahya Khan before the elections in December, the powers of the President had become even more sweeping than they were under Ayub. Therefore, if Mujib was unable to accept Ayub's offer of office, how could he have accepted it under Yahya Khan's more draconian regime?

One can only conclude that Yahya Khan's purpose in making the statement was to rouse the ambitious Bhutto against Mujib. Bhutto had other reasons already to be nervous about Mujib's potential power. He knew, as he says in *The Great Tragedy*, that several West Pakistan leaders were willing to support Mujib in the national assembly "because they also wanted secession of their provinces." His stated reason is fallacious. He knew that under the Legal Framework Order Yahya Khan could stop any constitution which he did not like. But Bhutto feared his isolation in the national assembly.

If independence had been Mujib's real aim, the game that would have suited him most would have been to go into the national assembly without disclosing his hand, mobilize support for full autonomy for the provinces with the help of West Pakistan leaders, and use the resulting decision either way: if Yahya Khan accepted it, Mujib could have used it as a stepping stone in the manner alleged by Bhutto; if Yahya Khan refused, Mujib could have proclaimed independence with much greater justification. But he could not have given up autonomy, even if he did not aim at independence, until the power structure in Pakistan was completely overhauled. With the constitution remaining as undemocratic as it was and the power complex in the west remaining what that was, Mujib's power at the centre would have hung by the slender thread of a four per cent majority for the east in the national assembly. This, as Kamal Hussein, Mujib's principal adviser on constitutional matters, explained in an interview in Dacca, would have been a dangerous position for Mujib to be in. The west would have only needed to buy or win over a few East Pakistan members of the assembly to throw Mujib out. Therefore, either he had to ensure a democratic system throughout Pakistan or at least autonomy in the eastern wing before accepting office at the centre.

Mujib said in the interview that he warned Bhutto in Dacca in the last week of March 1971, that unless the two of them joined their forces, Yahya Khan would destroy them turn by turn, first using Bhutto against Mujib, then other West Pakistan parties against Bhutto with the backing of the army and other elements of the oligarchy, and finally the oligarchy against the West Pakistan parties themselves. More specifically, Mujib proposed that he and Bhutto should jointly demand transfer of power to the elected representatives in the two wings; this done, they would work out a confederal arrangement between the two wings. Bhutto more or less confirms this in *The Great Tragedy*. He also confirms that Mujib was not only willing to shoulder responsibility at the centre but demanded it in addition to autonomy for East Pakistan under his Six-Point Programme. But by that time Bhutto had already played into the hands of Yahya Khan. He had provided Yahya Khan with the excuse he needed to present the army as the only force left for saving Pakistan.

It was after Bhutto had threatened a country-wide agitation if the national assembly were convened without prior agreement between him and Mujib on the latter's Six-Point Programme that Yahya Khan felt bold enough to announce postponement of the assembly without consulting Mujib, the majority party leader, and announced a new date which was contrary to Mujib's repeated demand for an earlier session. This must have convinced Mujib that it would be pointless to assume power at the centre without consolidating his base in East Pakistan first.

But in spite of this service Bhutto was reduced to a sorry plight as he brings out in his own testimony. He says, for example, that Yahya Khan left Dacca without informing him and that he learnt of the President's departure only from an Awami League emissary who himself had only learnt of it long after Yahya Khan had left for Islamabad. That the President did not tell Mujib before he left is understandable; Mujib was to be the main victim of Yahya Khan's next move and could not be given advance warning. It is more revealing that Bhutto also was left in the dark. However, delaying wisdom till later, Bhutto still chose to go along with the army. When General Tikka Khan struck in Dacca, Bhutto said : "Thank God, Pakistan has been saved." A few weeks later, with guerrilla activity still rising in Bangladesh, Bhutto said that only a few pockets of resistance now remained.

What is more important for the present theme, whatever the

implications for Indian security, is not that Bhutto was made powerless or proved wrong but that the final manoeuvre by Yahya Khan, the brutal crackdown by the army, converted what had been one day a most hopeful prospect for India into what became the next day a threat to her survival. The prediction by the greatest Muslim leader of India's movement for independence, Maulana Abul Kalam Azad, in *India Wins Freedom*, that the two wings of Pakistan would never be able to remain together was about to come true but in a manner which could have imperilled India's own independence.

India was too deeply immersed in her own affairs in the winter of 1970-71 to grasp the full meaning of what was happening across the border. Indian politics, on the boil for the preceding two years, was crystallizing into a dazzling recovery led by Mrs Gandhi. Little else concerned her until the first wave of refugees hit eastern India in the first days of April. There had been a few warnings in the preceding winter months but none of them roused India into full awareness. There was, for instance, a suspiciously vigorous effort by Pakistan to get permission for resuming overflights across India. These had been suspended by India following the hijacking and burning of an Indian plane in Lahore, and India had refused to allow them again until Pakistan paid compensation and handed over the hijackers. The suspension was proving extremely irksome for Pakistan. It was forced to divert its inter-wing flights to a roundabout route via Colombo, which meant delays in the urgent task of building up its army in East Pakistan. Colombo was helpfully conniving at armed forces personnel travelling disguised as civilians, but it could not reduce the flight distance. India would have been in an awkward situation if Pakistan had agreed to the two Indian conditions. She would have had no reason left for refusing the overflights. But Pakistan did not because Bhutto, now publicly feuding with Yahya Khan and widely suspected of having a hand in the hijacking, would have made political capital out of this "surrender."

Instead of accepting the Indian conditions, Pakistan tried to bring Russian pressure to bear upon India. To win Russia over, Pakistan made token "repentance": Pakistan accepted an Indian suggestion that both sides should withdraw their troops from the border; they had been brought forward by both once again on account of the tension following the hijacking. The trick succeeded and Russia urged India in the name of the Tashkent Declaration to reciprocate by allowing the overflights. At one stage the Soviet Ambassador in New Delhi nearly succeeded in persuading the Foreign Office to relent. But the Indian Ambassador in Moscow dug his toes in against any opposite "surrender." Called to the Kremlin for several discussions, some of them acrimonious, he declined to sit down with the Pakistan Ambassador as Moscow suggested. "Another ambassador may do that, not this one," he said. Moscow was ultimately forced to convey its helplessness to Pakistan. But while the intensity of Pakistan's pressure upon Russia made India suspicious it did not stir her into any precautionary, let alone preventive, action.

The same thing happened with a second warning of danger. Early in March and in protest against an army attack on a gathering of students, Mujib launched a movement of civil disobedience and non-violent non-cooperation which was greater in its sweep than similar movements by Gandhi in the 1930s which had forced the pace of India's freedom movement. It not only encompassed the whole population but also the entire civil administration, including all Bengali agencies of law and order such as the police and a para military force, the East Bengal Rifles and, extending into the army, the East Bengal Regiment, the only Bengali unit in the Pakistan armed forces. In other words, Mujib created a total confrontation between the whole of East Pakistan and the West Pakistan armed forces there.

Other law enforcing agencies having defected to Mujib, it was clear that it would be the army that would act, and that it would act ruthlessly, being commanded now by General Tikka Khan who replaced the very popular Admiral Ahsan on 2 March. Tikka Khan brought to his post as the Martial Law Administrator and Governor a reputation for brutality in a similar role in Baluchistan. Being fanatically Muslim, he would be especially hard on Hindus, and some of his wrath would be turned upon India because Mujib's movement had always been sympathetic to her. These omens too were not read in India until too late.

Because of unpardonable lacunae in her intelligence apparatus, India was out of touch with what was happening in Dacca. Until the very last moment India half believed that there would be some settlement; Yahya Khan, it was thought, would not throw away the only chance he had of keeping Pakistan together and Mujib had already said he was more in favour of substantial autonomy than complete independence. India accepted the impression given by the Russians and the Americans, who were in touch with Yahya Khan as well as Mujib, that the differences had been narrowed down and both powers were helping to narrow them further. As once again a couple of months later, India ignored the logic of the situation, from which it was plain that Yahya Khan would have to be far more self-effacing than he was to accept anything which would also be acceptable to Mujib.

Therefore India did not realize clearly enough, or not sufficiently in time, that Pakistan would not only suppress the rebellion but solve its domestic political imbalance by driving out enough East Bengalis into India and bludgeoning the rest into political quiescence for a few generations at least. Mujib, as he confirmed later, suspected this much in a flash when Yahya Khan suddenly "agreed" to all his demands, including those he had put down only as bargaining counters, and then within hours of doing so secretly left for Islamabad. But Mujib could not convey anything to India. He was immediately imprisoned.

The fact that a military build up was taking place was known in New Delhi. Apart from reports in the foreign press, Mujib himself confirmed in a public speech on 7 March that a heavy transfer of troops from West Pakistan was secretly taking place. It was important for India to prevent suppression of the Bangladesh movement and to forestall the danger of a three-front war for herself. She also had the means for forestalling it. Twice before, India had successfully forced Pakistan to backdown by concentrating troops on the border. First in 1951, when Pakistan attempted a repetition of the tribal invasion of Kashmir four years earlier; next in 1965, in the interval between the clash in Kutch and the September war. It is likely that by posing a credible threat to the western wing in February 1971, India could have forced Pakistan not to transfer forces to the east. Indian Government sources have privately maintained that this could not be done because the army was stretched out in law and order dispositions throughout the country for the elections in March. But it is difficult to believe that so much of the army had become an adjunct of the police force that it could not even have made a show of force on the border.

As soon as the first wave of refugees came in, India began to face a many-layered crisis. The financial burden of refugee relief was the least part of it, though a World Bank estimate quoted in the *New York Times* put the cost at $700 million in a full year or roughly half of India's total expenditure on defence in 1970 (and twice the direct and immediate cost of the war in December). More serious was the disruption of the economy and security of the whole of the eastern India region extending from Bihar to the borders of Tibet and Burma. At the best of times this is the most unstable part of the Indian political and economic structure. At the close of the 1960s it was especially so on account of the supercharged political unrest which had gripped West Bengal. An East Bengal rumbling with a suppressed revolt would only fall into the hands of extremist radicals, and that would drag the whole of this region down; crushed under the heel of the West Pakistan Army it would simply become another kind of a risk for India, not a less serious one: another enemy base.

At another level there was a risk to the whole of India's newly emerging domestic polity; the first sign of it was cracks in Mrs Gandhi's image as a decisive and resolute leader. Her colleagues in the cabinet and in the party began to criticize her hesitations, though as yet in muffled voices. Externally, India's credibility sank as everyone witnessed her helplessness in a matter which vitally affected her while the East Pakistan Army, defying the logistical nightmare of operating 4,800 sea kilometres away from the base of its strength, crushed a united movement of 75 million people. The position could not be more absurd for India. She knew what she wanted : democratic rule in East Bengal because that would mean rule by an Awami League government; only under such a government would the refugees, whether Hindus or Muslims, feel safe enough to go back, and under such a government they *would* go back, regardless of the conviction held in many countries till months later that Hindu refugees would never go back to Muslim East Bengal, democratic or not. But how to make East Bengal democratic?

From the very beginning, two of Mrs Gandhi's senior cabinet colleagues, the Finance Minister, Chavan, and the Defence Minister, Jagjivan Ram, opposed by the Foreign Minister,

Swaran Singh, but supported with technical arguments by two retired Generals, Harbaksh Singh and Kaul, pressed Mrs Gandhi to resort to armed action. But Army Headquarters had reservations, and these commanded attention not only because they came from people upon whom the responsibility for operations would rest but because the Chief of Army Staff, General Manekshaw, had never been the one to shirk action if he considered it feasible; as General Officer Commanding, Eastern Command, he had strongly urged action in the east in 1965 and in 1967 had boldly given the Chinese a bloody nose when they intruded into Sikkim.

In personal discussions with Mrs Gandhi he advanced three reasons for his present hesitation: that in undertaking any action while the Tibetan passes were still open or about to open with the melting of the snows, India would run greater than normal risk of temporary loss of territory to the Chinese; that, at all times, a campaign in the east, a country which is simply a network of rivers, must keep clear of the rainy season; that therefore the campaign, if started before the monsoon must be quickly concluded and for that he must have a greater superiority in numbers over the enemy than would be available if action were taken immediately. On the first point he received the assurance, which General Chaudhuri also had in 1965, that fear of temporary loss in the north need not deter India from facing up to any situation which Pakistan might create, but he carried the day with the argument that since India was being urged to take the initiative and not, as in 1965, simply respond to an initiative taken by Pakistan, she should take it at a time when the risk of any loss in the north would be at the minimum, that is when the northern passes were snowbound and the Chinese unable to intervene while a campaign in the east was swiftly fought.

On the second point also he was persuasive. Additional forces had been deployed in eastern India because of the elections; with them, the force available against East Pakistan could be taken above the division plus strength with which India normally faced East Pakistan. But Pakistan was also now much above the division plus it normally had in that wing; it was now believed to have over four divisions. Having been reinforced in a hurry and partly by air these divisions did not have their normal complement of armour and artillery. But the war in East

Pakistan was expected to be fought with lighter weapons than in the west. Advantage in armour would not help India much if she did not have a sufficient advantage in numbers for a quick victory. She could acquire it, perhaps within a few weeks, but by then the monsoon would not be sufficiently far away and India could be in difficulty if the rains broke a little earlier than normal.

The clinching argument against early action, however, came from Mrs Gandhi's civilian advisers, especially D. P. Dhar, both when he was ambassador in Moscow and later when he became the chairman of the Policy Planning Committee. It firmly rested upon a political consideration: the external and domestic political viability of Bangladesh when it became independent. If India intervened before the necessity for doing so was clearly established in the eyes of the world, Bangladesh would be regarded as an Indian invention and refused recognition by almost all countries.

For its internal viability, Bangladesh would need a political leadership which was cohesive enough to fill the gap until the return of Mujib, which was itself at that time a most uncertain event. His whereabouts and fate had been in grave doubt since his arrest on the night of 25 March, and it was not known for certain whether he had been arrested or killed outright on some pretext. The thoroughness of the genocide by the West Pakistan Army had torn enormous holes in the leadership structure of East Bengal. Those who were left were yet to emerge as a team of inheritors. It was only later, and in the course of extended discussions between D. P. Dhar and the surviving leaders of the Awami League, that a committee representing all parties of East Bengal was formed for coordinating the struggle for Bangladesh during its most intense and painful phase which was yet to come.

Out of these diverse considerations, a sequence of Indian strategies grew, some political and some military, each with its own objectives and time frame. Some of them grew up side by side; others in a sequence—one coming to the fore as another faded out. But none of the strategies which was acted upon was ever wholly absent from Indian thinking. At no time, for example, even in April or May, did India rule out war, whether declared by India or Pakistan, if all other means failed. When India told the Provisional Government of Bangladesh as early as June that it would be recognized in the course of December, she did so in the clear knowledge that this might lead to war. But even while completing preparations for it India did not consider war inevitable until the failure of Mrs Gandhi's meeting with Nixon a bare month before the actual outbreak of hostilities. Within each phase, military or political, there were subordinate alternatives, different levels of campaign for different objectives.

There were two main causes of this complex and multi-layered evolution of the Indian response.   First, it took time to assess the military capabilities of the guerrilla movement in East Bengal, and military experts took a little longer to assess it correctly than para military and political experts, which is not surprising; and second, the public response to the East Bengal tragedy was initially so great in so many countries that the Government of India took time in shedding the hope that international pressure would do the trick by itself.   Military strategy therefore replaced the political only by stages.   What was only a contingency military plan about the end of July became a subordinate alternative by the end of August, a senior alternative by the end of September and by the middle of November it was the only way.   For convenience of narration and analysis, however, on the pages which follow each phase is being treated as more distinct in its timing and sequence than it actually was.

Before the end of May, Mrs Gandhi and her closest advisers had mentally accepted the possibility of war; by the middle of July they saw it as probable.   But the ruling philosophy almost up to the middle of August was nearly wholly political, with room in it only for a para military sub-plot as a pace-setter for events. India's objective in this phase was very simple : any political solution, ranging from autonomy to independence, which would be freely accepted by the Awami League leaders elected in December; if it had their approval it would also persuade the refugees to go back, and it would not fall short of the pledge given by the Indian Government in Parliament, that it would help East Bengal attain a democratic way of life.

In its first phase this was a passive philosophy.   There was some hope in Delhi until about the middle of April that Yahya Khan, still believed to be more sinned against than sinning, would, realizing how seriously he had blundered in accepting Tikka Khan's assessment that the Awami League movement could be crushed within a matter of days, would realize the error, it was thought, and would stoop to win a settlement with the Awami League and keep a satisfied East Bengal within Pakistan. But as the terror continued, this hope evaporated. India then turned to mobilizing international pressure, and here India's political leadership committed the second of its only two lapses from the hard headed realism it showed in the entire management of this crisis from the time India was fully roused to it.

Most governments, including the USA's, responded well to India's diplomatic approaches so long as they were under the impression that India expected support for only very limited aims: that the West Pakistan Army should end the terror it had let loose in East Pakistan, that Yahya Khan should grant moderate autonomy to East Pakistan and that he should not execute Mujib. But this impression could not endure, nor did India intend it should. Even preliminary consultation with the leaders of the Awami League who had taken refuge in India convinced Indian leadership that "moderate autonomy" would not do any more. East Bengal would no longer accept what it might have in March. It now demanded almost complete independence, and this became the unstated target of India's international diplomatic campaign. But at this the minds of most governments boggled, including the Soviet Union's, and India found all of them reluctant to apply the degree of pressure Yahya Khan would need for conceding such an aim. They certainly had the means to apply the requisite pressure. But their problem never was how to apply it but how far and to what end.

From this point on, a vicious circle took over: the more international pressure proved ineffective, the closer Indian thinking moved to the only alternative—war; the more India thought of war the more she alienated official thinking in other countries. A comment often heard in India in the early summer was that if Mrs Gandhi wanted the world to pay more heed to her warnings of "disastrous consequences" of the failure of international opinion, she must make it clear that India would then have to take recourse to war; otherwise it would be thought her threats were only a means of securing more international aid in the name of refugee relief. But exactly the reverse was true. The more India made it clear that she was not ruling out war, the cooler was the reaction of most other countries. India's mistake lay in not realizing this and investing disproportionate time and effort in the hope that international opinion would, by itself, bring independence to Bangladesh.   When India integrated this effort with the alternative, war, as she did from early August onwards, it began to pay, as later pages explain.   But most governments recoiled when India brought them to the precipice of Bangladesh's independence, especially if secured with the help of the Indian Army.   Their reasons varied but the effect was identical for this country.

The attitude hardened in many countries when in the last week of July India refused to have UN observers on the Indian side of the border with East Pakistan.   Along with Mrs Gandhi's blunt statement at the end of November that India could not expect justice from the UN, it became one of the causes of the thunderingly adverse vote which India faced in the UN Assembly when the war broke out.   India argued that no observers were needed in an area which was being visited daily by foreign journalists and almost every week by a variety of foreign delegations, including some from the UN.   But those so inclined were only confirmed in their suspicion that India had something to hide there, perhaps evidence that, as alleged by Yahya Khan, the rebellion in East Pakistan was being instigated by India.

India's principal objection was that by such methods what was a case of genocide by the West Pakistan Army, resulting in demographic inundation of eastern India, would be converted into another Indo-Pakistan feud and relegated to the limbo where all the old feuds between the two countries are rotting already— in some rubbish heap of UN documents.   But this made the uninformed suspect that this must in fact be just one of those innumerable disputes.   The objection was also seen as inconsistent with a statement by the Indian Foreign Minister in Parliament on 28 June that at some future date India would be willing to take the problem of the refugees and Bangladesh to the United Nations. The statement was hedged with many qualifications but even then was strongly at variance with the known direction of Indian policy; it did not help to enlarge the credibility of Indian statements.

On the other hand, Yahya Khan scored in many capitals which were predisposed to believe him, especially Washington, with statements which, for all that India knew them to be deceptive, appeared plausible to those who did not know the local scene very well. He said he would take back the refugees, but he added there were only two million of them; this would leave eight million in India's lap. He promised to call the national assembly to meet but this was now only a rump; the majority of its members had either been killed or driven out of the country, nearly a 100 had been declared unlawful by Yahya Khan in a first short list with promise of another, and of the seats thus declared vacant, more than half had been filled by "uncontested" elections held under the army's boot. A civilian puppet was appointed Prime Minister in Islamabad and another as Governor of East Pakistan in place of Tikka Khan, but all power remained respectively with Yahya Khan as the President in Islamabad and with Tikka Khan first and then General Niazi as chiefs of the eastern army. In October Yahya Khan announced that the national assembly would meet in December but without the Awami League, which he had declared illegal soon after the army struck in East Pakistan, and without the National Awami Party, Bhutto's main opponent in West Pakistan, which was shortly to be declared illegal. Even so, the decisions of the assembly would be subject to his approval.

But Yahya's most persuasive trick was that soon after some of these announcements were made criticism appeared in the Pakistan press that these were dangerous concessions to rebels who were masquerading as democrats. Since the press was then under the direct and strict control of martial law authorities, this criticism could have appeared only with their approval and could be meant only for convincing distant observers that he was becoming dangerously liberal in his old age. The Indian Ambassador in Washington warned his government that with its willing suspension of disbelief in Yahya Khan the US Government was ready to be persuaded and to impress upon India that she also should be. This cancelled out the reassurance value of an earlier report by him that according to a recorded decision in the State Department, "if the United States had to choose in future between India and Pakistan, it will choose India." Against this background a report, disturbing for India, appeared in the Pakistan press that Yahya Khan had invited Nixon to mediate between India and Pakistan.

On every count that mattered, India found Washington dangerously unfriendly throughout this crisis. When Kissinger came to New Delhi in the first week of July, he warned Mrs Gandhi that China would intervene on behalf of Yahya Khan if India intervened on behalf of Mujib, but he added reassuringly that although as between India and Pakistan the USA would be neutral it would support India in the event of a Chinese attack. But when he met the Indian Ambassador on his return home from his secret visit to Peking, he said the USA would stay neutral in the event of a Chinese attack, and he accentuated his expectation that China would intervene against an Indian intervention. When he and Nixon met Mrs Gandhi in Washington in the first week of November he changed his assessment again (in the meantime he had made his second visit to Peking). Now he considered a Chinese intervention unlikely but he underscored the unavailability of US help if the Chinese did come down the Himalayan passes again.

US prognostications about China were of less interest to India— she could have no more read China through US eyes than heiroglyphics through a distorting prism—than the reasons why they oscillated so much. After Mrs Gandhi had visited Washington the established Indian reading came to be that at no time was there any chance of the USA assisting India against China. The domestic mood against foreign involvements would not allow that, apart from Nixon's overpowering bias in favour of Pakistan and the investment he was making in his new China diplomacy. The only reason why Kissinger suggested the contrary in July was that with this assurance he would be able to make India more receptive to his advice that India should keep out of Pakistan's domestic crisis. Since this did not pay—Mrs Gandhi gave no assurance either to Kissinger or Nixon that India would not intervene— the opposite tactic was tried, of warning India, in the hope that it would deter her, that US assistance would not be available. Since India did not show proper fright even now, and Mrs Gandhi said even more firmly in Washington than in New Delhi that she did not think the Chinese would move, the real US assessment of Chinese intentions was given out while US neutrality was emphasized in order not to cause any offence in Peking and to preserve such chance as there yet might be of deterring India.

The US Government was more constant in what it said about Pakistan; in New Delhi and at home Kissinger consistently said that given time the USA would bring Yahya Khan round. But equally consistently India's assessment continued to be that what he meant by this was very different from what India wanted. He confirmed in New Delhi that no US representative had been able to meet Mujib, let alone ensure his release or negotiations for a settlement with him. Mrs Gandhi told Kissinger in New Delhi that if Mujib were released and discussions held with him, there was some chance as yet of a reasonable settlement. Kissinger said the US could give no assurance on that, and Mrs Gandhi bluntly warned him that in that case India would have no alternative but to step in with assistance to the Mukti Bahini.

Mrs Gandhi repeated her plea with Nixon in November, although she added that by then she was much more pessimistic about a settlement than in July. She also stated, more clearly than to Kissinger, that if the international community proved unwilling or unable to act effectively India would have no option but to act on her own to look after her essential interests. But she was unable to shift Nixon out of his position, which continued to move around three points, each more unacceptable to India than the rest: that both sides should withdraw their troops from the border, that there should be bilateral talks between India and Pakistan, and that in the meantime UN observers should be posted on both sides of the India-East Pakistan border for the (unstated) purpose of ensuring that India did not assist the rebellion in East Pakistan. This position differed from Kissinger's in July only in that Nixon said more emphatically that Yahya Khan was moving in the right direction and should be given more time.

Nixon did not specify the time he thought Yahya Khan should have, but by any reckoning it would be enough, as Mrs Gandhi saw it, for a three-fold American objective: that the opportunity should pass, may be never to recur for another year at least, for India to give sufficient assistance to the Mukti Bahini at a time when the risk of a Chinese intervention would be at its minimum; that the Mukti Bahini should be sufficiently softened up by the West Pakistan Army and demoralized by the absence of adequate Indian support; and that Yahya Khan's regime should be rescued out of the crisis. The net consequence for India would have been that the bulk of the refugees would have indefinitely remained a burden upon her; they would have gone back to Bangladesh but not to East Pakistan.   In a brief outline the Indian Ambassador in Washington had given a similar assessment of American aims the previous month, when he had reported Nixon's willingness to be misled by Yahya Khan's spurious democratic credentials.   Mrs Gandhi was now able to see these aims in their fullness and at first hand.   Nixon was to claim later in a message to Congress that he had put a time bound programme for a political settlement to Mrs Gandhi.   But this was specifically denied by Mrs Gandhi within two days of her meeting  with Nixon and no one had contradicted her then.   In the course of an NBC interview on 7 November she was asked: "Did the United States suggest some plan of action which you felt you could not accept?"   Mrs Gandhi replied: "No plan of action has been suggested to us."

Mrs Gandhi explained to Nixon also, as earlier and with greater success to the British Prime Minister and the French President, that although it was probably too late already, there might yet be some chance of a political settlement if negotiations were held with Mujib.   But she added that he would negotiate only if he were first released unconditionally.   She did not think, and told Nixon so, that Mujib would negotiate under the duress of continued imprisonment, and even if he did he would be repudiated by his people and any "settlement" made by him in these conditions would be torn to shreds in the streets of Dacca. Nixon claimed that pressure was being put upon Yahya Khan, and with some success he implied, to negotiate with Mujib.   But when these reports reached New Delhi senior American diplomatic officials known to be shocked by Yahya Khan's actions commented that this was most unlikely.   They did not think that Yahya Khan would commit political suicide, which must surely follow if he released Mujib, and that the State Department and the White House had every reason to know this.   Mujib also confirmed in the interview he gave me in Dacca that he did not sense at any time that Yahya Khan would release him and no one on behalf of Yahya Khan, Bhutto or anyone else, approached him with any suggestion for a negotiated settlement.   He saw Bhutto only after his release, and Yahya Khan never after 24 March.

Another claim by Nixon, repeated at the meeting with Mrs Gandhi, was contradicted by Bhutto although it was received by India with credibility when Nixon first made it. Nixon said American intervention had saved Mujib from execution even though it had not secured his release till then. But Bhutto disclosed after he became President of Pakistan that Mujib was about to be executed on 16 December but was saved by Bhutto. But it was Kissinger who brought out the hollowness of American claims regarding efforts made on behalf of Mujib. At a White House meeting on 5 December to decide US strategy during an impending Security Council meeting on the Indo-Pakistan war, Kissinger said, as quoted by Jack Anderson: "We will go along in general terms with reference to political accommodation in East Pakistan, but we will certainly not imply or suggest any specifics such as the release of Mujib."

Consistently with such a stand the US Administration, inspired in this by Nixon himself as reported in the US press, publicly opposed and in private diplomacy sought to reverse, while refusing even earlier to go along with, a decision by the Pakistan Aid Consortium to withhold further aid to Pakistan unless it reached a political settlement with the east. The administration also allowed previously committed US arms shipments to continue despite the precedent set by the US itself in 1965 when economic aid as well as previously committed supplies of arms or spares were immediately discontinued for both countries upon war breaking out between India and Pakistan. The administration justified its opposition to the consortium decision both on the ground that this amounted to using the leverage of aid for influencing the recipient's domestic political policies and for the reason that by continuing aid the United States would retain some leverage in Pakistan. On this the *New York Times* commented on 30 June: "You cannot have it both ways."

More ominous than the consistency in Nixon's preference for Pakistan, especially for Yahya Khan, were the variations in the attitude of the US Administration. It supported Yahya Khan more when he appeared to be winning than when he did not. The initial US assessment was that resort to armed action by the West Pakistan Army would mean immediate loss of the eastern wing, which would either join India or become independent (it never rated the chances of a pro-Chinese takeover as high as some in India did); therefore it urged Yahya Khan all it could up to 25 March to come to terms with Mujib. At that time it also considered Mujib to be a safe bet for America. After all, he was brought up in politics by Suhrawardy who, as the Prime Minister of Pakistan, had once said the Americans would find "no more faithful friend than Pakistan." In fact, so close were Mujib's relations with the Americans in Dacca that there were rumours of his election being financed by them and, as Mrs Gandhi said during one of her speeches in Washington, Mujib was once alleged to be an "American stooge."

When Yahya Khan struck despite American advice, the first official reaction in Washington was very adverse. But it began to improve after the end of April when it looked that the army had mastered the first flush of protest. It faltered for a time in the face of the outburst of American public opinion against General Tikka Khan's terror, or when it began to appear that the army would be in difficulties as the monsoon rains came down. But it more than recovered when, with the rains over and American public opinion also diverted to other issues, the army proved that it was still in command. There was the same up and down curve during the war in December and, as seen from India, there was a distinct possibility that if General Niazi had not packed up so soon and the Indian Army had been held a little longer at the gates of Dacca, more would have been heard of the Seventh Fleet.

However, what distressed India more was not American hostility but Soviet ambivalence. Not only was Soviet support expected more; it was needed more. Its absence hurt doubly. Once war became a clear possibility, the question which worried India more than almost any other was where would the balance lie between the probability of Chinese support for Pakistan (it was only in the autumn that the probability was downgraded to a remote possibility) and the possibility of a Soviet desire not to lose Pakistan. New Delhi was not inclined to doubt, as it had not since about the end of 1969, that if it had to choose between India and Pakistan, Russia would choose India, especially if China took a hand in tipping the scale of Russian priorities. For the present, however, the choice was between Yahya Khan and Mujib, not between Yahya Khan and Mrs Gandhi, and Russia seemed not to think that there was much to choose between the former pair in terms of Soviet priorities although Yahya Khan undoubtedly had been guilty of unspeakable crimes which had drawn scathing Russian criticism, but nothing more tangible.

American fondness for Mujib at the start of the year was Mujib's first disqualification in the eyes of the Russians, his formerly right of centre policies another. But the third and most important was that to the Russians he did not appear to be the man of tomorrow. Like the Americans, they too thought it possible that Yahya Khan would re-establish himself in the east, and that would leave out in the cold those who had backed Mujib; the Russians were reluctant to take this risk in an area to which they attached some importance because of China's proximity and earlier interest in it. Hence their anxious advice to Yahya Khan and Mrs Gandhi not to let the situation get out of hand.

Podgorny's letter on 2 April was the first strongly worded foreign letter to reach Yahya Khan. But it did not go far in urging autonomy for Bangladesh, much less independence, and even as it was it was not followed up by the Russians for quite some time. Political parties in West Pakistan, such as the National Awami Party, were basing their policies on a clearer expectation that Pakistan would break up than the Soviet Union was. On the other hand within a few days of signing the Indo-Soviet Treaty the authoritative Soviet journal, *New Times*, offered a similar treaty to Pakistan, pledging Soviet support for the territorial integrity of Pakistan if only it would leave SEATO and CENTO.

At the Inter-Parliamentary Union Conference in Paris in the first week of September the Soviet Union opposed an Indian resolution condemning Yahya Khan but supported an American resolution, strongly opposed by India, which called on both India and Pakistan "to exercise restraint." Britain and a number of other countries represented at this conference showed much more sustained sympathy for the Indian position than the Russians did. As late as the last week of November authoritative commentators in the Soviet press were strongly urging India and Pakistan not to run the risk of war and President Podgorny used the strong expression in New Delhi on 1 October: "We consider the further sliding towards a military conflict must be prevented." The Soviet Union was firm in condemning the West Pakistan Army's atrocities in the east and in demanding a political settlement, more firm than all other countries except Britain and

France—and West Germany until it showed disappointment over Mrs Gandhi's refusal to rule out war during her talks with Brandt. But on the means of achieving such a settlement, or on what India should do if there was no settlement, Russia's position remained very different from India's.

The Russians never doubted that India was faced with a terrible problem and that no one was doing enough to ease it for her, let alone to solve it. On this they were clear before and elaborately clear during Mrs Gandhi's talks in Moscow at the end of September. India also had the confidence that if in pursuit of the means chosen by her she ran into trouble the Soviet Union would help her in every way it could. Conversely, the Russians had the confidence, justified alike by the Indians and by later events, that India would choose the means with a full sense of responsibility. It was this mutual trust which made it possible for the two countries to sign the Indo-Soviet Treaty at the time they did. They signed it in the clear knowledge that it would increase the likelihood of war because, with the fear of Chinese retaliation taken care of by the treaty, every Indian would expect and demand that the government take military action if no other means availed India. Far from discouraging this expectation, both Indians and the Russians made it stronger by demonstrating that the treaty was in operation already. Indo-Soviet talks in the last week of October were officially described as being in terms of the treaty; it was disclosed soon after that a Soviet military team would visit India shortly to assess India's needs; India's Foreign Minister announced that India could count on Soviet aid; the Soviet Foreign Minister declared that no country could now decide its policy towards India or the Soviet Union without taking the treaty into account. But in spite of all that, what the Russians really expected and desired India to do they made very clear during the talks Mrs Gandhi had with the Soviet trio, Podgorny, Kosygin and (especially) Brezhnev.

The Russians were tireless in trying to persuade Mrs Gandhi out of any intention to intervene militarily. That even Brezhnev did so was a particular disappointment for Mrs Gandhi. India, unlike some western countries, did not see Brezhnev as someone apart from the other two Soviet leaders. In the Indian experience the three were a troika, though it was known in New Delhi that with regard to the rest of the world there was a sort of division of labour between them. But Brezhnev's increasing lead over the other two and his forceful impact upon the government's policies from his position in the party were fully appreciated. Therefore it had been noticed with some satisfaction that he was the least inclined to tolerate China's influence in Pakistan and in the present crisis was more fully alive to the danger India faced and the bonus China would get if Pakistan succeeded in imposing the burden of its own problems upon India. Mrs Gandhi expected that he would more readily see India's urgent need to take effective measures; more readily than Kosygin in particular who was the author of the Tashkent Summit and for more than five years had been committed to the idea of carrying Pakistan along with India. At Mrs Gandhi's insistence the dates of her visit to Moscow and of Brezhnev's tour of eastern Europe were adjusted to ensure that the two would meet and he would join his two colleagues in their joint discussions with Mrs Gandhi.

But when the discussions began all three of them advised India against any military action. Insisting on an analogy which was rather inept because of the diametrically opposite attitude of the entire population, they urged Mrs Gandhi to remember Viet Nam. (When Mrs Gandhi pointed out that Pakistan might attack India instead, Brezhnev again said "Remember Viet Nam," though here, it is thought, he meant that while military action should be avoided, if it had to be taken it must be brought to a swift conclusion.) But until the very end, until confounded by clear evidence to the contrary, they were unconvinced that India had either the military sinews or political nerve for the kind of campaign she would have to conduct. Their perception of India's domestic political viability and of Mrs Gandhi had immensely improved since the elections in March; but a military campaign and the trans-border responsibilities it might involve later on were a different matter; they were most uncertain how India would measure up to these.

In particular they must have wondered, though this is only a surmise, whether India would have the confidence to remove sufficient forces from the northern front to bring the campaign against Pakistan to a swift conclusion. If India showed the slightest evidence of being bogged down, would China remain reluctant to intervene, and what would be the American role, in which pro-Pakistan sympathies would now be buttressed_by an increasingly pro-Chinese stance?   This was worrisome.

These doubts were the substance of their misgivings about the consequences of an Indo-Pakistan war, even assuming that it led to the separation of East Pakistan.   If the consequences were uncertain, was the risk of war worth taking in the first place? If it was not, was India wise in giving  any assistance to the Mukti Bahini if there was a risk that this would provoke Pakistan into the kind of retaliatory attack upon India which Mrs Gandhi herself had  indicated as probable in the course of her talks? These questionings made her discussions with the Russian leaders a most strenuous exercise for Mrs Gandhi, and it is a tribute to her unyielding will that she stood up to it in separate as well as simultaneous confrontations with the members of the troika.

Ultimately, Mrs Gandhi's perseverance won.   She succeeded in convincing them on three major points:  that the people of Bangladesh had a deep and durable commitment to freedom, were willing to make heavy sacrifices for it, and were increasingly becoming more battle worthy; that Mujib had a firm hold on the imagination of his people, and if only he could return he would be able to lead a united nation; and that independent Bangladesh under  Mujib would not be pro-western or  pro-Chinese.   More immediately important was the recognition she forced out of the unwilling troika that India had the right to choose and was determined to adopt any means she might have to for resolving the crisis which had arisen for her.   In the joint statement issued after her visit, the right was written into a unilateral Indian para, while in the very next—a unilateral Russian para— the Russians stuck to the position Podgorny had taken in his letter to Yahya Khan on 2 April.   But the Russians had to take "into account" the firm position Mrs Gandhi adopted.   It is for this reason, as India understands it, that although in many statements right up to the end of the war in December the Russians continued to oppose the use of military means both by India and Pakistan, they gradually began to disinvest in the unity of Pakistan after the end of September.   They made only one statement thereafter in support of it—in the joint communique they signed with Algeria early in October. But they probably did so for the reason they gave Mrs Gandhi and which she found convincing, that the Algerians had insisted they would otherwise issue a much stronger statement unilaterally; of all the Arabs the Algerians remained the most hostile to India for assisting in the break-up of Pakistan.

Mrs Gandhi's visit to Moscow marked the opening of India's final effort, and at the highest level, to find a non-military answer to her problem by mobilizing international pressure against Yahya Khan. By the time it reached its apogee, in Washington, early in November, the visit could be said to have been made too late. With only one month remaining, not the most willing government in the world could have marshalled its diplomatic forces adequately for reducing the obstinate general in Islamabad. But this is not so. Not until the last ten days of November did India expect a war so soon. She certainly did not desire it so soon. The beginning of January would have suited India better; the snow on the northern passes would have been thicker by then, the ground in East Pakistan would have been harder after the rains, which in this season had gone on, unexpectedly, right up to the end of October, and in every respect India's preparations would have been more complete than they were when Mrs Gandhi set out. This would have given the world time enough, two months at least. Secondly, those who needed time and were prepared to use it had been given time enough by earlier events; since April or May there had been no reason for them to be ignorant of what was happening in East Pakistan or what India was facing.

Therefore, what was needed now was not persuasion by a higher level emissary from India but clearer warning of where India stood. This was the only pressure remaining to be applied upon the will of the other countries, and Mrs Gandhi would not have been in a position to apply it until she knew India's position herself. It was not much before Mrs Gandhi set out that India had a reasonably clear idea how far and to what end she could use the alternative of military intervention if pleading for diplomatic intervention by other countries did not get her very far.

By the middle of July, four hard decisions had been clearly taken by the government. They had surfaced in the Prime Minister's thinking even earlier but took a little time to become committed policies of the government. The first was that the refugees must go back; India would not be indefinitely saddled with them. The second, which followed, was that power must pass to the Awami League leaders, within or without Pakistan as they may accept but with the assurance given them by India that should they opt for independence they would have India's support; by June India had told even the Provisional Government of Bangladesh, formed in April, that she would recognize it some time in December. Third, for bringing about transfer of power to the League, India should not hesitate to use her forces, whether directly or indirectly through assistance to the Mukti Bahini, but first should concentrate on mobilizing international pressure. And fourth, in order that the resulting political regime in the cast might have the widest internal and international acceptance, the severity of Pakistani atrocities and the burning desire for freedom among the people of Bangladesh should be allowed to stand out clearly in the eyes of the world and in the minds of the people of East Bengal.

But the most activist decision in this, willingness to use force, was lacking as yet in its guiding mechanism; no one could say how far it should go and what course it should follow. It had been accepted in April or May that the eviction of Pakistani forces in the east would not be possible in the circumstances which existed then. But in what circumstances would it be possible? Could it be at all achieved at one go, or should India accept an intermediate objective? Assuming she should, should it be given as an aim to the armed forces or left to the Mukti Bahini? If the latter, should India confine herself only to giving assistance, and if so should it be given only at the border or deep inside, and only by India's para military forces or also—or only—by the regular army?

Two schools of thought contended in New Delhi during this period, one advocating and the other opposing the liberation of a large slice of territory in which a provisional government should take over and await recognition till India felt she could face the risk, as she felt she could some time after December, that Pakistan might declare war following recognition of Bangladesh by India.

The most the army was prepared for at this stage was to beef up and speed up "Operation Jackpot" for training more guerrillas and inducting them into East Bengal, not participating itself in a partial liberation plan. It was for this that it incurred the gossip which went round Delhi in the course of the summer that General Manekshaw was running cold in the feet. But he had sound reasons for his hesitations. His unstated argument was that when the chips of international diplomacy were down India's political leadership would not show the will to retain what was won in a limited move; it would be Haji Pir again on a bigger scale, with a bigger loss of army lives in vain. Suspicion about the will and stamina of the political leadership has never been much below the surface in the armed forces. But his stated objection was more specific. The undefined and porous border of a "liberated" area would be under constant attack by the Pakistan Army, which would be able to bring in reinforcements since, without a regular war, India could not blockade the coast. This would be a most enervating position. The initiative would remain with the Pakistan Army; at a time of its choosing it would force India to choose between going in in full force to defend the provisional government or let it be extinguished by a superior enemy force.

But the army found its best ally in a political argument: that so long as the Pakistan Army held out in Dacca and Indian forces were seen to be the main defenders of the provisional government, Bangladesh would not even stand out as a clear emotional entity, let alone a legal or diplomatic one.

The opposite argument was that with full scale commitment of the regular forces deferred in any case until early next year, India could not sit idle in the meantime. For Indian forces, regular or irregular, and even more so for the Mukti Bahini guerrillas, there must be a definite aim and objective which was attainable not too far hence; otherwise their will would disintegrate. As for the position being enervating, it would be so for the enemy too and by the sheer attrition to which he would be exposed 4,800 kilometres from the base of his main strength, he would be forced to come to a settlement with Awami League leaders. Besides, with the help of the BSF the Mukti Bahini had already captured some well defined enclaves in the north-eastern and south-western corners and shown it could hold them against counter-attacks by the Pakistan Army.

In the end it was Pakistan which resolved this controversy for India. It resorted to steps which made total liberation in one sweep an attainable objective. In the course of early summer, India gave out hints that capture of a slice of territory as compensation and for rehabilitating the refugees on East Bengal soil might well be an immediate Indian objective. One of the hints was an official note to Pakistan which, as annotated by an official source for the Indian press, could only bear this meaning. Simultaneously there was a hint of a more menacing variety: the training of East Bengal guerrillas on Indian soil was rapidly stepped up as they were found to be eager, highly motivated, and, as their increasing operations deep inside East Bengal suggested, quick to profit from the training given them in more sophisticated sabotage and more organized fighting. Yahya Khan took the hint and on 19 July he declared that he would launch an all-out war if India tried to capture any part of East Pakistan as a base for a "puppet" government. But militarily more important was his deep conviction, and that of his generals in the east, that this is all that India would do. The conviction led him and them to take the decision which opened the gateway to Dacca. Believing that the Indians would only capture the rim, Pakistan moved its forces out to the rim—and not only moved them, but dug them in there.

In the course of May and June the Pakistani Army, now enlarged from one division to a little over four, fanned out from the few towns and cantonments into which it had been hemmed in during April by the first flush of guerrilla insurgency. It completed the operations before the rains. As its hold on the countryside improved, it started sending out to positions closer to the border units of Pakistani para military forces, such as the Razakaars, with some leavening of regular elements too. But from early August onwards it carried out a move of critical significance which sealed its fate. It moved out in bulk towards the border, building up strong defensive positions in and around a ring of towns stretching from Jessore in the south-west to Rangpur and Dinajpur in the north, Mymensingh and Sylhet in the north-east, Comilla and Maynamati in the east and Chittagong in the south-east. Enough stocking up was done in all these towns to make each garrison self-sufficient for a couple of months at least.

This move, completed by about early October, made sense from the viewpoint of the appreciation Yahya Khan had made about India's maximum goal. If encroachments, forays and nibblings were all that the Indians would do, it would be best to plug their routes of ingress, and to do it in strength so that every foray could be punished severely. By strong counter forays into Indian territory, the enemy should be constantly kept off-balance and

prevented from building up his raiding parties and bases. Terror
and light forces could be used in combination to hold the interior
once outside infiltrations were checked at the border.    The contrary strategy of building up an inner fortress would have a triple
disadvantage: the rimland would be lost, the enemy would acquire a closer approach to Dacca, and the world would see that
Pakistan had no control over large chunks of its territory. Of
course Yahya Khan knew, and had said, that any Indian attempt
to take even a part of East Pakistan would lead to an all-out war.
But this, he believed, would be a war in the west; for a variety of
reasons, especially fear of Chinese counter-intervention, India
would not march its army into the eastern wing.

From India's point of view the move-out had an overwhelming
double advantage.   Infiltrators would still be able to get in,
since the entire population would be on their side—no guerrilla
movement anywhere has ever had it so good in this respect—
and once in they would have only a softly held interior to play
havoc with, preparing it for the day when the Indian Army
would make an all-out assault. Secondly, it would be easy to cut
the spread out Pakistani shield into sectors by cleverly placed
slicing movements and thrusts, and soon there would be no coordination left in the enemy force because a quick fall back on
Dacca would be prevented by the nature of the terrain and poor
logistics.   This tilted the balance in Delhi heavily in favour of an
all-out army operation, aiming at total liberation at one go.

So neatly did Yahya Khan's thinking fit into Manekshaw's
planning that in retrospect it would seem the Indian signals
about a limited aim were only a stratagem; but one must put it
down as one among many lucky breaks which the Indian side
had in this war because no one even privately claims credit for it
among all those responsible for the higher conduct of the war who
were interviewed in confidence during the work on this book.
The limited aim was seriously considered and information about
it was not deliberately leaked.   It only so happened that the
enemy response was such that it helped to lift the aim of Indian
military planning to a higher level.   Pakistan had every reason
to realize later that it had underestimated Indian intentions.
But by that time it was too late to reverse its deployment plan.

But it should be explained that the dichotomy between the two
Indian strategies, the large and the limited, was by no means

total. Just as the political and military strategies, although alternatives, grew up side by side, so did the strategies for limited and total liberation.   It was under the command of the army that the Border Security Force, which had been substantially expanded, was operating inside East Pakistan in April and May. Next, attacks ranging deep into East Pakistan had been the accepted strategy ever since it was decided, soon after 1965, that India would not abstain in the east if a war broke out again.   The most important new element in this strategy, a multiple prong aimed at Dacca from the east by a new corps formation, was rapidly built up during all those weeks when it was being debated in New Delhi whether Dacca should be the objective at all as yet, and at least from early August if not a week or two earlier a full-scale war was clearly contemplated as a possibility by the political as well as military leadership.   The likelihood of Pakistan launching it in desperation increased as its operations against the Mukti Bahini proved unavailing, and as early as June the Commander of India's Eastern Command in Calcutta was alerted that this might lead to a major war. But it was not until about the end of September that he was told he need no longer think of capturing a lodgement area only.   On the other hand the idea of taking such an area, never abandoned right from the time in June and July when the BSF and Mukti Bahini began to show they could capture and hold it, would have held the floor for some  time longer if Pakistan had not struck on 3 December.

It is to the credit of the political, civilian, and military managers of this war on the Indian side that once they were shocked into a full alert in April they always had more than a couple of fully worked out plans.   It is the emphasis on any one of them at any given time that distinguished it from the others.

Once total liberation became militarily feasible, and as India's pleadings with the world increasingly proved unavailing, the previous four decision plan was revised and uplifted.  No part of it was rejected; that was not necessary.  But it was incorporated into a larger whole.  The first element in it was made sharper still.  From the second, the possibility of the Awami League agreeing to remain within Pakistan was retained only as historical junk; there was no longer any possibility of it. The third was elevated from assisting the Mukti Bahini and other guerrillas to absorbing them  in an overall Indian military scheme.   It was decided that the fourth had achieved consummation because anyone not convinced so far was not going to be until presented with a *fait accompli*. The enlarged new plan stood as follows:

1. India must try to convince other countries that a political settlement could mean nothing less than independence now.

2. Since few countries did much about the previous lower level objective, India must prepare to make every effort required for ensuring full independence on her own.

3. Since this would inevitably mean India's armed intervention, military preparations for it must be completed very quickly.

4. Consistently with the security of India's northern and western fronts, the maximum force level must be built up in the east for the speedy campaign required by the given geopolitical circumstances.

5. Therefore the risk of providing any provocation in the north even by mistake must be strictly avoided, which partly explains the (unconvincing because untrue) slant in all official Indian publicity about the Indo-Soviet Treaty, that it had nothing to do with the particular circumstances in which it was signed.

6. For the same reason there should be no Indian adventure in the west—a decision about which much was to be heard in December—but use should be made of the present opportunity to make this front as secure against future attacks as possible.

These were the aims which the political leadership gave the armed forces. The Joint Chiefs Committee, and particularly General Manekshaw, who came closer to functioning as India's Chief of the Defence Staff than anyone else before him, devised a matching military strategy (which is better discussed in the next chapter). But there was one objective which straddled politics and war: that India should not appear to be the aggressor.

It was accepted now as a high probability that there would be a war. Mrs Gandhi did not hesitate to admit in public that she contemplated it; the admission was plain in her replies to questions at her "Meet the Press" interview during her visit to Washington. But it was as likely—probably more—that Paki-

stan would start it.   The problem was how to make this likelihood a certainty.

In part this was a very specific and concrete military problem.
The Indo-Soviet Treaty envisaged assistance in the event of
aggression against either country, not by it, and India did not
wish that its expectation of Soviet support in the event of Chinese
intervention should be weakened by any Soviet suspicion that
the war was started by India.   In the discussions which preceded
the signing of the treaty the Soviet Union concurred with the
Indian view that the treaty would apply if Pakistan, with or without Chinese support, attacked India in retaliation against Indian
assistance to the Mukti Bahini; the Soviet Union regarded the
Bahini as a liberation movement and  support to it as just and
defensible.   But aggression by India in the accepted sense of the
word might have been viewed by Moscow in a different light.

In part, however, this was a moral problem, and this aspect
of it was neither dubious nor unprecedented.   Henry L. Stimson recalls in his *Diary* that before wheeling America into World
War II, Roosevelt asked his cabinet: "Where moral objectives
make American involvement in war against an  amoral
enemy desirable, how can the enemy be manoeuvred into firing
the first shot?"   Later, in 1946, Stimson said to a Committee of
the US Congress: "We realized that in order to have the full
support of the American people it was desirable to make sure
that the Japanese be the first to start fighting so that there should
remain no doubt in anyone's mind as to who were the aggressors."
India's objective was similar.   Only it proved easier of achievement.

The moral condemnation of Pakistan had been more nearly
universal than any country's.   A state of near civil war had
spilled over the border from East Pakistan into India and now it
was genuinely difficult to see where East Bengali actions ended and
Indian began.   Even clashes clearly recognizable as Indo-Paki-
stani were escalating in a manner that it was a matter of opinion
as to who began them and who stepped them up.   But above all
that, it was obvious to those who cared to see and understand the
facts that India had no interest in starting a war just then whereas
Pakistan was facing an increasingly tight choice between waging
an open war against India and losing East Bengal to a confusing
mixture of Indians and East Bengalis.   These factors would drive

Pakistan, not India, to a declaration of war.

But as an added precaution Indian forces on the border, ably assisted in their designs by Pakistani provocations, fought a number of retaliatory and initiating actions in the course of November which made the choice before Yahya Khan unbearably tighter. The biggest of these was fought at Boyra, in the Jessore sector north-east of Calcutta on 22 November, in which the Pakistanis lost 13 tanks and three Sabre jets which were shot down by a flight of four Indian Gnats. This was the equivalent of the Kutch action of 1965—but in reverse; it was Indians who were doing the testing this time. The meaning of the test went home in Pakistan when, in reply to Pakistan's charges of Indian aggression, an Indian spokesman said: "It is Bengali guerrillas who are described as the Indian Army."

On 23 November Pakistan declared a state of emergency. Two days later Yahya Khan described the military situation as "very bad" and then added his famous prophecy that "ten days hence I might not be here. I will be off fighting a war." Indian pressure thus succeeded in triggering off a declaration by him which, in retrospect, became a self-indictment when on 3 December Pakistan launched the war with a pre-emptive air strike effort.

## Military Options

Before the Joint Chiefs of Staff Committee could even begin to prepare India's strategy, they asked the one question to which no one had an answer yet: When would the war be? India's intelligence apparatus was now far superior to what it had been ever before. The whole intelligence community had been brought together under a single apex of tight coordination presided over by the Vice-Chief of Army Staff. Alongside, there was a first class Research and Analysis Organization, and going right down the military and civilian pyramids there was close intelligence coordination between the three services and between them and the civilian machinery, including the BSF. But the question the Chiefs were asking was bigger than all of them put together could answer with the precision required. Later in the year they were going to be able to refine their predictions. In fact, they were going to be able to focus on three narrow areas of high probability—the early days of November, January or December, in that order. But earlier in the year it was not possible for them to predict the quarter or the month, let alone the week.

Yet, in a theatre of war dominated by snow conditions on the Himalayan passes and tropical rain conditions at the southern end, everything depended upon the time of the year, from national strategy to tactics at the level of brigades and battalions. The weather could take a major hand in deciding such a large scale question as to whether the Chinese could come in and in what strength. It could decide the intermediate scale question as to the lines of thrust which the enormous rivers and waterways of East Bengal would allow the theatre commander to exploit. It could also decide such questions of detail as to whether the corps commanders could count on ground communications or would have to depend upon air transport, or whether the ground conditions would allow brigade or battalion commanders to use heavy, medium, or amphibious armour.

Two key elements of the probable Indian strategy in the east depended upon the time available before the operations began, whether by India's choice or Pakistan's. First, the building up of a new corps formation to the east of East Bengal, which was to be the most important single attack element. Second, the training and deployment of the rapidly developing guerrilla forces which were to play a part which has yet to be fully appreciated though it has a far reaching meaning for India.

It could be foreseen even in April that war fought before the monsoons or after or at the turn of the year could be three different kinds of war. But which kind would it be? India's own preference was the end of the year or a couple of weeks later. The snow factor in the north would then be at its most favourable, the rain would no longer be an impediment in the south, the ground would have hardened sufficiently after the preceding monsoons for the Indian advantage in armour, acquired after the stepped up deployment around East Pakistan, to be in full effect. But the chances were that the enemy too knew all this very well and would not be sitting idle to let India pick up the time of her choice.

From the likelihood that the enemy would take the initiative and the possibility that he would take it quickly arose two problems for India. First, her forces had to be on balance and ready even while doing the extensive reorganization and building up that her ultimate plans required. This was especially difficult for the eastern sector of the eastern theatre, opposite the Dacca-Sylhet-Comilla triangle, where an existing corps had to be split into two, a new corps headquarters had to be raised and forces looking to the north and north-east towards Tibet had to be turned a hundred and eighty degrees to look south and south-west but all the while retaining capability to face the Chinese at short notice should the need arise. The second difficulty was that all build up had to be surreptitiously done and none of it done so far in advance of the probable date of deployment in action that it may be done at leisure. In India's given conditions a war with Pakistan always involved tricky problems of internal security. The build up could not be attempted too openly, nor accomplished so far in advance that it should give away the probable plan to the enemy. The forces could only be moved up to lay-back positions well in the rear, but there kept at maximum readiness for immediate movement. Units for which there was inescapable need at the front had to move under the colours of units already known to the enemy to be posted forward.

A simple answer to the second problem would have been to deploy for the eastern theatre forces so overwhelmingly superior in numbers compared with the four divisions plus which the enemy had that it would not matter how well or how much in advance he knew what Indian dispositions were or were going to be. In other words carry out an enlarged version of the standing contingency plan which had been ready since the second war in 1965. But this answer was now irrelevant for three reasons.

The standing plan only envisaged the capture of as good a bit of East Pakistan territory as possible for use in bargaining for any territory that India might lose on the western front. (Since 1965 India had been so impressed by the strategy behind the abortive thrust of Pakistan's 1st Armoured Division that she could no longer rule out its success in a future war.) Now, however, all Indian planning had to look to the possibility that the objective might be the total liberation of Bangladesh.

Secondly, India's political leadership had now prescribed the objective that the western border must be made as secure as possible against future attacks. For that, some territorial adjustments would have to be ensured to make the border more defensible, and a political settlement secured with Pakistan which would at long last eliminate the Kashmir dispute. But none of this would happen unless some critical areas of Pakistan were captured which could be bargained against a durable settlement, and unless extensive damage was done to the enemy war machine to discourage him from waging war again. In other words it required that India must maintain in the west a high force level for an offensive defensive.

But the most crucial reason was the ambiguity of China's intentions. If China moved at any time between April and June, it would catch India at a severe disadvantage. Ground conditions along the border would not hamper it, it would capture territory which India would not be able to recover while facing two enemies, and the two enemy situation would become perpetual for India if China, by maintaining controlled tension in the north, prevented the Indian build up required in the east for eliminating one enemy. This would also be the time of maximum danger for Indian forces already sent into the eastern sector because the only road which linked them with the rest of the country, from Silchar in Assam to Aijal and Agartala, was exposed all along its entire flank to disruptive forays from East Pakistan.

But fortunately, the time up to the start of the monsoons passed reasonably well. This was probably because, apart from China's own problems if it chose to intervene, which will be discussed later, Pakistan, it appears, had not asked for any help till then. Until the end of May, Pakistan put its trust in the assurance General Tikka Khan had given in the last week of March that the guerrilla movement could be quickly suppressed. "Give me a few days," he is reported to have said. By now, it was true, a few weeks had passed but only, it was thought, because of the support given to the guerrillas by the perfidious Indians. A few weeks more and the job would be done. The calculation was going well for Pakistan in May, which was a worse month for the Mukti Bahini than April had been. It was only from about the middle of June onwards, with rains impending which might hamper the Pakistani Army more than the native guerrilla, that Pakistan began to lose this confidence.

Once the rains came down, India was not in a position to do very much anyhow, not in the areas of forward build up at any rate. Therefore, from June onwards she could concentrate her thinking on what she should do if war broke out at any time after early October. India did not desire that the inconclusive guerrilla warfare which had gone on throughout the monsoon and by the beginning of October was already six months old should become endless. Prolonged guerrilla movements, especially if not approaching success under their initial leadership, are often captured by more radical forces than India would have been happy to see prosper either in East Pakistan or Bangladesh. But the replacement of guerrilla war by a regular war earlier than October would have suited her even less. Now she could think of the replacement with an easier mind.

Pakistan's calculations also appear to have focused on this period from early winter onwards. Its reasons for not thinking of an earlier attack can only be surmised. The most important appears to have been Yahya Khan's hope, exactly corresponding to India's, that he could persuade other countries to pressurize India into desisting from supporting the guerrillas. That is why he was using the numerous devices he used to convince the world that he was willing to make a reasonable settlement with East Pakistan. But about the time when winter began he seems to have despaired of this, again as India and about the same time, and turned his thoughts to diplomacy by other means. India's suspicions, aroused in July by Yahya Khan's declaration that any attempt to capture an area for lodging a "puppet" government in Bangladesh would mean an all-out war by him—and aroused precisely because such was one of the Indian intentions at the time —were confirmed early in October when Pakistan moved its troops forward to the borders of West Pakistan, having done so already in the eastern wing. India drew the attention of the Soviet Union. The Soviet Union also took its own soundings and twice in October, through the Soviet press, criticized the movement. In the third week of October it drew the attention of Washington and urged it to counsel restraint on Pakistan. Washington's response was "unhelpful," according to the Soviet press, but early in November the US Embassy in Delhi also warned Washington that war might be imminent.

As India assessed her chances in a show-down, she first had to speculate on China's intentions—there has never been room for more than speculation on this subject—because on that would depend the intentions and capabilities of the immediate adversary and the most important single military question for India: whether she would have to fight a war on one, two or three fronts.

One set of indicators was statements by Chinese and Pakistani leaders, from which, if accepted at face value, only one conclusion could follow—that massive Chinese support for Pakistan was a near certainty. On 13 April the Chinese Prime Minister promised all help to Yahya Khan in maintaining the "territorial integrity of Pakistan" against all "external interference" and the "handful of people" in the east which is all that he saw in the nearly universal rebellion. China's most ardent supporter in Pakistan, Bhutto, declared on 30 April that China would intervene, the Pakistani Ambassador in Peking hailed Chinese support, and on 19 July, in an interview with the *Financial Times*, London, Yahya Khan said: "Pakistan will not be alone if India forces a war upon it." At the beginning of November, Yahya Khan told *Newsweek* that war with India was imminent and China would supply arms and ammunition. On 9 November he stepped up his expectation and told the Columbia Broadcasting System that "China would intervene if India attacked Pakistan." About the same time the acting Foreign Minister of China at a banquet for Bhutto in Peking promised that "should Pakistan be subjected to foreign aggression, the Chinese Government and people will, as always, resolutely support the Pakistan Government and people." Returning home from this visit, Bhutto assured the people: "We have achieved concrete results."

But contrary indications were also available, including some from Pakistan and China. There was no joint statement at the end of Bhutto's visit to Peking. Foreign correspondents based in Rawalpindi reported almost unanimously that Bhutto had returned without any specific commitments or assurances by China. The correspondent of the *Times*, London, quoted Bhutto as saying: "The question whether China would take any diversionary action in the north was 'a superficial matter'." China watchers in Hongkong reported that China was keeping its options open, and analysts of the Chinese press noted far fewer hostile references to India at this time than in 1965, when China had done little enough to help Pakistan.

But as these indicators were contradicted by statements for the record by both countries, India had to rely more on her own appreciation, political and military. Of the political indicators, the most important was the Chinese desire to become a legitimate member of the international community, playing a role through the United Nations rather than in military engagements. More important, however, were the military indicators, calculations about which took into account both possibilities, a Chinese intervention by air or by land. The first possibility did not appear to cause too much anxiety. Despite the development of a new airfield at Hotien, in Sinkiang, at only 1,800 metres and therefore free of the atmospheric limitations which afflict airfields on the Tibetan plateau, and despite the expansion of an old airfield at Cheng-tu in eastern Tibet which is connected to a railhead, it was calculated that the Chinese air force was not a serious threat. Most of the important targets in northern India are in the radar shadow of the Himalayas from all positions to the north of this barrier. The intruder would be at a serious disadvantage against the defending aircraft, many of them faster than what the Chinese have and which, in contrast with 1962 and 1965, would now be fully aided by a radar network. Hit and run bombing raids could still occur. But the damage they could do would not be great so long as public morale did not crack and the political leadership stayed firm in its will. The Chinese would not have to face the problem of the shadow, or not so much, along the north-eastern approach into India. But so long as only one approach needed to be covered, the IAF could spare resources for it while still taking adequate care of the Pakistan Air Force.

Calculations, more complicated, about the chances of a Chinese intervention by land were derived from India's experience of the 1962 and 1965 wars. The 1962 war contributed the spectacle of a Chinese withdrawal which was as precipitate as the massive intervention only a few weeks earlier; the second war contributed China's refusal to intervene even after moving one division to the Ladakh border.

It was broadly known even in 1962 that fear of being cut off by snowfall on the Tibetan passes contributed to the Chinese decision to withdraw in 1962. But this was too general a conclusion to be useful in particular situations. However, by 1965 the

role the weather had played in 1962—or would in future—
had been better understood. The two main roads available to
the Chinese in 1962, over the Bum La and Se La passes, were in
no condition on the Indian or the Tibetan side to take large
scale movement with heavy snows impending. Snow would not
make them impassable for long periods at a time but disrupt
planned movement, especially of supplies; nullification of Chinese
capability was not expected but its considerable diminution was,
placing the invader at a serious disadvantage if confronted with
a sizeable opposition. By the end of that November, India was
in a position to move approximately three full divisions to the
front within another month, the full force originally intended
to be assembled under the new 4th Corps formation. This
was not a prospect which the Chinese could have relished.

The snowfall is not equally heavy on all the eastern passes;
it is about the least on two of the eastern most, Khinzemane and
Dichu. But the terrain on the Indian side nullifies this advantage.
On the Tibetan side, lateral communication is easy across the
flat plateau. On the Indian side the country is deeply furrowed
by high ridges enclosing sharp valleys, most of them running
north-west to south-east and nearly at right angles to the Tibetan
border. They compartmentalize the country into separate
gullies so that exit usually has to follow the route of the ingress;
troops which come in by one pass cannot be easily diverted to
another for withdrawal. Therefore, unless the majority of the
passes are open it is not easy to send in more than a few invading
columns or to coordinate those that come in into an effective
force. The defender can put up selective concentrations
against them. Hence the great importance of holding Se La in
1962, which the Indians abandoned in a tragic state of panic and
confusion.

India's experience of China in 1965 offered two more indicators.
East-west movement in Tibet was still not very easy and though
still superior to the Indian was not superior by as much as in 1962
because of road development in India since then. But China
was now very well off in Tibet for roads radiating to the border
from bases in the rear. Therefore it had the capacity to move
forward very fast in parallel columns, each from its base to its
allotted sector of the front. Border positions were normally
held in battalion strength, but stocked up for sustaining a couple

of brigades. Normal brigade positions relatively in the rear were similarly stocked up for much bigger forces. Therefore, the Chinese could build up very rapidly.

Now, it might have been for purely political reasons that China decided not to come to the aid of its ally in a more sizeable way in 1965. But there was nothing to prevent it from giving a more threatening posture to the division it did move to the Ladakh frontier. With the experience of 1962 still raw in her mind, India would have been put in a fix by the slightest gesture of a threat, and China could have made it at minimum cost to itself and maximum advantage to Pakistan's second and third plans even if the first proved a flop (which it might not have if credible Chinese encouragement to Pakistan had made the restive elements in the Kashmiri population a little bolder).

But China did not move; neither here nor in any other sector. Why?

There could be only two reasons for it. The one believed more likely in New Delhi—possibly because it confirmed the appreciation made on the eve of the 1965 war which has been discussed on earlier pages—was that China would not make any overt move, howsoever small, unless assured of sufficient superiority to guarantee success; even a small move can escalate, and then China would be in difficulties if it did not have the forces required for assured victory. In the global circumstances that China faced at the time it could not have assembled on any one sector a force which would be overwhelmingly superior to a force India could now be expected to put together while it traded territory for time.

The reason believed less likely, but important nevertheless, was that the logistical plan which India suspected the Chinese had in Tibet was not so formidable as was earlier thought. It was adequate for a very rapid defensive build up—which suggests that the division which was moved to the Ladakh border was brought forward only to deter any adventurous thought the Indians may have had—but not for a sustained offensive of the kind China would need against the improved Indian defence capability. On this precedent some of the stepped up movement seen on the Tibetan side of the border from September onwards in 1971 was put down as precautionary reinforcement of border positions and patrolling to keep the Indian side under observation where rather large scale movements were taking place though they were only movements of withdrawal of Indian forces.

In a combined reading of the Chinese logistical and force level requirements, it was estimated that for anything like the scale of operations which China would wish to mount, if it mounted one at all in spite of its new diplomacy, it would need to complete forward build up, on a scale large enough to be clearly observable, before May for any action before the monsoons, before July for action immediately after the rains, and by October for action intended immediately before the winter snows. This last would need to be very sizeable and carried forward quickly into captured areas south of the passes to sustain troops through the winter—unless only a hit and run offensive was intended again, and that would not work in India's new military and psychologically reinforced condition. Early snows can be as early as November, while by early December they are normally so thick that no campaign can be planned without taking the risk of severance into account.

The latest intelligence analysis made just before the monsoon began was that the Chinese garrison in Tibet facing India was a well balanced force of 150,000 men. It was known from earlier assessments that between a third and half of this force, depending upon the level of Tibetan protest—very low as the 1970s began—was normally deployed for maintaining internal security and between two-thirds and half for a role on the Indian border. But since Indian dispositions were also co-extensive with the whole of the border, the Chinese could not afford to leave any sector of the front too thinly held. The maximum force they could assemble for any offensive role on one of the three main sectors—the eastern (NEFA), the central (UP-Tibetan border) and the western (Ladakh)—was estimated to be about three divisions. This position had been regarded with some equanimity since the completion of India's first five-year defence plan in about 1969. It was thought that with the forces India had strung out all along the border, and with the steady improvement in lateral communications since 1962, India could assemble at any given point a sufficient force to contain a three division assault, and could do so within the reaction time she would get from first indications of any significant Chinese deployment.

But with a war impending in the east which India would have to fight mainly with forces withdrawn from the north, India's problem was now much more complicated. India's normal force allocation against East Pakistan was only one division, for the north it was eight or nine. Now these figures had to be reversed in order to find for the east the force level needed for the kind of operations required there. And yet security had to be ensured in the north as well, and against an enemy who was inscrutable for all the speculation one could make about his political motivations. This called for the closest coordination between intelligence and operational plans, something which had not happened in India before. The Indo-Soviet Treaty was a safeguard against any major national level threat by China. But it was considered necessary that the magnitude of conflict which China could generate within the force level available to it in Tibet must be contained by India with her own resources first, if necessary by accepting initial loss of territory.

Specifically, India's problem therefore was three-fold: to anticipate in time where, if anywhere, the Chinese would build up; to have in all the sensitive areas sufficient forces locally committed which would prevent a Chinese walk-over while sufficient forces were rushed to the threatened sector from the eastern or any other theatre to hold the Chinese assault; and so to deploy the forces withdrawn from the north that they could turn back in very quick time. The last point had implications for the schedule of withdrawals as well as the manner of deployment. The more sensitive the area the longer India had to delay withdrawal from it, deployment in depth of the troops withdrawn from it had to be held over till the very last, the withdrawn troops being used in the meantime as reserve so that they could be turned back as soon as needed and with as little damage as possible to operational plans in East Pakistan.

By the time the monsoons ended a withdrawal and redeployment plan had been drawn up in consultation between Army Headquarters, the new Central Intelligence Committee, and the three theatre commands, Western, Central, and Eastern. The strategic concept behind it was that for a sufficient time, but as brief as possible, India should disengage from the northern front and finish off the job on the eastern first; thereafter, the forces borrowed from the north should be sent back to it if necessary or, if possible, switched to the western front to help finish the war quickly there as well. After that they would be free to go back north with no risk remaining either in the east or in the west.

The tactical plan behind the borrowings was that as the season for any sizeable Chinese build up in any sector of Tibet came to an end, the reserves allocated for it were to be withdrawn and deployed as reserves for the nearest sector of the East Pakistan front, leaving the committed troops in the affected sector of Tibet in a holding role for any surprise move the Chinese might make. As the season for a limited Chinese build up came to an end in any sector, the committed troops for it were to be withdrawn and held in reserve for the nearest sector of the eastern front, the troops previously borrowed as reserves for it being moved forward. After the snowfall on the passes became heavy enough to foreclose any threat for a period of time in any sector the committed northern troops now held as reserve for the eastern front were to be moved forward in the nearest eastern sector. In each phase of the eastern deployment of troops borrowed from the north, their commitment in depth was to be avoided as long as possible, just as their withdrawal from the north was also to be avoided as long as possible—the most sensitive sector being touched the last.

The scope for miscalculation in this was thought to be limited to marginal failures of intelligence or weather forecasting. It was not feared that the need for reserves would arise in any sector when even the troops committed to the ground had been withdrawn from it. But committed troops might have to hold on for longer and might have to yield more ground than would be necessary if the reserves were at hand. Or the Chinese, discovering the absence of even troops committed forward, might exploit an unexpected gap in the weather and more readily make a raid in some size than they would otherwise.

This danger would be greatest in the central sector. Although the objectives China would regard more important are mostly in the eastern and western sectors, there were constraints operating there of which the central sector was relatively free. The eastern, being closest to the eastern theatre of war, could be most quickly reinforced. The western has no sensitive targets to offer which are worth a raid; a raiding party can get lost in the wastes of Ladakh. But in the central sector there are passes leading into India which are both low in altitude and latitude. For example Manna Pass, at 3,048 metres leads on to Joshimath which is only 1,800 metres and gives access to some of the most important among Hindu centres of pilgrimage. They are of no immediate importance, not to a raiding party at least; but even temporary enemy occupation thereof could cause a disturbance in the Hindu ethos and a tremor in every village in northern India.

The intelligence-operational plan of withdrawals and redeployment and the risk of any loopholes in it imposed upon the eastern theatre of war the most rigorous single determinant apart from the nature of the terrain: a time frame. It had to have a plan of operations which could be completed very quickly, but with a flexibility which could accommodate a different combination of possibilities on the northern front. There were several reasons for the importance of speed: the probability of international pressure, upon which Pakistan was banking, which could bring Indian intervention to a halt and probably also force India's withdrawal before anything of value was accomplished in the east; the possibility of some overt intervention by the USA, of which first indications were available by about the end of November; the risk of some significant Pakistani success in the west which might need to be countered before it got out of hand. But the most important was that forces borrowed from the north must be returned before weather conditions changed significantly, or earlier if anticipations proved to be more than marginally faulty. All borrowings must be for the minimum period, which meant that a smooth slot had to be prepared for each formation which was expected, so that it could slip in with the minimum dislocation to itself or other units. Before they left their northern locations many units had to be retooled for the great difference between facing an enemy in the mountains and another in an almost tropical, alluvial plain heavily interlaced with rivers and streams. At the same time the plan into which the borrowed units were to fit had to be such that it would survive not only premature withdrawal but even the absence of the expected unit.

There was a pendant to this problem, the Ledo Road. Ever since 1962, when the problem began to be studied seriously, it has been recognized that geographically the easiest access into eastern India is by General Stillwell's old road through northern Burma. It has no snowfall at all, the highest pass on it being only 500 metres high, and it is the shortest route between major Chinese army bases in Yunan and Indian oilfields in northeastern Assam. Ever since Kosygin told Mrs Gandhi during his visit to New Delhi in 1968 that China's offensive capability had been greatly reduced by shortage of oil, Indian military planners have wondered whether the Chinese would succumb to the temptations of this target.

But there are two restraints on this danger; in 1971 both were operative a little more than earlier. Ledo Road is in serious disrepair. Although important for the Burmese Government as a route into some very thinly administered and usually rather disturbed areas in northern Burma, it has been allowed to fall into decay, probably to deny its use to China. At least a couple of months of intensive work are needed to fit it up even temporarily for sizeable army traffic. Such intensive work cannot be done surreptitiously, and Burma would not authorize its repair by China. Apart from Burma's own reasons for it, the country's relations with India have been such of late that it will not willingly allow on its soil activity hostile to India—it has cooperated with India in quelling the Naga insurgency—and China would not force a passage through an unwilling Burma unless its own vital interests were at stake. In the circumstances of 1971, when China was trying to make its new image stick, it would not have invaded Burma in cold blood whatever the provocation India offered Pakistan. But even if it did, repair work on the road, easily detectable, would have given India some warning, and there was no sign of it in October 1971, the critical time of appraisal for India.


Pakistan of course would have preferred its problem in the east to remain its internal affair; the four divisions it had there would have ultimately suppressed the Mukti Bahini if India had denied sanctuary, encouragement and assistance to it. At the level of preference, India would have preferred East Pakistan's problem to remain East Pakistan's internal affair without the western wing pumping in three extra divisions; the Mukti Bahini would have ultimately finished the lone division Pakistan normally maintained there. But once the affair became bilateral, it was Pakistan which preferred its further escalation; India did not. The Indo-Soviet Treaty can be termed political escalation of the conflict by India. But its immediate military purpose was only to discourage China from jumping into the fray.

In this respect, India's and Pakistan's preferences in 1971 were exactly the reverse of their respective preferences in 1965. India would have been best off in 1971 in a one front war confined to the east, and even there would have preferred, at least for some more time, the limited aim of partial liberation. She knew she would be less well off in a two front war and worse off with the third front, in the north, also becoming involved. Pakistan would have been in a hopeless position in a one front war, had some expectation of compensation in the west in a two front war, and if China opened a third front in the north—well, then anything could happen. On the other hand in 1965, Pakistan preferred a war limited to Kashmir, and it was India which stood to gain by escalating it. There has been much speculation whether Pakistan sought escalation in 1971 only to bring international peace-makers into the game or for some more tangible gain. This is best discussed later in the light of the operations as they developed. But that escalation from one to two fronts and hopefully three was its immediate purpose is not open to doubt.

Pakistan saw political as well as military advantage in escalation. It hoped to submerge its military disadvantage at each level in a real or imagined advantage, at least relatively speaking, at the next higher level. Politically it hoped to force China to translate its words into deeds. In this its ambition was to emulate India. By bringing matters to a head, India had forced the Soviet Union to accept an Indian position which, if matters had remained at a low key, the Soviet Union would have continued to drown in a torrent of comforting but not otherwise very helpful goodwill. In other words, she forced the Soviet Union to take sides as between India and Pakistan and to accept the implications and consequences thereof.

In hoping to force China to make a military commitment to it, Pakistan was overlooking China's limitations, and as a hard headed customer China was not going to go along with this ploy. It had the Indo-Soviet Treaty to consider, as also the needs of its own new diplomacy and its difficulties in assembling a large enough force at any one point on the Indo-Tibetan border. Perhaps it had also to consider that helping Pakistan to defeat India would appear to many countries to be the same thing as helping Pakistan to continue its colonialist rule over East Pakistan.

It is not at all likely that Pakistan had any hopes of support from the Soviet Union either; even the expectation that the Soviet Union would continue to restrain India must have abated after Mrs Gandhi's visit to Moscow. But Pakistan expected of the USA, just as India expected of the Soviet Union, that it would give effective help if the war situation became very dangerous for it.

How far the USA encouraged Pakistan behind the scenes in this expectation is a matter open only to surmise as yet. But developments which occurred during the war confirm that the expectation was not based only upon a unilateral calculation by Pakistan that the United States would be pushed into giving material support if the crisis were escalated. It would at least be willing to bail out Pakistan from a serious crisis, and perhaps be willing to do something in time to help Pakistan to get the better of the crisis. Indian military and political policy was being evolved with this possibility clearly in mind. That is why neither politically nor militarily India reacted either in panic or haste when a task force of the US Seventh Fleet appeared in the Bay of Bengal. The cool firmness displayed exceeded the precedent set in facing up to the Chinese ultimatum in 1965.

The bilateral military balance between India and Pakistan was very different from what it was in 1965. Pakistan was appreciably stronger in military terms than in 1965 although it had lost much of its advantage over India and politically was far weaker than India or itself at the time of the 1965 war. In 1971 Pakistan had in the west ten infantry divisions, two armoured divisions, two infantry brigades, two armoured brigades and two other regiments of armour. India had 12 infantry divisions, including two under Southern Command in Rajasthan, one armoured division, two infantry brigades, two armoured brigades and one para brigade. India's advantage in infantry was thus offset by disadvantage in armour. In the east, India had seven divisions against Pakistan's four plus, but she also had a very large deployment of guerrilla forces which were at various stages of combat readiness and had diverse roles to fulfil according to their capabilities. In the air India had a decisive numerical superiority (eight to one in the east) although the Pakistan Air Force had some machines of greater sophistication and power than any in the IAF. India now had 45 squadrons in all of combat and transport aircraft against Pakistan's 13, compared with 34 and 12 in 1965. The IAF had replaced most of its Vampires, Toofanis, and Mysteres with the superior Russian built SU-7. The former had come down from 11 squadrons in 1965 to two this time; the SUs had gone up from nil to six squadrons. The MiG-21 squadrons had gone up from one to eight, Pakistan had also acquired 90 MiGs since 1965, but all of them were MiG-19s of Chinese make, inferior to the MiG-21s now being made in India. The MiG-21 is also superior to F-104 but the IAF had nothing to compare in speed and electronically controlled fire power with the 24 Mirages of the Pakistan Air Force. In deep penetration bombing capability both sides were weak and numerically at near parity as in 1965.

The improvement in India's radar detection system, which was interrupted when the United States withdrew its assistance in this field after the Indo-Pakistan war of 1965, had been resumed since then and by 1971 was substantially better. Seventy-five per cent of the planned improvement was in position, and on the western front in particular India was well covered from Kashmir to the Arabian Sea coast. A more substantial and immediately useful improvement, however, was the addition of an extensive network for detection from the ground by a well-trained observation corps in areas exposed to enemy air attack or requiring close air support for ground action by the army. Here India benefited from an example Pakistan had set, and improved upon the exemplar. Pakistan had good ground detection and coordination in 1965; India had none. In 1971 India put down a much better version of it. But only just in time. When the war broke out, the observation corps had only just become operational, and that too with point-to-point communication facility improvised by the Posts and Telegraphs Department while the air force waited for a more sophisticated electronic system for which orders had been placed but which had yet to arrive.

In naval power also, India had a decisive superiority. She was at or below parity in submarines because Pakistan had heavily invested in them at the expense of surface vessels, a course many of India's naval experts had favoured when, under Nehru's preference for visible naval power, an aircraft carrier was bought instead ten years before. But apart from the classic units of surface naval power like cruisers, destroyers and frigates, and the aircraft carrier which convincingly demonstrated its worth in the Bay of Bengal in the 1971 war, India had enormously improved its surface strike capability with the purchase of missile boats from the Soviet Union which showed their power in the dramatic and in some ways decisive raid on Karachi.

Within this framework of global and bilateral calculations, some a matter of political judgment, others of quantitative analysis of capabilities as interpreted by each side according to its understanding of the nature of this war, each side set up its objectives and the strategies and dispositions required for attaining them. Some of the strategies were entirely new, devised in the light of the latest circumstances, some required only the pulling together and fitting in of ideas which had been worked out much earlier and had already been given shape in terms of organization, equipment and disposition on the ground.

Pakistan was not without a few keys it could turn even in the east to widen the conflict with some hope of advantage to itself. Of its four divisions plus, Pakistan had concentrated almost three against India's weakest flanks: the Siliguri corridor in the north and the whole of the poorly consolidated eastern flank which stretches east and south from the corridor to where Tripura joins Burma. Indian political, administrative, and military resources along this enormous rim have always been stretched to the limit by the ever present Chinese threat, by Naga and Mizo insurgencies, and by the general absence of cohesion here. Military build up related to the crisis in East Pakistan had only just begun. Political and administrative weaknesses were as yet unremedied.

Pakistan had concentrated most of the armour it had in the east in the bulge of East Pakistan which juts north from a constriction between Hilli and Gaibunda towards Sikkim and at the nearest point is only 32 kilometres from the Chinese at Nathu La. The military cantonments of Rangpur, Saidpur, and Dinajpur even normally held the bulk of such Pakistani armour as was in the east, both because this is the only country suitable for armour and because of the temptation offered by proximity to the

Chinese. Now they held much more of it. The obvious danger for India was that an armoured thrust, before it could be held, might cut this territory, open a corridor for the Chinese and invite them into territory under its control; an Indian counter-attack on these Chinese forces would mean a Sino-Indian clash of India's making, not China's.

Much of Pakistan's infantry was concentrated at strongpoints, especially Sylhet, Mymensingh, Akhaura, Comilla, Maynamati, and Laksham—that is, opposite the soft underbelly of Assam and the still softer western flank of Tripura. If it struck north, northeast, or east in sustained raids in any kind of strength, Pakistan could not only disrupt areas which are prone to disruption in any case but also disrupt the solitary road from Silchar to Agartala down which all the build up of the new Indian corps formation in Tripura had to take place and which was at many points within range of Pakistani guns.

A third but more improbable Pakistani thrust could be from the area of Jessore, another strongpoint, towards Calcutta. Pakistan knew from recent experience that enemy forces had also concentrated here in strength. During a number of clashes in November the Mukti Bahini, the Border Security Force, and elements of the Indian regular army had established an enclave at Chuadanga and kept the whole area from Kot Chandpur north of Jessore to Satkhira in the south in a constant state of eruption. Therefore, it could not have had expectations of any territorial gains here. But the area being very close to Calcutta, even temporary intrusions could produce interesting repercussions in India.

However, in the eastern theatre as a whole Pakistan's hopes had to be mainly defensive. Each of the three offensive possibilities was really the obverse of a defensive intention—in the north to put the Indian armour concentration in the corridor off balance, in the east to disrupt India's offensive build up, in the west to cause political dislocation and rock the overall Indian military planning. The main anchor of its hope in the east was the knowledge, which Pakistan would have surely had, that India would be fighting with borrowed forces which could be withdrawn from the northern front only for the duration that China allowed. They would have to go back, and without getting very far into East Pakistan, if the extra three divisions Yahya

Khan had put down there gave a good fight and his other hopes did not let him down.

As seen from Dacca, the most important among these hopes was that India would not wage full scale war upon the eastern wing. General Niazi and General Farman Ali, the military and political chiefs of Pakistan's eastern army, were saying to foreign correspondents even as late as the last week of November that India would not dare to do much more; the world would not allow her to. As seen from Islamabad the picture was rather different by now. By about the middle of November Yahya Khan was reconciled to and preparing for a kind of war, as confirmed by the dispatch of the submarine *Ghazi* to get the Indian flagship *Vikrant* which would obviously mean that both sides would throw in all they could. If he still did not change the dispositions in the east it was only because he had a different hope in his heart: he was banking on the orderly withdrawal of his force to the west intact. Light is shed by this calculation upon certain obscurities of later events.

Indian strategy in the east was exactly the reverse. It aimed at a knockout blow. Made as secure against a surprise Chinese attack as she possibly could be by bold military planning, careful calculation and timely diplomacy, India drastically revised and enlarged her standing contingency plan for East Pakistan, making it equal to the enlarged objective of the total liberation of Bangladesh. The contingency plan had provided for two main thrusts, each supported by armour, one directly east from the major Indian base near Calcutta and the other moving south from the Siliguri corridor from positions which had been developed from the late 1960s onwards to prevent a link up between the Chinese and the Pakistanis. The objectives of the thrust from the north were to disorganize Pakistan's armour formations and if possible to capture territory for widening the Siliguri corridor at least for the duration of the operations if not permanently. The objectives of the thrust from the west were to disrupt any Pakistani build up for a thrust towards Calcutta and, more importantly, to capture sizeable Pakistani territory for later bargaining. The area south and west of the Padma offered Pakistan the easiest access to what were the main Indian forces in the east until 1971. It was also the most feasible single territorial objective for India, especially the half of it west of the Madhumati.

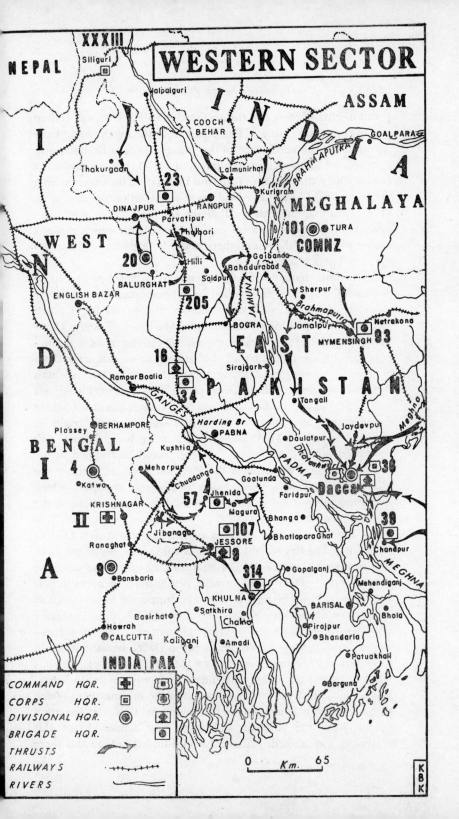

But neither of these two thrusts fitted in with the revised Indian aim of capturing Dacca. The thrust from the north would have encountered the confluence of the Jamuna (as the Brahmaputra is called below the Assam border) and the Ganga north-west of Dacca where they meet to form the Padma. The advance from the west would have been held up at the Madhumati first, then at the Padma, and then Dhaleshwari. All these rivers are formidable barriers, with an expanse and depth which make it impossible to ford them, and there could be little hope of capturing any major bridges intact.

Both components of the contingency plan therefore had to be downgraded. They were retained for two important reasons. They would help to cut up the enemy forces, as General Jagjit Singh Aurora, General Officer Commanding-in-Chief, Eastern Command, developed his slicing moves, by-passing enemy strongpoints, as he intended, instead of wasting time on capturing them or wasting troops on investing them. Secondly, the northern thrust would help in the defence of the Siliguri corridor against a possible Pakistani attack and widen it against possible Chinese intervention. A substantial body of Pakistani troops could be cut off west of the Madhumati if their main base, Jessore, was by-passed quickly. Similarly, another could be trapped in the north, including the bulk of the Pakistan armour, if either the Hilli-Gaibunda gap were closed or Bogra were captured, which is the most important single hub of land communications in the whole of Bangladesh.

But higher priority was given to two important new lines of advance. The first would come down from the north but from positions to the east of the Brahmaputra, not from the west, the Siliguri side. This would involve heavy investment in a new logistical build up because it was to be supported from Tura and other bases in the Garo-Khasi-Jaintia hills which in the past have not been important areas of army deployment. But, if successful, it could develop a credible threat to Dacca because it would have only one enemy strongpoint on the way, Jamalpur, which it was known was not heavily defended, and only one main waterway which is not very wide, a branch of the Brahmaputra which in Bangladesh is known as the Brahmaputra itself after the main stream joins the Jamuna and takes that name. Once this waterway was crossed, Jamalpur would be left behind and there would be no other natural obstacle before Dacca. It would also help to cut off the Pakistani brigade at Mymensingh, an important centre of communications and commerce in the eastern half of Bangladesh and, with Sylhet, the most important north of Dacca.

The second drive, planned to proceed from the east in multiple prongs, was given the highest priority in logistics, in objectives and in allocation of resources. It was entrusted to the new corps formation, the 4th, anchored at Agartala and given three main lines of advance: first, south-east to Comilla and beyond that (*a*) to the banks of the Meghna, north-west of Comilla at Daudkandi and south-west at Chandpur, to threaten Dacca from the south; and (*b*) directly south to Chittagong and further south to Cox's Bazar to cut off escape routes to the sea and over land to Burma; second, directly west, past Akhaura, by the shortest route to the banks of the Meghna, the last main water obstacle before Dacca; and third, north-west to Sylhet, past Maulvi Bazar.

Sylhet, Akhaura, Comilla and its twin cantonment, Maynamati, and further south Laksham were known to be well stocked up and strongly fortified; they held the main concentrations of the enemy forces eastwards of Dacca and, with Dacca, accounted for more than half of the total Pakistani forces in the eastern wing. This entire force and the whole area east of the Jamuna and Padma would be cut off from any escape to the sea by water or land, and would be further divided into smaller sections by the second and third prongs and the branches of the first. The most important of these thrusts was to be from Comilla. It would place the Indian forces in an arc around Dacca, from Chandpur in the south to Ashuganj in the north-east, with only the Meghna and the narrow Lakhia as the final obstacles between them and the capital.

The daring shown in undertaking the build up of the 4th Corps at Agartala owes a great deal to a fortunate coincidence, one of the many with which India was favoured in this war. The Chief of the Army Staff, General Manekshaw, had been in the east for six years as General Officer Commanding-in-Chief, Eastern Command, and his successor as GOC, General Aurora, had worked under him first as Corps Commander and then as a Deputy Chief. Both understood the needs and prob-

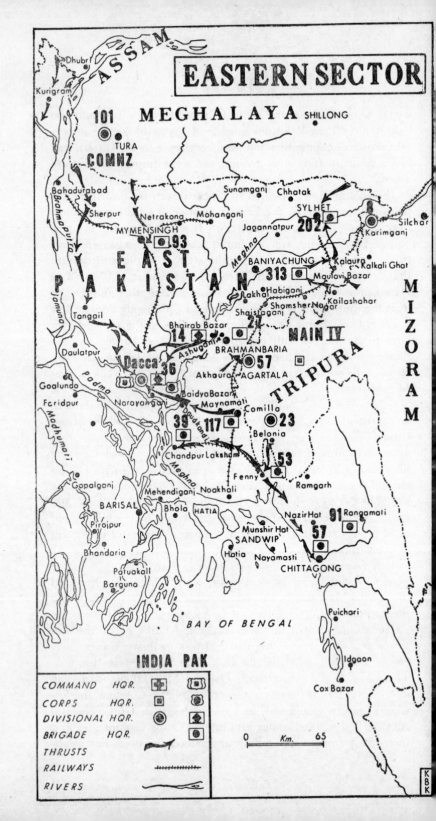

lems of the eastern theatre extremely well and quickly reached complete understanding about the importance and requirements of this new dimension which was now added to the old eastern plan. General Aurora had also been commander of the 33rd corps, from which the 4th was to be initially carved.

The carving, the raising, the building up and deployment of the new corps had to be undertaken while the whole area of its logistics, deployment, and responsibility was already in a state of acute abnormality. It was headquartered farther away from its command headquarters than any other operational corps during this war, and it was linked to its command headquarters over lines of ground communications which were either primitive or vulnerable and in many stretches both. This line ran first from Calcutta to Siliguri through some areas of acute political disturbance; then from Siliguri to Silchar in southern Assam, crossing the main Brahmaputra *en route*, through territory where general logistics are highly undeveloped; from there south to Agartala over a single road which had no black top until the decision was taken to build this corps and then had to cope simultaneously with the enormous refugee exodus in addition to the requirements of the armed forces. After leaving Silchar the road plunges towards the border and thereafter at many points down to Agartala it is exposed to enemy guns and hostile eyes. By the time the build up began Pakistan's artillery had already got into the habit of firing on this road, and yet the movement of the three divisions constituting the corps not only had to be completed on schedule but kept as secret as possible.

Withdrawals from the Nagaland and Mizo hills for building up the 4th Corps faced the added problem of local insurgencies there. Therefore they were among the last to be withdrawn and the first to be returned to their areas. The added double precaution was taken of intensifying operations against the insurgents before withdrawing these units so that the insurgency would remain dislocated for some time to come, and the colours of the units which were withdrawn continued to be deployed by the troops which remained so that the fact of the withdrawal might not become too conspicuous. In fact the troops withdrawn from Nagaland barely had the time to go into deployment before the Pakistan Army on the eastern front surrendered. The only other unit to share this unenviable distinction was the brigade which was withdrawn from Walong, probably the most sensitive sector of the northern front, next only to the sector opposite Nathu La. Walong is opposite and very close to the main Chinese base in Tibet, at Rima, which is well serviced by a good network of roads, including one which comes down directly to Walong and then goes on to the oilfields at Digboi.

Air support, both in strike and transportation roles involving actions which the IAF had never conducted before, was allocated for all the four drives into Bangladesh but especially for the drive down from Jamalpur in the north and for the multi-pronged advance from Comilla in the east. It was the Jamalpur drive which was given the crucial support of a para drop, India's first in combat conditions, which speeded up the fall of Dacca. Most of the helicopter flights of the IAF were placed at the disposal of 4th Corps Headquarters. This amounted to 12 machines in all for the whole theatre: a pitiable number for a general who at the peak of the operations was to command 130,000 men under arms, said to be one of the largest forces ever assembled under a single commander. But they were to perform untiringly and without them, as Aurora admits in a high tribute, some of his most crucial operations might have proved a flop.

Virtually operating as a theatre commander, not as the commander of the eastern army only, Aurora placed three requirements before the IAF. The first, the obvious and classic one of offensive air support. Aurora wanted his formations to travel very light for the sake of mobility. He asked the air force to take over as much of a flying artillery role as possible; there would be situations in any case in which guns which could take to the air would be needed more than those held up on river banks or bogged down in flooded and soft alluvial ground. The second requirement was transportation. With high mobility an indispensable part of Aurora's plans, and given the obstacles on the ground to rapid movement in bulk, troops would outrun their logistical support and would be held up unless supplied by air. This is where he needed helicopters the most. The third supporting role he required was a compartment of the second— evacuation of casualties, because, again in the interests of mobility, auxiliary field formations such as medical were going to be kept to the minimum.

The air force had its problems. It had hardly any airfields to the east of East Pakistan, especially south of Shillong, which it could use for its strike or transportation support roles. Without them, it could not shuttle across the theatre. Flights which took off from Indian airfields in West Bengal would have to fly all the way back which meant twice across the whole theatre if the flight was in support of ground operations east of the Jamuna-Padma line. IAF aircraft were to improvise arrangements for flying casualties back from captured airfields in Bangladesh on their way back from strike or transportation sorties; the casualties would be flown to these airfields by helicopter. But this imposed limits upon the operational capability of fixed wing aircraft and helicopters. More important, the IAF could not attack enemy sea ports to the south and east; they were out of its reach from Shillong as well as from Calcutta.

In coping with these drawbacks the planning of the eastern campaign became a fully coordinated affair of the three services and India's first experience of such an exercise. That the coordination was achieved, how far, on account of what factors, and against what limitations are matters which have lessons for the future organization of India's defence apparatus. More was called for here than that Aurora should have combined use of the forces of the three services allotted to his theatre.

East Pakistan was divided into two parts by an east-west line drawn through Dacca. All the areas to the north of the line, including Dacca, were made the responsibility of the Indian Air Force, to the south the responsibility of the naval air arm. This was even better than the navy expected. The Chief of Naval Staff, Admiral Nanda, had insisted from the very beginning that unlike 1965 the navy must be fully in play this time and accordingly it had been allotted three principal roles: to protect Indian merchant shipping and keep the sea lanes open for essential Indian traffic; to deny the use of the seas to Pakistan for naval as well as trade purposes by blockading both wings; and to undertake offensive forays on the coasts of both wings. To be invited to help the air and ground arms was an added bonus.

Pakistan's more positive hopes rested entirely in the west, where its aim was to profit from its advantages in logistics and punch and in a swift manoeuvre to capture some significant areas of Indian territory and then bargain them for getting Indian troops to quit East Pakistan and disgorge whatever they might have captured there. The troop dispositions it made in the west neatly corresponded to these hopes and aims.

The northernmost areas in Kashmir on the Pakistan side of the cease-fire line were manned by Northern Scouts, Gilgit Scouts and Kohat Scouts, forces corresponding to the Indian Border Security Force and other para-military formations. The deployment of the regular Pakistan Army began south of Tithwal.

It is doubtful whether Pakistan had any strong expectations of success in infiltrations across the cease-fire line; what it could not do in 1965, when it had the advantage of secrecy and surprise and a great deal of unrest on the Indian side, it could not do now when it had none of these advantages; with slaughter of Muslims by Muslims in the east, Muslim emotion in Kashmir against the Hindus of India were largely neutralized. Therefore, whatever Pakistan had to do in Kashmir it had to do through its regular forces—a severe limitation seeing how the hills just swallow up forces. Nevertheless, it put down two infantry divisions in Kashmir, the 12th in the north and the 23rd in the south. The 12th was so disposed behind the Haji Pir bulge and the Kahuta area that it could either move north towards Uri or south towards a more conspicuous target, Poonch. The 23rd could either move north to reinforce the 12th or south for a role in the Chhamb area with forces drawn from some very large concentrations built up in the Kharian-Sialkot area, the largest of Pakistan's cantonment complexes.

In the last days of November, a great deal of Pakistan vehicle movement was seen, four or five times more than even winter stocking up would require; it was particularly heavy in the Haji Pir and Kahuta areas. But the movement could have had no serious purpose apart from deception because there are no attractive *and* attainable objectives here.

South of Kashmir, Pakistan had all its old advantages: near parity with India in numerical strength, an edge over India in firepower and armoured mobility, internal lines of communication running all along and just behind the front, a strong line of

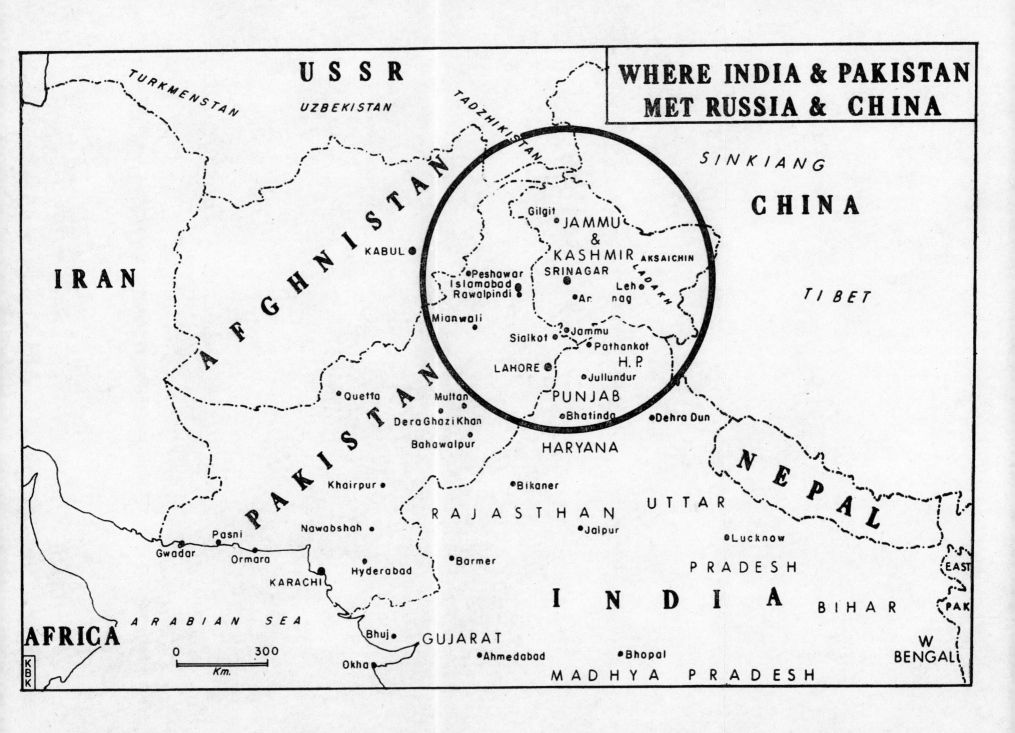

WHERE INDIA & PAKISTAN MET RUSSIA & CHINA

defences based upon the Ichhogil system which had been further strengthened since 1965 and given more depth, and belief in the superiority of the Pakistani soldier over the Indian which 1965 had not demolished.

Since 1965 Pakistan had built up another strongly defended area, in the Shakargarh bulge, which is north of the Ichhogil line and separated from it by a narrow gap equipped with a bridge at Dera Baba Nanak over the river Ravi which forms the border along this stretch. The defence system in the bulge partly covered the approach India used in 1965 for the tank assault in the Phillora-Pasrur area to draw Pakistan off its Chhamb offensive. Thus, as it stood in 1971, the bulge could be compared to the Ichhogil system a little further to the south: it provided a barrier in the middle which the enemy would find very expensive to break and, given Pakistan's mobility in the rear, the possibility of developing alternative thrusts to the north or south.

This meant that not only in central Punjab but in much of northern Punjab as well, Pakistan did not fear a major Indian thrust except possibly through the gap at Dera Baba Nanak. Indian thrusts into West Punjab, the most important part of West Pakistan, could only be launched in three areas: first, south of the Ichhogil, immediately south or a little further down, below the Ferozepur area; second, north of the Ichhogil system through the Dera Baba Nanak gap; third, just north of the Shakargarh bulge from the south-western corner of Jammu which contains the Chhamb-Akhnoor corridor made famous by the 1965 war. If the main Indian strike forces could be led into and held along any two of these three lines of attack, there could be an opening along the third which Pakistan could exploit, given its advantage in north-south mobility and the assumed superiority of its strike machine. If an Indian thrust developed in the southern area, south of Ichhogil, Pakistan would be free to try an armoured attack through Dera Baba Nanak or through the Chhamb corridor again. Alternatively, if the Indians could be engaged in and committed to either or both of the two northern openings, Pakistan could strike in the south, in the Ferozepur-Fazilka area.

This required Pakistan to ensure two things: that of its main strike formations, the 6th and 1st Armoured Divisions, one should cover the two northern gaps, which are close to each other, in an offensive defensive disposition, the other should be opposite the gap in the south, with facilities for each to reinforce the other very quickly; and second, that it should produce sufficient and convincing action at one end to draw India into a commitment there, and then exploit the opportunity which would open at the other. Pakistan was to meet both these conditions.

Pakistan had divided the western front into four main sectors: Jammu and Kashmir, with responsibility mainly along the cease-fire line but coming down up to Marala headworks, south-west of Chhamb; the Sialkot sector covering the area from the head-works up to the northern end of the Ichhogil canal defence system and including the Shakargarh bulge, but also with corps level responsibility for Jammu and Kashmir; the Lahore sector with responsibility for the whole of the Ichhogil system up to just north of Suleimanki; and the Multan sector which covered the rest of the western front right up to the sea, although there was an almost independent divisional headquarters at Hyderabad. Because of the advantage of fast communication lines running close to and parallel to the front, any sector could lend troops to or borrow them from the next sector on either flank.

In addition to the 12th and 23rd Infantry Divisions in Jammu and Kashmir there were three infantry divisions, the 15th, the 8th and the newly raised 17th, one armoured division, the 6th, and one independent armoured brigade, the 8th, in the Sialkot sector, which offered various combinations of offensive and de-fensive possibilities. The 15th Infantry Division was in the northern part of this sector and the 8th in the southern, both fully committed to ground defence. The 17th Infantry Division minus one brigade was lightly committed while the 6th Armoured Division and the 8th Independent Armoured Brigade were so engaged that they could be switched to an offensive role if an opportunity offered.

The Lahore sector, because well covered by the Ichhogil system, had more infantry than armour—two divisions of infantry, the 10th and 11th, one infantry brigade drawn from the 17th Division in the north, and only one independent armoured brigade, the 3rd. The infantry was fully committed for the defence of this prime target. But because Lahore is the hub of an extensive network of communications, these troops could be moved either north or south if the Indian battle plan showed no threat to Lahore.

Deployment was at its thickest in the Multan sector, both on account of the extensive area of its responsibility and the variety of possibilities it offered, even better than those in the Sialkot sector. It had the 7th Infantry Division, which came down from its normal peace time station in Peshawar just when the war broke out, the 18th Infantry Division, the newly raised 33rd Infantry Division, two independent infantry brigades, the 105th and the 25th, and the 1st Armoured Division, Pakistan's prize strike force, and two other regiments of armour. The 18th Infantry Division, both the infantry brigades, and the two extra regiments of armour were fully committed. A brigade of the 18th Infantry was put down in the Rahim Yar Khan area where the railway line to Karachi runs closest to the Indian border, the 33rd Infantry was placed at Rohri, opposite Sukkur, another hub in the communication corridor between Islamabad and Karachi. It was free to move north or south. One brigade of the 18th Division was placed at Chor, along a road and an abandoned railway running from Barmer in Rajasthan to Hyderabad, north-east of Karachi and the second most important town of southern West Pakistan. The 1st Armoured Division was completely free and since it moved in mid-October from its normal peace time station, Multan, to its known forward assembly area, the Changa Manga forest, it had been slowly forming up, with the minimum of fuss and noise, in its launching areas.

Apart from local reserves which sector commanders can always raise by revising local dispositions, Pakistan thus had the following main formations in more or less reserve dispositions, ready to be disengaged from their light local duties to more serious action wherever required: the 1st Armoured Division and the 7th Infantry Division, close to each other and opposite the Fazilka area of Punjab and the Ganganagar area of Rajasthan; the 33rd Infantry Division minus one brigade; the 17th Infantry Division minus one brigade; portions of the 23rd Infantry Division; to some extent the 6th Armoured Division and the 8th Independent Armoured Brigade. These were the elements with which it could hope to develop the alternative thrusts outlined earlier.

Backed by reserves which were based in Sialkot, it could produce enough action to show that it was trying once more to spring the old pincer on Kashmir. The northern prong would be without the benefit of infiltrators, but would be compensated by the greater reliabilty and offensive power of regular forces. The southern would not have the 1965 opportunity of cutting off the north-western areas of Jammu province, let alone the whole of Kashmir. India had since built alternative roads leading to the north. But if it penetrated deep enough it could pose a credible enough threat from the north-west to the defences of the Jammu city area which normally look south-west towards Sialkot. Not a fanciful idea as events were to show. It offered a better opportunity than the only alternative in the north, to move the 23rd northwards to combine with the 12th for an assault across the cease-fire line either towards Uri or Poonch. A limited offensive in the Chhamb salient would also serve the important defensive purpose for Pakistan of disrupting any Indian offensive towards an area of great importance to Pakistan.

South of Kashmir, Pakistan had two possibilities, either able to draw upon Sialkot in the rear depending upon which looked more promising. The first was to use as the shield the strong defensive system built up in the Shakargarh bulge and to use as the sword a balanced force of armour and infantry—the 6th Armoured Division and the 8th Independent Armoured Brigade, lying lightly engaged in Sialkot, were available as the driving element of this force—and make a thrust either south-east to attack and if possible capture Gurdaspur or north-east to the rather vulnerable road running from Pathankot to Kathua to Sambha to Jammu, most of it just outside the north-eastern perimeter of the bulge. Disruption of Indian logistics to the north could be one gain (not very important unless combined with a strong action in the north with significant territorial ambitions); another could be to capture any of these places which, especially Pathankot, would be worth using as bargaining counters in later negotiations with India.

Secondly, south of the Shakargarh bulge Pakistan could exploit the advantage that at Dera Baba Nanak it has a readymade bridgehead across the Ravi. It has an enclave on the Indian side; therefore both ends of the bridge are secure in its hands and the Sialkot concentrations are only a short distance behind over a good railway system, one main and one supporting line. Tactically an ideal situation, but it has a serious strategic disadvantage: a Pakistani thrust here would unite enemy forces instead of dividing them. India has always had, south of Kashmir, two important areas of deployment: one immediately south of Kashmir, which supports the Kashmir forces from below and confronts the Pakistani forces in the Sialkot area; the other south of there up to the Lahore-Amritsar axis. A Pakistani attack out of Dera Baba Nanak would be jointly attacked by both these forces. Instead of dividing them it would be squashed by them. Therefore the purpose of any Pakistani effort here would be only to probe Indian intentions or at best to make diversionary noises.

Pakistan's main opportunity lay further to the south, with supporting tactics at the northern end. If action at Chhamb, with or without activity at the northern prong resting on the cease-fire line, or if any drive launched out of the Shakargarh bulge, or preferably both, induced India to commit enough of its strength in these sectors, it would be very well worth a try to launch an armoured attack in the south and do what Ayub could not in 1965. Pakistan could repeat or modify Ayub's plan—that is, aim, as he did, to get behind Amritsar or, with a comparable but different ambition more to the south, aim at the softly held Indian territory from Fazilka to Ganganagar, east of which lie the adjoining border lands of Haryana and Punjab. This advance would have to cover a long distance to reach any prize targets, longer than Ayub's thrust would have had to, but would lie over areas which have always been lightly held by Indian troops, as the enemy knew from every appreciation since before 1965. There were no irremediable defects in Ayub's idea; the causes of its failure were purely local and almost adventitious. There could be hope that in its modified form it could be repeated without repeating the flaws.

Further to the south, Pakistan's chances would be bleak. It had no major launching areas opposite Rajasthan which could sustain an offensive across the expanse of the desert. Nor are there targets which would be worth the effort.

The Indian aim in the west had to be something more than merely to hold off the enemy. In terms of the aims given it by the political leadership, to which the Defence Minister, Jagjivan Ram, added another by his repeated declarations that this time the war would be fought on enemy territory, Indian forces had to fight an offensive defensive war with four objectives. First, to inflict as much damage on the Pakistan war machine as possible in order to eliminate its offensive potential for some years at least, a repeat of the only aim India had in 1965. Second, to crush the Shakargarh bulge, which was a Pakistani club with nails jutting into a sensitive area of Indian communications leading north to Kashmir. Third, to push the cease-fire line in Kashmir sufficiently far to the west in certain areas to eliminate Pakistani bulges into Indian territory, to join up certain Indian bulges to make a more defensible straight line, and to strengthen the line by aligning it with some natural defences. And fourth, to capture enough worthwhile territory in Pakistan for using it as a bargain to impose a political settlement which would be advantageous to India, and for this to aim especially at some sensitive targets such as either the Marala canal headworks south-west of Chhamb which regulate releases not only into the Ichhogil canal defence system but also other extensive irrigation channels, or at points on the railway line which runs in an arc north-south-south-east and connects Rawalpindi with Karachi, giving the whole of northern and central West Pakistan its only outlet to the sea.

It was generally thought that India was in a better position this time than in 1965 to hold enemy territory against international pressure and for long enough to secure a satisfactory settlement. Once the chips were down the Soviet Union would hesitate, to say the least, to apply pressure upon India on behalf of Pakistan. The United States, which reinforced Russian pressure in 1965, had made itself irrelevant to India in diplomatic and political terms. Senior army command had its misgivings for a time about India's political stamina, misgivings which had been carried over from the day when India gave up at Tashkent territories won with difficulty in the Haji Pir bulge; they rankled again at the thought of the price which might have to be paid in cracking the hard nut of the Shakargarh bulge. But the misgivings did not last; they yielded to the evidence of the political leadership's resolution not to give up gains without securing a durable frontier in the west.

With this assurance at the back of its mind, the senior Indian Army command considered the relative advantage of three different territorial targets: the areas opposite Chhamb, the Shakargarh bulge, and vital communication targets in central and southern Sind opposite Rajasthan. Chhamb was important to each side as a barrier against a thrust by the other which could be menacing. A Pakistani thrust could threaten Jammu. An

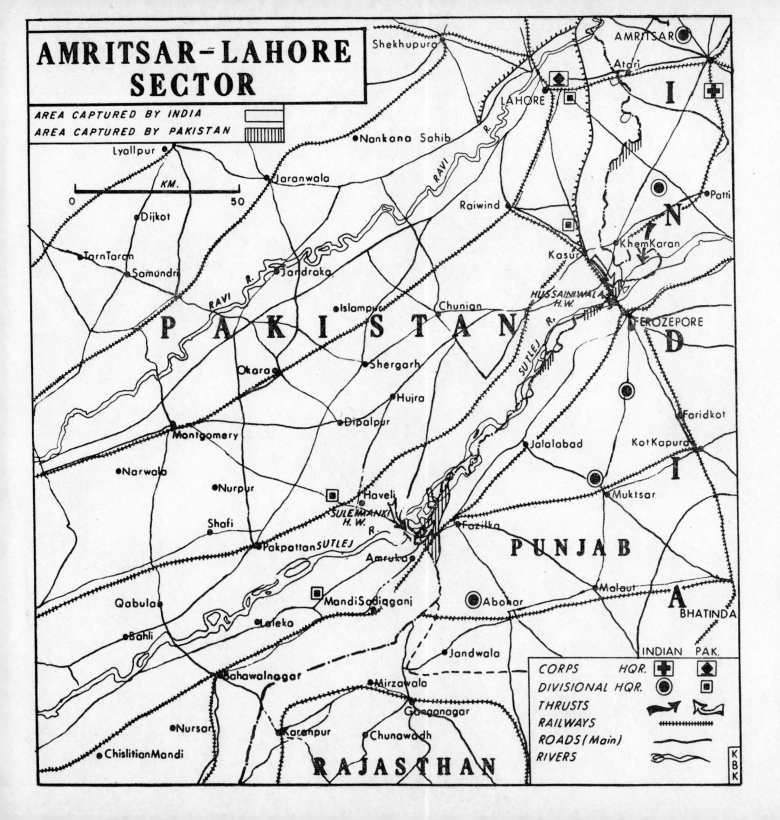

# AMRITSAR–LAHORE SECTOR

AREA CAPTURED BY INDIA
AREA CAPTURED BY PAKISTAN

KM.
0          50

Shekhupura
AMRITSAR
Atari
LAHORE
Nankana Sahib
Lyallpur
Jaranwala
Raiwind
Patti
Dijkot
RAVI R.
KhemKaran
TarnTaran
Kasur
Samundri
Jandraka
RAVI R.
I N

PAKISTAN

Islampur
Chunian
HUSSAINIWALA H.W.
FEROZEPORE
Okara
Shergarh
SUTLEJ R.
Hujra
Dipalpur
Jalalabad
Faridkot
Montgomery
KotKapura
Narwala
Muktsar
Nurpur
Haveli
I
Shafi
SULEMANKI H.W.
R.
Fazilka
PUNJAB
Pakpattan SUTLEJ
Amruka
Malaut
Qabula
MandiSadiqganj
Abohar
BHATINDA
Laleka
Bahli
A

Jandwala

Bahawalnagar
Mirzawala
Nursar
Karanpur
Ganganagar
Chunawadh
ChislitianMandi

RAJASTHAN

| | INDIAN | PAK. |
|---|---|---|
| CORPS HQR. | ✚ | ♠ |
| DIVISIONAL HQR. | ◉ | ▣ |
| THRUSTS | | |
| RAILWAYS | | |
| ROADS (Main) | | |
| RIVERS | | |

KBK

Indian thrust, if it reached the Marala headworks in the southwest, could threaten Sialkot from the rear and, only a short distance further to the west, cut the Islamabad-Lahore-Karachi main railway line. On the whole a Pakistani thrust was less practicable in 1971 than in 1965. A breakthrough to Akhnoor would not be as useful as in 1965 because of the alternative Indian routes to Kashmir developed further in the rear. Even the lesser objective of going much beyond Chhamb would be difficult to attain because since 1965 India had built a very strong line of defences to the rear of Chhamb, integrating it well with natural obstacles. Pakistan, on the other hand, did not invest much in fixed defences because, going by its experience of 1965, it regarded Chhamb as a defence problem for India, not an offensive opportunity. Therefore it must have given Pakistan great cause for anxiety when it discovered that in the Chhamb area alone India had assembled a whole division, the 10th, where in 1965 it had only a brigade, and a whole brigade, west of the Munnavarwali Tawi, where it had only a battalion in 1965.

Shakargarh offered the negative advantage of eliminating a Pakistani threat to Indian communications with Kashmir through northern Punjab. Behind it, but further from this direction than from Chhamb, and across territory laced with strong defences, were more important targets, Pasrur, Sialkot and the railway line between them and between Sialkot and Lahore. Gain had to be carefully measured against cost. On the whole the negative advantage appeared more important than the positive.

The Dera Baba Nanak gap was not very attractive for India. It gave access to important areas, was not as heavily defended as the Shakargarh salient, and if a thrust through here went deep enough it could by-pass the defences of the bulge from the south and not only take them from the rear but also threaten the Sialkot complex from an unexpected direction. A good strategic situation but tactically weak. The key to such a plan was the bridge, and it was held by Pakistan. All the effort which went into the building up of such an important thrust could be frustrated by Pakistan by blowing up the bridge.

On the other hand Rajasthan offered an invitation to Indian ambition. Indian build up could take place here without enemy interference, and, once accomplished, could make a bid for the

lifeline of Pakistan. The western bulge of Rajasthan over a
long stretch of its length is less than 160 kilometres from the railway between Karachi and central Punjab and, apart from the
desert terrain, is separated from the line neither by natural nor
manmade obstacles. Indian troops here would be nearer Karachi
than Pakistani troops at their southernmost cantonment, Multan,
would be. They would also be nearer Karachi than Delhi, and
only about a third as far away as Karachi is from Islamabad or
only half as far as Karachi is from the main centre of Pakistan's
military power in central Punjab. This is what kindled an idea
first in General Chaudhuri's mind in 1965 and next in Manekshaw's in 1971. That neither got very far with it is no reflection
upon the validity of the idea.

The Indian battle order on the western front was in response to
all these threats and opportunities. How good the response was
the operations were to show. The front was divided into two commands, the Western under Lieutenant-General K. P. Candeth,
and the Southern, under Lieutenant-General G. G. Bewoor.
Western Command had three corps headquarters under it: the
15th Corps at Udhampur, commanded by Lieutenant-General
Sartaj Singh, with consolidated command of all forces in Jammu
and Kashmir, including an infantry division, the 3rd, which
faced Tibet in north-western Ladakh; the 1st Corps at Pathankot-
Sambha, under Lieutenant-General N. C. Rawlley, responsible
for the whole area south of Kashmir up to Dera Baba Nanak,
just below the southern edge of the Shakargarh bulge; and the
11th Corps under Lieutenant-General K. K. Singh at Jullundur-
Kot Kapura, with responsibility from Dera Baba Nanak up to
the Rajasthan border. Rajasthan itself was under Southern
Command, which had set up an advance headquarters to cover it.
In 1965 Southern Command troops here were directly under
Army Headquarters. This time they were not, but still had no
regular corps headquarters above them. They operated directly
to the advance command headquarters. The 15th Corps had the
19th, the 25th, the 10th and the 26th Infantry Divisions under it
and the 3rd Independent Armoured Brigade. The 1st had the
39th, 36th, and 54th Infantry Divisions and the 2nd and 16th
Armoured Brigades. The 11th had the 15th, 7th, and 14th
Infantry Divisions, the 14th Independent Armoured Brigade and
the 1st Armoured Division, the Indian answer to the Pakistani

attack spearhead of the same name. The Indian 1st was lying somewhat to the north of the Pakistani 1st and about as close to the border from its side, each eyeing the other and waiting for it to make the first move. Southern Command had two divisions under its advance headquarters, the 12th and 11th, and some *ad hoc* forces.

Of all the Indian forces on the western front, including the two divisions in Rajasthan, those which could be described as offensive reserves were the 1st Armoured Division, held as Army Headquarters' reserve, corresponding to the Pakistani 1st Armoured's position as GHQ reserve; and the 1st Corps, which was a reserve under Western Command, corresponding to such command reserve forces of Pakistan as the 7th Infantry Division, the 17th Infantry Division minus one brigade, the 33rd Infantry Division minus one brigade, portions of the 23rd Infantry Division, the 6th Armoured Division and the 8th Independent Armoured Brigade. Since Pakistan's objective was to seize territory quickly and then negotiate from a strong bargaining position, it needed a strong offensive reserve, but since India's objective also was to conduct an offensive defensive, its needs for effective reserves were great. That is why, and also in response to a very strong Pakistani build up which India discovered only when the last hour was ticking away, the 10th Infantry Division under the 15th Corps, which was initially intended to be in an offensive posture, and the whole of the 1st Corps were retained in a more or less uncommitted posture until Pakistan disclosed its hand. Just before the war started, India moved a brigade from the division in Ladakh to the Indian area opposite Bahawalnagar in Pakistan when her suspicions about the movement of the 7th Pakistan Infantry Division and 1st Armoured Division became even stronger; another brigade was moved from the 1st Corps to the Poonch area of the 15th Corps.

After the 10th Division was placed temporarily and at the last minute in a defensive role, the only Indian forces left which were committed to an offensive role from the very start were the two divisions under Southern Command. However, more typical of the total Indian posture in the west was the 1st Corps, which stood flexibly around the Shakargarh bulge, waiting to see what moves the enemy would make. It was entrusted with the limited offensive objective of blunting at least, if not eliminating, this menacing fist.

In the air, Pakistan hoped to play a trump—a pre-emptive air strike.  It was intended of course that the strike should catch India unawares, but by a brilliant piece of deductive logic India's Air Headquarters, now under Air Marshal P. C. Lal, the cleverest head there is in the three services commands, had not only worked out that there would be an air strike but very nearly the time of the day and the day of the year when it would come.  The starting point of the Air Chief's reasoning was the appreciation made by the Joint Chiefs of Staff Committee, which based itself on a firm conclusion presented by the Central Intelligence Committee, that Pakistan would try to make a quick capture of territory for use as a bargaining counter.  The Air Chief argued that for a quick victory on the ground the PAF would try, as the IAF would in its place and was going to, to gain control of the tactical air quickly; its aim would be to join the Pakistan Army's ground offensive and speed it up, which it would not be able to do unless the IAF was kept out of the air over forward areas as much as possible.  Therefore it would try to knock out India's forward airfields and would seek to do so in a pre-emptive strike, having profited since 1965 from the example Israel set in 1967.

The second conclusion at Air Headquarters was that for two important reasons Pakistan would not attempt a daylight pre-emptive.  Moonlight was considered to be important for Pakistan because with it Pakistan would neither need night bombing facilities, with which it was known to be not very well provided, nor the use of flares, which would have required its aircraft to fly at some height and expose themselves to what they were known to be afraid of, India's ground defences, especially Russian missiles.

Pakistan's second line of reasoning was reconstructed by weighing other pros and cons of a daylight versus a moonlight pre-emptive.  A daylight pre-emptive would be more worthwhile for Pakistan if a heavy attack in the morning were repeated at short intervals.  For this, however, Pakistan would have to be willing to pay a heavy price in aircraft losses, which it would not be because it knew that it was already inferior in numbers.  It would also require for such a pre-emptive much surer knowledge of Indian air dispositions, which it would not have because the IAF had only just carried out an extensive reorganization.

With the moon as the fix, Air Headquarters chose the three six-day periods, three days before the full moon and three days after, of early November, December and January as the most likely periods of attack. These three periods were prominently marked up on air alert and surveillance work charts at Air Headquarters. Early November was considered too soon because readings taken in late October did not show the kind of activity in Pakistan which must precede an imminent war. Early January was considered too late: Army and Air Headquarters agreed that Yahya Khan could not bear much longer the situation which had now developed for his army in East Pakistan, and that he would not like to let the weather foreclose any chance there might yet be of a Chinese intervention. As events were to show India was to profit enormously from this pin-pointed anticipation of the so-called pre-emptive.

India's strategy could not envisage making a pre-emptive in the west because it would have preferred to avoid a war on two fronts; even in the east it would have preferred the low-grade war to go on for some time more. But in preparation for the day when Pakistan might opt for a more straightforward war, the IAF had drawn up an elaborate strategy and had extensively reorganized itself for it. To offset India's relative disadvantage in armour and the absence of any compensating advantage in numbers in the west, and to deny Pakistan the advantage it had in internal lines of communication running parallel to the front— in fact, to convert this into a disadvantage for Pakistan—the IAF decided to cast itself in an entirely new role.

Apart from its own customary roles of attacking enemy strategic targets and preventing such attacks on its own side of the front, the Indian Air Force took on close air support to ground forces as its overriding new function. As quickly as possible it was to gain control of the tactical air over the ground combat zone so that Indian troops could proceed without enemy air interference and enemy troops could be denied the advantage of air support and air cover. Far more than in any previous conflict it was to place enough strikes at the army's disposal and to function virtually as the air arm of the army. Pakistan had tried this tactic with success in 1965, making Indian ground command envious when they saw enemy commanders summon up effective air suport at will; they pressed for the same coordination on the Indian side in any future conflict, and the IAF more than met their expectation, again improving upon the Pakistani model.

Tactical ground support at the front was also to be part of the objective of strategic attacks in the rear on Pakistan's air installations. While their primary aim would be to damage enemy air power, a secondary aim would be to keep the PAF on the defensive, tied down to its rear bases and unable to give air cover and support at the front. This was to have interesting repercussions, most profitable for India, upon relations between the enemy army and air commands.

The second main role given to the IAF was to disrupt the enemy's main lines of communication by taking advantage of the fact that the main railway running from Karachi to Rawalpindi lies broadside to the Indian border almost along its entire length and is equally vulnerable along most of the critical stretches; India's forward airfields are spread out in a string parallel to it from north-western Rajasthan to the Kashmir border.

The requirements of close air support called for some reorganization, operational and structural, on the part of the IAF. Operationally this meant a somewhat greater centralization than in 1965, a development which appears to be contrary to the general trend in this war towards delegating authority downwards. But it was in fact a direct consequence of the strategy evolved by the Chiefs of Staff. The essence of the strategy was the complete contrast between Indian intentions in the east and west—to overrun East Bengal and to hold the enemy in the west, the latter objective calling for stolid defence in some sectors, diversionary offensives in others and feints in still others. Accordingly, the objectives of the air action on the two fronts had to be different too, as also on different sectors of the western front, so that the purpose of the army might be fully met without the enemy being able to infer from the kind of air action undertaken which was an offensive and which a feint. Only Air Headquarters, which received the army's plan in August, knew sufficiently what was the strategy of Army Headquarters. Therefore Air Headquarters not only sent down broad objectives this time, as it always does, but also broad indications about operational plans, which are usually left to the commands. The detailed working out and execution of the plans was, however, left to the commands.

Structural changes were made in regional commands of the IAF, adding a functional element to the organization in order to make air support to ground operations more effective. For a number of years the IAF was a single command service. When this command was divided, the only concept adopted was regional. First two commands, Eastern and Western, were set up and later a Central Command was formed, based at Allahabad. But there was no great distinction in functions among them. On account of the Chinese threat to north-eastern India, Eastern Air Command, with responsibility for covering the northern front as well as East Pakistan, was located in Shillong. Some coordination was later provided when both Eastern and Western Air Commands placed advance headquarters with the two corresponding army commands, Eastern Command in Calcutta and the Western in Simla. But now, not only these advance headquarters were strengthened; responsibility for all strategic bombing operations and for maritime reconnaissance as well as transport operations was transferred to Central Command, and Western and Eastern were freed for maximum concentration on air defence and tactical operations in support of the army. A tactical air centre was attached with each army corps or independent division, and, for still closer coordination, the IAF Forward Air Controllers who help to direct the close support aircraft on to their targets were given representation with each brigade.

From May onwards the IAF placed heavy emphasis upon training air crews in accurate navigation at low altitudes, quick identification of camouflaged enemy ground positions and other small-sized targets, short-distance coordination with Forward Air Controllers and observers on the ground, and first glance understanding of the ground situation when opposing armed forces are engaged in close combat. Simultaneously, IAF ground staff assembled full facilities for quick rebuilding work at forward airfields—fast drying cement, stone, bulldozers and teams of workmen. The result was that even damage caused by direct hits—and there were many, including some with delayed action bombs—was repaired within hours.

To forestall damage to aircraft, all those not absolutely needed at the front were removed to middle and rear bases, and those retained at the front put in blast proof pens (which since the war have also been reinforced against direct hit damage). Even so, some loss of forward air capability as a result of the pre-emptive was assumed as inevitable and provided against; selected forward airfields were equipped as staging points so that even if in any sector full capability airfields were not available forward, actions could be kept up from airfields in the rear. Retaliatory bomber strikes were stacked up only in the rear, at Central Command airfields like Kanpur and Agra.

The contrast between the opposing strategies was greatest at sea. Pakistan's had only a single and relatively simple element: attacks by submarine, the one naval arm in which it was stronger than India. Since 1965 Pakistan had been investing heavily in fast moving Chariot and Midget submarines. It stationed the faster submarines off Bombay and sent to the Bay of Bengal its biggest, the *Ghazi*, obtained from the USA for training purposes before 1965 and retained since then. (No submarines were based in East Bengal ports, a fact known to Indian Naval Intelligence.)

It was discovered only after the war, from its logbook after it was sunk, that the *Ghazi* left Karachi for the Bay of Bengal on 14 November and that on 24 November it was asked to arm all weapons. But towards the end of November a message to it from Karachi was intercepted which told its commander that the Indian flagship, the *Vikrant*, was in Visakhapatnam. The message gave no clue as to the whereabouts of the submarine. But the Indian Navy had anticipated that it would be in the Bay because it was the only one which had the endurance to operate at that distance, and that its target would be the aircraft carrier. In 1965 also it was sent after the same target and posted off Bombay, where the *Vikrant* was known to be. But Pakistan did not know that the ship was in dry dock. It engaged the *Brahmaputra* instead and claimed it had sunk the frigate. But, in fact, it had itself sustained some damage without hurting the *Brahmaputra* and had to be sent to Turkey for repairs.

In the Indian strategy the navy had a more complex role, covering not only the three classic roles of naval attack and defence, contraband control and defence of Indian merchant shipping, but also a most unorthodox one described on later pages. The dispositions of the navy corresponded to these tasks. It was divided into three task forces, one for the Arabian Sea, the second for the Bay of Bengal, and the third to be placed off the southern tip of India, ready to move east or west as the situation might require. The slower and older ships were placed on contraband control duty, the newer and faster on anti-submarine patrols. But most of the gun power was concentrated on the west coast because little warfare was expected in the eastern waters. Eastern operations were based at Visakhapatnam—the first operational role for this new eastern naval base, home of the submarines recently bought from Russia—and the western at Bombay but with ports along the Kathiawar coast allotted a role—another first—the importance of which was to be unfolded later.

The *Vikrant* was allotted to the eastern waters. By a fortunate coincidence it happened to be where it was going to be needed. The *Vikrant* and five frigates, along with six helicopters, had been detailed in April to assist the Ceylonese Navy in keeping a watch on the island's coast during a serious insurgency there and in the midst of reports that Chinese or North Korean ships were running arms to the insurgents. By the time this task ended in June the monsoon was about to begin and the *Vikrant* was dispatched to its normal monsoon home, the Bay, where it is more sheltered than in the Arabian Sea from the disturbances of the season. By the time the monsoons ended the danger of a war with Pakistan appeared above the horizon and the flagship was directed to remain in the east. Had it not been for this danger signal the *Vikrant* would have gone in for refitting and would not have been available for several months. From early November the flagship was kept on a number of evasive detours and never in any one port for long. Its last anchorage on the mainland before the war was in Visakhapatnam, and when it set out from there as well, deceptive traffic was simulated in and out of harbour to make inquisitive eyes believe that it was still in dock. Pakistan was obviously convinced by this: hence the message to the *Ghazi* at the end of November.

Since Pakistan's new subs were so fast that they could race any Indian ship to Karachi, India decided to hide some of her own smaller and faster anti-submarine warfare ships and missile boats in the lesser known ports of the Kathiawar coast, which are closer to Karachi than Bombay. The role intended for them was to intercept any enemy submarine which disclosed its presence by attacking any Indian Naval or merchant vessel in the crowded sea lanes around Bombay. But in fact, this turned out to be the foundation building tactic for the boldest single action by Indian arms, next only to the lightning strike on Dacca—the brilliantly planned and executed naval attack on Karachi by missile boats. Loving care went into the planning of this attack at the training school at Cochin for several months. Because the Russians, from whom the missile boats were bought, had never used them in an offensive role, the school had to plan such a use from scratch, discovering new possibilities of range and accuracy in the missiles in this process. Various configurations and approaches to Karachi had to be worked out for the attacking force before the right one was found. Mock trials were carried out off Bombay on 4 November. Even then final details were held back, to be added only in the knowledge of the exact sea conditions which would exist at the time of attack. These were written in on the night of 30 November, while those who still wavered in their faith in the boldness and novelty of this attack were offered change of command by the Naval Chief, who was personally the driving force behind the concept.

Towards the end of June the Indian Navy started building up, practically from scratch, a naval control of shipping organization for wartime coordination between merchant shipping and naval plans for protecting it. An ordinance empowering the navy to exercise control over the scheduling and routing of merchant ships was passed only in the last week of November. In the meantime, in anticipation, practically the whole organization had been put down on land and water. The pattern of shipping was studied for weeks to prepare for the protection of the expected average number of ships in harbour, in the approach lanes or further out. The likely areas of congestion were located and flagged and special arrangements made for their protection. While maximum dispersal and diffusion of merchant shipping was insisted upon, it was recognized that some concentration would be unavoidable and protective arrangements would be necessary. It was thought that Pakistan would try to deter foreign shipping from Indian waters by sinking some in circumstances in which it could expect to escape the blame.

But it was also thought that the greater the evidence of Indian preparation, the greater would be the confidence with which ships of other countries would continue to go in and out of Indian ports.

Persian Gulf routes, on which the greater part of Indian shipping plies, presented a special problem because of their nearness to the Pakistan coast. Therefore, an Indian flotilla had to be sent out towards these waters as the danger increased, and as war became a near certainty after mid-November Indian ships were directed not to take this route. Direct protection was afforded to Indian shipping only in areas close to Indian naval deployments. But some remote protection was also given by so disposing some naval ships that they were interposed between the likely lines of enemy attack and the lanes most frequented by Indian merchantmen. Particularly vulnerable areas were combed before ships were allowed through them. Where areas of maximum danger overlapped areas of unavoidable convergence, shipping schedules were modified to avoid bunching together.

By extensive training and publicity campaigns, fishermen and sailors along the west coast and aircrews flying over vulnerable areas were educated how to spot enemy submarines. Posters were distributed carrying pictures of the *Ghazi* in various profiles. It is possible that some of this information reached the ears of the enemy and deterred him from using his submarines as fully as he might have. At any rate, the success of these measures is proved by the fact that the daily average of dockings at Indian ports remained unaffected throughout the war. An Indian guarantee to shippers all over the world that their customary ports of usage on the Indian coast were safe was accepted at face value.

As soon as war broke out, India announced a blockade but quickly modified it to contraband control, which is more flexible and allows the imposing authority to decide whether to board a particular ship or not. A blockade might have exposed India to an awkward choice if an American or Chinese ship had decided to run it.

## Final Aims

By the time November turned to December, both sides had taken complete readings of each other's intentions within the limits of comprehension available to each, and suiting their troop dispositions to their resources and their natural or man-made advantages and handicaps, had adopted aims and postures which, if over simplified a little, stood out as follows:

## India

*East*

1. To pierce through the weak spots in the enemy's shield in order to disrupt his war control completely and cut him up into several pockets.
2. To by-pass enemy strongpoints, leaving them to be decimated later.
3. To deprive the enemy of all his means and routes of escape.
4. To squeeze Dacca in a tight grip of hostility, with complete control of the environment—land, water, and air.
5. To force surrender upon the enemy, or else to drive the final knife into his shrinking heart.

*West*

1. To wait for the enemy to show his hand first.
2. Thereafter to launch limited offensives with specific objectives, while containing his strikes.
3. To launch out from Rajasthan and cut through to the railway in southern Sind.
4. To eliminate the Shakargarh bulge, combining territory with attrition as the aim of India's strike corps, the 1st.
5. To hold the 1st Armoured Division in retaliatory reserve as long as possible.
6. As the war draws down in the east, to switch troops to the west for speeding up attainment of the prescribed objectives.

*In the Air*

1. To gain total control of the air in the east as quickly as possible and all across the theatre, adding its fastest element to the theatre commander's tactics of mobility.
2. To gain control of the tactical air in the west for giving maximum support to ground operations both in battle front strikes and interdiction in the rear.
3. To attack enemy bases in the rear both for attrition and to keep him pushed back from the battle front.

4. To disrupt the enemy's lines of communication.
5. To support the navy in its forward role in the east and in its plan to attack the enemy's home base, Karachi, in the west.
6. To counter enemy air action over Indian territory in the rear.

*At Sea*
1. To impose a total blockade on all enemy traffic between the two wings and to cut them off from each other.
2. To impose contraband control on all other traffic to either wing.
3. To ensure the protection of Indian merchant shipping, both in harbour and at sea.
4. To attack the enemy navy at sea and in harbour, if possible striking at the enemy's home base, Karachi.
5. To extend air cover for ground operations in southern East Pakistan.

## Pakistan

*East*
1. To maintain offensive forays in the eastern sector, and to make them in the northern as well if the Chinese encouraged the opening of a corridor.
2. To hold the enemy as long as possible at the line of the shield built up close to the border, and to this end develop battles around the strongpoints built up along the edge of the shield.
3. To escape, if necessary, by land into Burma and by river and sea to West Pakistan.

*West*
1. To activate the entire front at once to conceal the sectors chosen for offensive strategy.
2. To spoil the probable enemy offensives from Chhamb in the north, and in the south from bases in Rajasthan.
3. To make an armoured assault on a selected sector either north of the Shakargarh bulge or south of the Ichhogil system.
4. To stage a powerful feint in the other sector to cover the real assault.

5. By these means to capture significant Indian territory in the west to bargain against what the enemy may capture in the east.

## In the Air

1. To deliver a knock-out blow at the enemy's forward air bases as Pakistan's opening attack.
2. To disrupt the enemy's bomber capability in the rear and, with it, his retaliatory capability.
3. To gain control of the tactical air for supporting ground operations.
4. To counter enemy air action over Pakistani territory in the rear.

## At Sea

1. To make submarine strikes against the enemy's navy, especially the flagship *Vikrant*.
2. To dislocate the enemy's merchant shipping traffic.

Some of these opposing objectives were moved up or down in the course of the war. Some stand out more clearly in retrospect than they did at the time. But not only were they written into the opposing strategies before these went into action; the writing on either side was not very difficult for the other to decipher at least as far as these main outlines went. Only two actions, one on each side, had a surprise element in them: the Indian naval attack on Karachi and (only to some extent) the pre-emptive air strike attempted by Pakistan. For the rest the surprise was only in the suddenness or scale of execution, or the choice of particular timing or tactics or the display of efficiency or ineptitude. The Pakistani attack at Chhamb was to be an example of suddenness and scale, the Indian river crossings at Ashuganj an example of efficient improvisation, the Pakistani attack at Longewala a piece of tactical daring and the Indian air effort in the west an example of concentration upon the chosen objective.

In keeping with these objectives, both sides also completed their final or nearly final dispositions about the same time, that is, in the last couple of days of November and the first one or two of December. On the eve of the war their battle orders were ready.

The Indian battle order in the east was:

1. 2nd Corps—Headquarters, Krishnagar;
   (a) 4th Mountain Division, Headquarters, Plassey;
   (b) 9th Infantry Division, Headquarters, Gopal Nagar.
2. 4th Corps, Headquarters, Teliamura;
   (a) 8th Mountain Division, Headquarters, Eraligul;
   (b) 23rd Mountain Division, Headquarters, Shanti Nagar;
   (c) 57th Mountain Division, Headquarters, Agartala.
3. 33rd Corps, Headquarters, Siliguri;
   (a) 20th Mountain Division, Headquarters, Atair;
   (b) Two loose brigades.
4. Transport and Communication Headquarters, 101 Communication Zone Area, Tura;
   (a) 95th Infantry Brigade, Tura;
   (b) 166th Infantry Brigade (inducted almost towards the end of the operations).

Thus, out of the seven divisions built up as India's Eastern Field Force, five divisions and two infantry brigades were borrowed from the northern front; only the 9th Infantry Division, which was the one normally allocated in the areas opposite East Pakistan, was not a mountain division. Nearly everything was withdrawn from the central sector of the northern front. A whole division was withdrawn from NEFA along with its divisional headquarters and artillery as well as general headquarters. A brigade headquarters was withdrawn from the Bomdi La area on 8 December and it hardly ever went into action. The forces protecting Bhutan were also withdrawn.

The Pakistan battle order in the east was:

1. Advance Headquarters, Eastern Command, Dacca.
2. 36th Infantry Division, Headquarters, Dacca;
   (a) 93rd Infantry Brigade, Headquarters, Mymensingh;
   (b) 45th Infantry Brigade (planned to be raised under the 36th Infantry Division but it did not come into existence).
3. 39th Infantry Division, Headquarters, Chandpur;
   (a) 53rd Infantry Brigade, Headquarters, Feni;
   (b) 117th Infantry Brigade, Headquarters, Comilla;

    (*c*)  91st Infantry Brigade, Headquarters, Rangmati (under raising);

    (*d*)  57th Infantry Brigade, Headquarters, Chittagong.

4.  14th Infantry Division, Headquarters, Ashuganj;

    (*a*)  202nd Infantry Brigade, Headquarters, Sylhet;

    (*b*)  313th Infantry Brigade, Headquarters, Maulvi Bazar;

    (*c*)  27th Infantry Brigade, Headquarters, Brahmanbaria.

5.  16th Infantry Division, Headquarters, Nator;

    (*a*)  23rd Infantry Brigade, Headquarters, Saidpur;

    (*b*)  205th Infantry Brigade, Headquarters, Khetlal;

    (*c*)  34th Infantry Brigade, Headquarters, Nator.

6.  9th Infantry Division, Headquarters, Jessore;

    (*a*)  57th Infantry Brigade, Headquarters, Jhenida;

    (*b*)  107th Infantry Brigade, Headquarters, Jessore;

    (*c*)  314th Infantry Brigade, Headquarters, Khulna.

This five infantry division force consisted of 12 infantry brigades and four divisional headquarters plus two infantry brigades and one divisional headquarters which were in the process of being raised.

The Pakistan battle order in the west was:

1.  2nd Corps, Headquarters, Sialkot;

    (*a*)  12th Infantry Division; ⎫
                                ⎬Both in Jammu and Kashmir

    (*b*)  23rd Infantry Division; ⎭

    (*c*)  15th Infantry Division;

    (*d*)  8th Infantry Division;

    (*e*)  17th Infantry Division;

    (*f*)  6th Armoured Division;

    (*g*)  8th Independent Armoured Brigade.

2.  4th Corps, Headquarters, Lahore;

    (*a*)  10th Infantry Division;

    (*b*)  11th Infantry Division;

    (*c*)  One brigade of 17th Infantry Division;

    (*d*)  3rd Independent Armoured Brigade.

3.  1st Corps, Headquarters, Multan;

    (*a*)  18th Infantry Division minus one brigade;

    (*b*)  33rd Infantry Division;

    (*c*)  7th Infantry Division;

    (*d*)  105th Infantry Brigade;

(*e*) 25th Infantry Brigade;

(*f*) 1st Armoured Division;

(*g*) Two regiments of armour.

The Indian battle order in the west was:

## Western Command

1. 15th Corps, Headquarters, Udhampur;
    (*a*) 19th Infantry Division;
    (*b*) 25th Infantry Division;
    (*c*) 10th Infantry Division;
    (*d*) 26th Infantry Division;
    (*e*) 3rd Independent Armoured Brigade.
2. 1st Corps, Headquarters, Pathankot-Sambha;
    (*a*) 39th Infantry Division;
    (*b*) 36th Infantry Division;
    (*c*) 54th Infantry Division;
    (*d*) 2nd Armoured Brigade;
    (*e*) 16th Armoured Brigade.
3. 11th Corps, Headquarters, Jullundur-Kot Kapura;
    (*a*) 15th Infantry Division;
    (*b*) 7th Infantry Division;
    (*c*) 14th Infantry Division;
    (*d*) 1st Armoured Division;
    (*e*) 14th Independent Armoured Brigade;
    (*f*) One Independent Infantry Brigade;
    (*g*) One Parachute Brigade.

## Southern Command, Jodhpur

(*a*) 12th Infantry Division;

(*b*) 11th Infantry Division;

(*c*) Some *ad hoc* forces.

India had a numerical superiority in the cease-fire line area, with four divisions and three independent brigades, including one armoured brigade, as against two divisions with Pakistan. Elsewhere under Western Command, India had near parity with Pakistan.

Formal and full war now only awaited some event or decision. Everything was ready for it.

Low grade warfare—of no mean order—had been going on for months. The protagonists in this were Pakistan's eastern army and perhaps a 150,000 or 200,000 East Bengalis who had taken up arms, and almost the whole population of 60 million or so which remained at home after ten million persons had become refugees in India, and which was at least non-cooperative and within its limits hostile. India's role in this combat was of a non-combatant though something more than of a second; one element of Indian para military forces, the Border Security Force, was actively engaged in it, but regular forces came into it only when border "incidents" broke out; some had the scale of regular military engagements.

This was a phase of the utmost complexity, both political and military, and it is doubtful whether it could have been sustained for very long. There was no clear demarcation of responsibility, no mutual acceptance of jointly recognized objectives, and room for misunderstandings and friction was large and still growing. But there are some very great achievements to the credit of this phase. The fortitude of a people crossed limits which have never been seen anywhere before, and individual bravery made heroes out of people who had never held a gun in their hands till then; were never thought capable of holding it by the West Pakistani rulers of their country. It was in this phase that ordeal welded a people into a nation and the foundations were laid of Bangladesh and of the remarkable victory of Indian arms in December.

The period also contributed new elements to Indian military experience and military thought: it taught the traditionalist Indian soldier the value of an unorthodox, irregular but highly motivated ally. This was the first time ever that soldiers who had received their training in military academies and regiments which are still more or less modelled upon the former British colonial army in India learnt how to train and coordinate with highly political guerrilla forces. The experience can transform India's military resources. But it did not easily fit into the framework of thought of senior Indian command. Unaccustomed as they were to close coordination with each other, they were still more unaccustomed to actions integrated with irregulars. The barrier of novelty was not easily crossed.

India's Border Security Force knew the game much better, and so long as the problem was only of coordination between it and the irregulars there was very little difficulty. Benefiting from its training and experience in trans-border activities, across the gulf of ethnic, religious and cultural differences, the BSF, and more so some of its specialized branches, worked out very successful techniques of highly controlled flexibility into which different kinds of tactics and objectives could fit. The Mukti Bahini and BSF jointly carried out some very successful raiding and holding actions in April, May and June: some of them so successful that the Pakistan Army was unable to dislodge them when, in the first phase of its outward movement, it fanned out of the cantonments to gain control of the country. But this did not help to build bridges between the regular Indian services, especially the army, and the Mukti Bahini although the BSF was already under the control of the army when it was hunting alongside the Mukti Bahini. This was because there was no tradition of particularly smooth linkages between the army and the BSF.

In the scheme of India's border defence, and as much on the Tibetan frontier in the north as on the western and eastern frontiers, and more so of course in such areas of border disturbance as Nagaland and the Mizo hills and parts of Kashmir, the BSF holds the ground until it becomes necessary for the army to take over. Even when that happens, the BSF provides a light forward screen to army positions which, rightly, remain in the rear until there is serious risk of open clash with the regular forces of the enemy. But in the transition from one situation to the other, it is often the BSF that, lightly armed (though lately it has been allowed to develop short-range rockets and train in the techniques for using them, a significant departure from previous philosophies), bears the brunt of the initial enemy thrust. On occasions it continues to do so while warfare develops to full proportions. In 1965 it was nine mixed battalions of the BSF and special armed police which, flown to Kashmir in a single day, first faced the infiltrators in Kashmir. In 1971 it held forward positions in the face of heavy enemy attacks in the Fazilka area before the army took over and some of its units continued to face the Pakistan Army even after that. But such is the orthodoxy of established military thinking that a proper and mutually acceptable place has yet to be found for such a mixture of actions. Despite the closer linkage between the two which has existed for some years by the army deputing a senior officer, at present of the rank of Major-General, to work with the BSF, marked differences continue between the BSF and the army about the status of the BSF. The BSF believes its role is akin to the army's; the army that it is little more than that of the local police.

The resulting frictions were aggravated in the first few months of the 1971 situation by a marked divergence in the estimate of the Mukti Bahini by the BSF and the senior commands of the regular army. During the weeks when there was a tussle between the limited and total objective schools of thought, the BSF was on one side, the army on the other, in the matter of their estimate of what the Mukti Bahini could contribute to either objective. The BSF thought, as should have been expected from its different background of training and more recent experience, that the guerrillas could do much more than the army thought they could.

Some of the advocacy on behalf of a role for the Mukti Bahini weakened its own case by exaggeration. It was argued, for example, in the course of April or the early part of May, that the Mukti Bahini by itself, given some assistance, would be able to liberate the whole country. But after March this was simply not so. Even before the military crackdown occurred on 25 March, Pakistan had built up much more than its normal division plus in East Bengal of well trained and very well armed forces. The Mukti Bahini would have needed at least twice as much strength, with matching gun power and tanks and a tremendous amount of training not only in bearing arms but in fighting regular engagements, to be able to cope with this very sizeable force. The kind of disruptive engagements in which the Mukti Bahini could have engaged the Pakistanis without the direct intervention of Indian armed forces could have proved quite harassing and damaging for the Pakistani forces, but by themselves could not have brought about their eviction even with regular marginal support along the borders by the Indian forces.

Where the Mukti Bahini directly came into the calculation at all another complication ensued: the Mukti Bahini's estimate of itself, as elevated still further by its nationalist fervour. This led to rumours, which did not help to make the relationship smoother, that the Mukti Bahini, and more so the more radical wings of the guerrilla movement, did not desire the presence of the Indian Army on what they believed already to be free Bangladesh. In fact, they believed only that the intervention of India's regular forces was unnecessary, not unwelcome; they could do the job themselves, they thought, if only India would give them the tools in greater quantity. This the Indian authorities were unwilling to do until they could be more sure of proper use of the arms; if the Russians had doubts regarding American influence on certain elements in the Awami League movement, India had some about the opposite influence on certain elements of the guerrilla movement.

But these problems had been smoothed out by the time the higher objective began to emerge in the government's thinking. In fact, the respect won by the Mukti Bahini for its high motivation and durability, and for its increasing ability to conduct more organized actions, was partly responsible for the army accepting in the third week of August the objective of total liberation in one sweep.

In the meantime, at camps run by the BSF, army trainers in BSF uniforms had been training since May thousands of guerrillas for induction into East Pakistan. One of the camps, in the Chindwara forest in Madhya Pradesh, was the same which General Wingate used in World War II for training his guerrillas for action behind enemy lines in northern Burma; it was from the forest here that his Chindits took their name. The training of the East Bengal irregulars ranged from unarmed combat to skilful sabotage by small teams of commandoes to action in groups of company strength. Their weapons ranged from knives to mortars. The objectives given them, in the formal language of their instructions, were:

Employment in their own native land with a view to: (*a*) initially immobilizing and tying down the Pakistan military forces for protective tasks in East Bengal; (*b*) subsequently, by gradual escalation of guerrilla operations, to sap and corrode the morale of the Pakistani forces in the eastern theatre and simultaneously to impair their logistic capability for undertaking any offensive against Assam and West Bengal; (*c*) to avail the cadres as ancillaries to the Eastern Field Force in the event of Pakistan initiating hostilities against us.

At the peak the numbers inducted from India, apart from large forces of freedom fighters who had never left East Bengal, was about 100,000. By mid-October, Pakistan's Eastern Command had begun to admit publicly a substantial increase in guerrilla activity since the beginning of the monsoons; it estimated the guerrilla force at the time at 50,000 which was probably an underestimate because very heavy inductions had begun at the start of October; they went on rising in intensity every day until the end of November.

In the first stage of induction, the Mukti Bahini forces were used only around the periphery of East Bengal, sabotage and disruptive work going on deeper inside at that time being largely the work of the freedom fighters operating on their own. But the peripheral actions were strong enough to force the Pakistanis to withdraw 16 kilometres inland from the border and to put their irregulars, the Razakaars, to fill the gap. But this only speeded up the deeper deployment of Mukti Bahini guerrillas. In the second stage they were sent a little deeper, with specific tasks assigned to them. In the third stage, which began when the outward movement of the Pakistani forces created a vacuum in the central region of East Bengal, organized units of the Mukti Bahini were sent out on more sophisticated operations and on a larger scale.

The forces inducted from India were of three categories. First, the Mukti Bahini itself, built around five out of the eight or nine battalions of the East Bengal Regiment (the remaining were immobilized in West Pakistan) which had defected in March; this force was increased to eight battalions, organized into three brigades, all of them armed with Chinese weapons. Second, 50 companies of East Pakistan Rifles and Ansars. And third, a very large force, which could be expanded to up to 100,000 of able bodied refugees, particularly students, who had volunteered from refugee camps but, for lack of further facilities, could not be built up into formations.

Various alternative ways of deploying the three regular brigades of the Mukti Bahini were considered: allotment of independent sectors to each of them, to see how they would do; allotment of a single consolidated area to all three of them, and dispersed coordination, in smaller units, with regular Indian forces in various parts of East Bengal. It was finally decided to allot all the three brigades to 4th Corps because most of these men, belonging to the eastern sector of East Bengal, had been trained in Tripura and Meghalaya and had acquired most of their battle experience also in that sector. East Pakistan Rifles and Ansars were distributed as sector troops in different parts of the theatre.

Before the crisis began, the Indian Navy was even less experienced than the army in the art of training irregular forces and coordinating operations with them. But by the time the war ended it knew more about water-borne guerrilla operations than most navies can claim to. It began with a group of eight men of the Pakistani Navy, led by a Chief Petty Officer who had defected at Toulon, in France, where the Pakistani submarine, *Mangrol*, was being fitted up. With them as the nucleus, the navy trained 300 carefully selected and highly motivated East Bengalis in sophisticated techniques of waterborne and underwater sabotage. They were trained to handle delayed action waterproof explosive charges, some of them made in India, with triggering devices of Indian manufacture, which were strong enough to blow holes in ocean going vessels.

With 8,000 kilometres of inland waterways in East Bengal, they had plenty of training ground available to graduate by stages to higher jobs. But Indian naval officers in charge of the operation decided to begin at the top, starting with ports like Chittagong and Chalna and Khulna and then going inland. It was thought best to take the maximum risk with the first bang so that international shipping might be scared off East Bengal ports before the Pakistani Army authorities got the chance to step up security at ports, which would make subsequent operations there more difficult. This involved induction from the sea and action by the navy in a state of undeclared war, despite the presence of about 60 Pakistani gunboats and 1,500 professional sailors in and around the ports chosen as targets.

On the night of August 15-16 five task forces of trained guerrillas were smuggled in to carry out coordinated attacks on the seaport of Chittagong and on the river ports of Chalna, Chandpur, Narayanganj and Barisal. In the remaining part of the month they destroyed or damaged 14,224 tonnes of shipping, including a Somalian freighter at Chalna, two coasters at Chittagong and three at Chandpur, two Pakistani freighters, one collier, six barges, three motor launches, and two pontoons at different places. The force was then withdrawn, regrouped, rearmed and inducted again in September. In that month they destroyed 6,096 tonnes of shipping, including three Pakistani ships, and damaged 25,400 tonnes including two 8,128-tonne Pakistani freighters and a British freighter. The *Daily Telegraph*, London, described these operations as "brilliant." The *Times*, London, as "fantastic." These damages led to a steep rise in insurance rates; they were raised from five pence to one pound for every £100 worth of hull.

In October a Pakistani freighter was sunk and some coasters were damaged. The total damage for October was 6,096 tonnes of shipping sunk and 11,176 tonnes damaged, and shipping insurance companies imposed a further 25 per cent increase in rates plus a charge of $1,000 per ship per day in port in East Pakistan. Night navigation was totally stopped thereafter and Pakistan adopted several other protective measures like convoy shipping, continuous patrolling, flood lighting and hand-grenade attacks on suspected persons near port peripheries. But the naval Mukti Bahini succeeded in capturing a few motor launches and armed them with infantry weapons for stepped up operations in November.

All guerrilla forces and reserves were sent in November, with improved mines, on board a large number of mechanized craft. They destroyed 26,416 tonnes of shipping in this month and damaged another 10,160 tonnes including another Somalian ship and a Greek freighter. The port directors at Chalna announced at this stage that foreign ships could visit the port only at their own risk. Altogether some 50,800 tonnes of shipping was sunk and 66,040 tonnes damaged.

# IV  The Triumph

# A Swift Victory

Late on the evening of 1 December, the Chairman of the Foreign Policy Planning Committee, D. P. Dhar, and the Chief of Army Staff, General Manekshaw, were travelling together by air to Chandigarh to call on the Chief Minister of Kashmir, who was seriously ill in hospital there. Just before they reached their destination Manekshaw looked out of the window at the quiet country spread out below them in bright moonlight and said to his sole travelling companion: "In a couple of days, perhaps at an hour like this, the whole of this peaceful landscape is going to be shattered by war."

Manekshaw was out only by a few hours. Pakistan made a compromise between moonlight and daylight, and close to sunset on 3 December, it launched its pre-emptive attack by air. Before the night ended, the war had spread to both theatres and all services.

Pakistan concentrated first on forward airfields. Nearly all of them were attacked, from Srinagar in the north to Barmer in Rajasthan. As night fell, Pakistani bombers took over and penetrated as far as Agra, the main bomber base of the IAF and at this time the strike base of Central Command. Agra was attacked thrice that night.

The size of the attack—small—and the damage it did—negligible—confirmed every anticipated reason why Pakistan would avoid a pre-emptive by daylight. But the speculation which had been rife in Delhi—that Pakistan would only stage a bang to draw the world's attention to India's doings was quickly put in its place as everyone discovered that the attack was well coordinated with other services. At sea, the *Ghazi* moved in within three miles of Vishakhapatnam. Two other submarines moved to positions off Bombay and one to another off the Kathiawar coast. On land the whole of the western front was activated at once. Even without these moves an air strike of this size could only have been a prelude to war. But Pakistan made sure that it would be seen as part of what was clearly intended as an all-out war, which for some time had been expected by everyone.

At the southern end of the western front Pakistan, showing very good understanding of Indian intentions, began to uncoil an armoured force which was to blast its way a little later into the offensive plans of India's Southern Command. In the next sector to the north, it made a strong probing raid from Suleimanki against Fazilka, and still further north against India's Ferozepur-Husseiniwala salient where an Indian enclave on the Pakistan side was quickly eliminated. Several probes were made in the whole of the central sector from the area opposite Khem Karan to the Pakistan enclave on the Indian side at Dera Baba Nanak. But the real punch of these opening moves was reserved for Chhamb and Poonch. The attacks in the central sector were no more than they were meant to be, probes to test Indian intentions; they lacked the size and intensity of anything more serious. Those from Ferozepur to Fazilka were also meant to be only probes. They were greater in size and depth only because they also had to serve their purpose as feints or, rather as temporary feints upon the real feint which was being staged at the northern end. Fazilka for a time looked like being in real danger, and the Indian sector command took the threat all the more seriously because of the suspected presence of the 1st Pakistan Armoured Division behind Suleimanki. But Pakistan had no intention of playing this card as yet. For the present it was concentrating on the northern sector.

Pakistan had assembled enormous firepower opposite the Indian salient at Chhamb—about 12 regiments of artillery, containing two hundred heavy guns and a large number of medium guns behind them, the 1971 counterpart of the 90-tank assault led by Yahya Khan in 1965. With these, Pakistan was to fire 60,000 rounds in less than two days. The build up to this size had gone unnoticed by India; the belated redisposition of the 10th Indian Infantry Division to an entirely defensive posture did not show awareness of this particular build up; it was carried out, or attempted, only in general anticipation of an attack about then.

On the other hand, along the northern prong, where an appreciable build up had been observed by India, perhaps deliberately exposed to the Indian eye, the attack was smaller. But it was strong enough, and pointed at the more important target, Poonch, not Uri, to give the attack at Chhamb the appearance of the stronger southern prong of a seriously intended pincer on Kashmir. Indian Army planners took satisfaction in this: despite the overall near-parity on the western front as a whole, minus Rajasthan, they had assembled decidedly superior numbers in Kashmir, expecting Pakistan to be as serious about it as in 1965; now they believed themselves justified.

India too retaliated, with all arms and in both theatres. The first arm to strike back was, unexpectedly, the navy. By sheer good luck it sank the *Ghazi* even before the Prime Minister came on the AIR at midnight on 3 December to announce that war had broken out, and before the IAF retaliation had crossed the border. Fairly soon after the PAF began the pre-emptive in the early evening, a destroyer slipped out of Vishakhapatnam for the East Pakistan coast to cover landings which were planned to be made there at Cox's Bazar a few days after the expected outbreak of war. Almost immediately after leaving harbour, its sonar picked up a hard echo. It asked Vishakhapatnam for instructions, Vishakhapatnam asked Delhi, and in accordance with the standing clearance given to the three Services Headquarters to retaliate in full against intrusions, the destroyer was asked to fire a full pattern of depth charges. The destroyer let off its charges, not knowing what its target was, and continued on its way to keep its rendezvous. A strong explosion was heard in Vishakhapatnam about an hour later. The navy had no other ships in harbour to investigate the explosion, and the first indication that it might have been the *Ghazi* came only when some fishermen picked up a life-jacket with US markings upon it. When divers went down they found the *Ghazi*, its rudder in a hard to port position, indicating fast manoeuvres in a state of distress. They also found signs that an explosion had occurred on it, but no clear evidence to show what had caused it; nor whether the *Ghazi* was instructed to attack, lay mines or reconnoiter. They brought up the log-book, which explained the movements of the submarine but not its mission—certainly it aimed to carry out in 1971 the attack on *Vikrant* it failed to make in 1965.

About the time that the *Ghazi* sank, its intended victim, the *Vikrant*, slipped out of the Andaman waters where it had been waiting for the war, and early the next morning its aircraft made India's first naval raid, at Cox's Bazar, and in the following hours the same day set fire to the oil refinery at Chittagong.

On the evening of the third, the IAF held back its hand for about six hours. Like the headquarters of the two other services, Air Headquarters also had advance clearance from the Cabinet to strike back in strength. But in a brilliant piece of tactical anticipation it decided to let PAF interceptors tire themselves out in protective forward patrolling since they would be expecting an instant Indian response. Then, at about midnight, its bombers took off, followed from the early hours of next morning by rocket firing fighters and fighter-bombers, and despite heavy losses inflicted by ground fire and stiff air opposition over PAF prize targets in the rear, it plastered all important enemy airfields and inflicted heavy damage on them, showing far greater intelligence about enemy dispositions than Pakistan showed about India's. On one side it went as far back as Islamabad, Sargodha, and even Karachi which had remained untouched in 1965 on account of its distance from the nearest Indian operational airfield. On the other side the IAF simply eliminated the PAF with strikes at main airfields and combat in the air. Half the planes Pakistan had in the east were destroyed on the ground or in air combat. The remaining were grounded because in sweeps covering the whole theatre all the main airfields, especially those at Dacca and Chittagong, were put out of commission by IAF MiG-21s carrying 1,000-pound bombs. By the forenoon of 4 December Pakistan knew for certain that the pre-emptive had failed. Perhaps the war was decided in these few hours.

On the ground in the west, the Indian Army held its hand a little longer still, taking in the meantime heavy beating at Chhamb. But on the night of 3-4 December, Eastern Command simultaneously launched all the planned drives into East Pakistan, concentrating first on extinguishing the risk of any serious Pakistani attack. Since the risk was the greatest in the eastern sector, that is opposite Tripura, the counter action was also the strongest there. Near its central sub-sector Indian forces encircled Akhaura, an important Pakistani base threatening Agartala, which is just opposite. In the northern sub-sector attacks were started towards Kalaura and Maulvi Bazar, to neutralize the danger of attacks out of Sylhet, and towards Shamshernagar to drive a wedge between the northern and central sub-sectors. In the north-western sector, below India's Siliguri corridor, Thakurgaon was captured which controls roads leading to the district headquarters, Dinajpur. In the western sector the rail junction of Darsana was captured, putting Indian troops in position for a drive to cut the headquarters of Pakistan's 9th Infantry Division at Jessore from its brigade headquarters at Jhenida. A number of pockets so far held by the Mukti Bahini and the BSF were joined up all along the front and 200 square kilometres of East Pakistan territory captured.

But the most spectacular retaliatory blow was delivered by the navy. On the second night of the war it made a raid on Karachi which, along with the failure of Pakistan's pre-emptive the previous night, must rank as two of the most important causes of Pakistan's defeat in the west. The raid began to go forward, according to plan, on the afternoon of 4 December, the Naval Chief sticking to his earlier assessment that Pakistan would be so busy with its ground and air offensive on the inner frontier with India, some 1,300 kilometres away, that it would not have much attention to spare for what was going on off its other frontier, the coast of Sind. He was reconfirmed in this by the absence of any enemy strike along India's west coast during the pre-emptive.

Preparatory to the attack, out of the naval ships on patrol duty in the northern Arabian Sea, imposing contraband control and protecting Indian shipping on the Persian Gulf routes, five large ships were selected for forming a decoy naval force, and between 30 November and 3 December they were placed in an area north-west of Karachi, 150 kilometres south of the Makran coast. Another force of five smaller but faster naval ships was formed up off the Kathiawar coast approximately 500 kilometres south-east of Karachi. An attack force of missile boats was towed up to different points on the Kathiawar coast and concealed among its numerous narrow waters. The manoeuvre did not remain hidden from the enemy. On 2 December a Canberra bomber of the PAF came up to Okha, chasing a missile boat. The boat escaped the enemy; so did the meaning of what the bomber saw.

Immediately after these dispositions were made the boats were fully fuelled up and placed on very fast evasive patrolling. After a study of the latest sea conditions, a course was selected for them which, at any time in the next few days, would give the boats such an approach to Karachi that their target, Pakistan's most important oil storage installations, would be distinguishable from the clutter of the harbour to the electronic eyes of the missile-firing guns.

It was calculated that naval ships protecting Karachi would be spread out in an arc around it, probably with about 150 kilometres between one ship and the next. As safety against them, both naval forces were given such a formation that either could converge on any enemy ship and pick it off in isolation from others if it discovered the attacking force before the missile boats could get to Karachi. The naval force placed off Makran, although only a decoy, was asked to make the first move; if the enemy detected it he would engage it, and the real attack force would escape attention. The missile boats and the ships accompanying them were to approach Karachi only after dark; it was known that the enemy's fighter attack planes did not have radar, and the bombers, which had it, would not be effective against fast moving targets.

It was also thought, correctly as events were to prove a few hours later, that if the Indian ships got in their blow first on enemy targets on land or at sea, the sheer unexpectedness of the raid would cause so much confusion that it would not be difficult to press the advantage. In last minute details of coordination with the IAF, it was arranged that a few hours before and after the naval attack, the IAF would attack both airfields at Karachi; the first time to keep the enemy either grounded or too busy to keep a watch on the coast, the second time to cover the Indian naval forces when they would be on their way back and vulnerable again in the early light of 5 December. On the afternoon of 4 December all formations were given the green signal.

Everything went right. Some better than planned. Even the diversionary naval force was not detected by the enemy. The IAF attack proved so effective that Karachi's defences were already in a state of confusion before the naval attack began. A Pakistani destroyer, the *Khyber*, which probably detected the south-eastern force but too late, gave away its own position and identity by exchanging radio signals with Naval Headquarters which wanted to make sure that the *Khyber* had not been frightened by one of Pakistan's own ships.

The *Khyber* was then given permission to attack, but while

looking for the Indian ships it attacked a ship of its own navy. When Indian ships attacked it, it broke into two. Another destroyer, the *Shahjahan*, came to its rescue but that too broke up under direct hits. But the element of surprise was still not dissipated. When the missiles struck Karachi harbour, the first enemy reaction was anti-aircraft fire and the second upward fire from shore batteries which were asked to turn their guns to the sky. The missiles were mistaken to be aerial rockets. The missile boats moved still closer inshore and emptied their magazines before turning back. By this time the diversionary force had been on its way home for a couple of hours already, and by the time the IAF made its second attack on Karachi, at 5.30 on the morning of 5 December, the second naval force was also 144 kilometres away.

The oil storage tanks at Karachi were probably first hit in the IAF attack late on the evening of 4 December. The minutes of the Washington Special Action Group meeting on 5 December which were disclosed by Anderson also appear to confirm this. But it was the powerful attack by the naval missiles, devastating in their inflammatory effect on any combustible target, let alone oil, which destroyed these vital tanks and, by making Pakistan cautious in the use of its heavy armour, which depends upon oil, helped to shorten the war substantially. With the coast of Pakistan under an effective blockade already, there was no hope of replenishment from outside, and another meeting of WSAG confirms this as well.

It was during this raid but in an engagement unconnected with it that the Indian frigate, *Khukri*, was sunk by a Pakistani submarine which is known to have been under the command of one of the ablest officers of the Pakistani Navy and a former Deputy Chief of the *Ghazi*. An Indian ship picked up the killer sub on its radio because the submarine did not maintain radio silence after the kill. It was given chase but it escaped because the Indian Navy could not combine speed, endurance and weapon power in any one chaser; a Super Constellation of the IAF which joined in the chase could keep track of the sub but had no means of attacking it, the ships which had weapons of attack could not keep pace with it, or not for long enough.

But the navy repeated the attack on the night of 8 December, this time approaching within eight kilometres of the harbour,

Its missile boats further damaged what was left of the oil installations and also attacked storages at Jewani and Gawadar, on the Makran coast near the border with Iran. Four Pakistani ships were sunk in this attack as well. The Russian Navy Chief, when he visited India after the war, was as surprised as impressed by the discovery of capabilities in a weapon supplied by Russians which, he said, the Russians did not know.

The navy proved to be completely effective, assisted again by Super Constellations of the IAF, in imposing a total blockade upon traffic between the two wings of Pakistan, and nearly total contraband control upon traffic between either wing and the rest of the world. It captured the first Pakistani ship and boarded the first foreign vessel within 24 hours of the start of the war, and thereafter no ship could ply between the two wings or to either of them except as allowed by the Indian Navy.

In the eastern theatre the navy fitted into the ground war with a click which must have been heard in Islamabad. The western sector was the first where serious fighting developed as the two-division 2nd Indian Corps under Lieutenant-General T. N. Raina, based at Krishnagar, 100 kilometres east of Calcutta, launched two thrusts in half division strength towards the enemy strongpoints of Jibannagar, Kot Chandpur and Chuadanga, a screen protecting the divisional headquarters, Jessore, and one of its brigade headquarters, Jhenida, and towards Kaliganj, on the railway connecting Jessore and Jhenida. The aim was to drive powerful wedges between Jessore and Jhenida and then to tackle each in turn; later Jessore was to be cut from its other brigade at Khulna. The two opposing strategies met their first serious test here: the Pakistani, based upon fixed defences and strongly built garrisons in or around major towns near the border, and the Indian, of by-passing and encircling moves in mobile warfare, the first objective always being to divide the enemy forces before testing their strength and to get behind the enemy screen before attacking it. The Indian won. Within the first three days not only was the outer screen punctured and its fixed supports overturned but Jhenida also fell and Jessore was made to feel so exposed that the next day the enemy gave it up without a fight, leaving behind some 6,096 tonnes of ammunition with which he was hoping to beat a frontal assault. The way the defences of Jessore were oriented made it clear that Pakistan was expecting an attack along the road and railway coming down from Bongaon, the nearest sector of the Indian border: Pakistan must have been confirmed in this expectation by the action at Boyra, near Bongoan, on November 22. But the Indian forces completely ignored this obvious axis.

The danger now was that the Pakistani divisional commander might try, as a large body of his troops was seen to be, to slip down the Madhumati and out to sea or to Dacca by boats which he might find at Khulna and Chalna. But the *Vikrant* stepped in with heavy air attacks on both these ports. Naval troops attacked Chalna by land while the naval Mukti Bahini intensified patrolling in the lower reaches of the Madhumati and its main branch, the Pasur. Their seaward retreat blocked by the navy, this Pakistani force, along with the brigade at Khulna, tried to make a stand on the west bank of the Madhumati along a stretch where a well fortified bund had gun emplacements overlooking the only road and railway from Jessore and was protected by the river on one side and paddy fields on the other. Indian troops found the approach difficult and called in the air force, which knocked out these defences with Gnat, Hunter, Sukhoi and Canberra strikes—one of the few occasions when Canberras were used in daylight in this war. The Pakistani troops broke cover and tried to move north in search of a crossing over the Madhumati further upstream. In the meantime, land elements of the Mukti Bahini helped to bottle up the divisional and brigade headquarters.

When Jhenida fell, the brigade headquarters tried to move back to Magura. But the opposing Indian brigade marched 50 kilometres across country during the night and captured Magura. Another Indian march over a still longer distance cut off the divisional headquarters' retreat to the east of Jessore and also the upstream escape of the brigade at Khulna. Information on both enemy moves came to the Indian forces from the Mukti Bahini, while information about their own forced marches never reached Pakistani intelligence although literally hundreds of people not only saw these marches but assisted them across sticky patches.

In the northern sector, south of India's Siliguri corridor, Pakistan offered very stiff resistance at Hilli where it expected a strong Indian attack to close the Hilli-Gaibunda gap and trap all Pakistani forces and armour caught north of this line. But the more it invested in the defence of Hilli the more it exposed the communication centre at Bogra, the real Indian objective which was in the rear. Anticipating the enemy reaction, the 33rd Corps Commander, Lieutenant-General M. L. Thapan, kept pressing at Hilli without meaning to take it by assault, while a force wheeling east and south from Thakurgaon occupied Bogra, seriously disrupting enemy logistics.

The real battle for Bangladesh was developing in the eastern half of the country, east of the Jamuna-Padma vertical divide, though the Jessore sector was much more in the news because of easy access from Calcutta. But the purpose of Indian drives in the eastern sector opposite Tripura was as yet hidden from view. It began to unfold itself only about the time that Jessore and Jhenida were falling; the north-eastern drive did not reveal itself until December 11.

In the meantime the land battle in the west was going much better for Pakistan. Its losses were heavy, but for equivalent gains. At the southern end of the front, the tank column driven towards Longewala achieved the greater part of its mission though nearly the whole of it was destroyed in the process. It consisted of a force of about 4,000 men with a regiment of T-59 (Chinese) tanks, a squadron of (American) Sherman tanks, a field regiment of artillery and another medium battery of artillery. According to documents captured from some of the tank crews after the battle, their objective was to disrupt the lines of supply of the 12th Indian Infantry Division between Jaisalmere, the launching pad for it, and Ramgarh along the route which the division was expected to follow in trying to reach the Karachi railway line in the Rahim Yar Khan area. The tank column had covered about 80 or a 100 kilometres and penetrated 16 kilometres into Indian territory before it was detected, and that too by a chance patrol, alerted by a villager who had heard the sound of the tank engines.

The surprise was probably achieved by routing the column through a country strewn with sand dunes and by denying air cover to it. But it remains a mystery why it was given no air cover even after its presence had been discovered. It is probable that Pakistan thought there were no aircraft at the nearest Indian airfield at Jaisalmere, which is also the probable reason why this airfield was omitted from those chosen by Pakistan as the targets for its pre-emptive attack on the evening of 3 December. Until shortly before the war began, Jaisalmere had not been in operational air use. Even then it had only a flight of four Hunter fighter-bombers, out of which one was not airworthy. But the three were enough to slaughter the tank column in the absence of any air opposition. Air attacks on the column began at 7.30 in the morning; by midday about 18 tanks had been destroyed and 25 by the end of the day. When units of the 12th Division caught up with the battle, they finished off the enemy force, or as much of it as had not fled back into Pakistan.

But by that time the column had succeeded in putting the 12th off-balance; it had to call back a column which had pushed out for Ramgarh before the Pakistani thrust was discovered, and it never got sent out again. However, in the counter-attack on the tank column, Indian forces captured 640 square kilometres of desert territory, against general absence of enemy opposition.

At the opposite end, Pakistan pressed home the advantage of surprise it had gained in the attack on Chhamb, and India had to abandon the town on 6 December. The battle was fierce. Pakistani troops as well as the PAF showed skill, resolution, and good coordination; the PAF flew 25 to 30 sorties a day in support of the ground battle. On the other hand, the Indians were without air support at this stage, the IAF being busy, according to its plan, with eliminating the enemy from the tactical air by knocking out his forward airfields before turning to active ground support. It gave what support it could spare but that was much less than what the army required. This was one of the only two phases of the entire war when there was some friction between India's Army and Air Commands and between Army Headquarters and senior commands in the field.

On the night of 7 December Pakistani armour pressed the attack beyond Chhamb and the Indian brigade had to be pulled back to the east bank of the Tawi. On December 8 India made a brief counter-attack and failed, and Pakistan followed up the Indian retreat in strength to establish a large bridge-head of over 8,000 square metres across the Tawi during the night. But what revealed the enemy's strategic intentions was not the establishment but withdrawal of the bridge-head.

On 8 December the Indian Air Force joined the battle and in two days it flew 200 sorties to this area. With SUs, Hunters and Canberras, the IAF struck with rockets by daylight and 1000-pound bombs by night. At the request of the army, it also diverted to Chhamb additional sorties from other sectors and in the course of the next day the scales began to turn in India's favour. On the night of 9-10 December India counter-attacked with two battalions of infantry, two squadrons of armour and all the artillery it could put together. But the attackers discovered that they were practically pushing at an open door. After investing immense effort and heavy casualties in men and armour in putting up the bridge-head, Pakistan quietly withdrew and the Indian attack met very little resistance.

But the Pakistani raid did its work. Made doubly credible by its size and by two supporting thrusts, one slightly to its right flank and the other at Poonch, it convinced the Indian command that Pakistan was now fully committed here to a large venture. On the night of 5-6 December, Lieutenant-General Rawlley, commanding the 1st Indian Corps, informed Army Headquarters that with Pakistan committed at Chhamb the Corps was beginning its attack on the Shakargarh bulge. As events were to show, this was a big enough task to tie down the 1st Corps here very fully for the next ten days.

South of this corps Indian and Pakistani force levels were more or less even. Although Pakistan did not have an independent theatre command opposite Rajasthan, it could still spare enough infantry and armour from the forces under the corps headquartered at Multan without losing its parity with India in that sector. From Pakistan's point of view the heart and purpose of this parity was the evenly matched confrontation between the two opposing 1st Armoured Divisions. Given Pakistan's confidence in its superiority in armour, combat between the two opposing strike divisions, with the other forces of both sides either more or less fully engaged or, if unengaged, equally matched, was the best that Pakistan could hope for. This was also the strategic aim of its dispositions and opening manoeuvres. Unlike 1965, the Pakistan 1st Armoured Division was not without hope of adequate infantry support. The 7th Infantry Division had already moved to its flank at Bahawalnagar from Peshawar, the 1st Corps at Multan had two more unengaged infantry divi-

sions and two infantry brigades, and to its left at Lahore there
were two other infantry divisions which were hitherto unengaged
because there had not been any serious fighting in this sector.
Therefore, Indian reactions and thinking in the land war on the
west had so far geared into Pakistan's plans to its satisfaction.

Could it be on the other hand that Pakistan's reactions and
thinking had geared into Indian military plans?

For example, could it be that by putting the 10th Infantry
Division at a place where it could seriously menace important
targets in Pakistan, India had forced Pakistan into a pre-emptive
effort at Chhamb, thus freeing the 1st Indian Corps for an offensive at Shakargarh while the Indian 1st Armoured was held as a
watchdog against the opposing 1st Armoured? Or that Pakistan, by seriously investing in an offensive at Chhamb, had freed
the 1st Indian Corps?

Events do not confirm either of these hypotheses. Five brigades
and a corps worth of artillery would have been too much for
Pakistan to put into a spoiling effort at Chhamb. On the other
hand, if Pakistan had intended to commit itself to a serious
offensive it would not have deflated its attack so readily. Its
withdrawal from the bridge-head across the Tawi corroborates
the testimony of prisoners of war that the attack at Chhamb was
not a serious offensive but more like a raid in strength. In greater strength than a spoiling raid, but not too extravagant for a
strategic feint which must convince. Despite the preceding artillery build up, the attack itself was launched at very short notice
and without the necessary reconnaissance in depth which would
have preceded an intended offensive. Pakistan was to show
opposite Rajasthan, at Naya Chor and Chor, that right up to
the end it could be very tenacious when it believed important
issues were at stake. It could even summon up a moderate
amount of air support. Therefore, it would not have abandoned
the bridge-head merely because the IAF had joined the ground
battle or India had counter-attacked with two battalions of
infantry and two squadrons of armour where Pakistan had five
brigades. On the contrary, the Pakistani attack would have
been stronger still if the 2nd Corps Headquarters at Sialkot had
meant it to be serious. It could have sustained the offensive,
apart from planning it more thoroughly. Sitting behind the
strongly defended Shakargarh bulge, 2nd Corps knew it was not

facing any imminent threat. Pakistan is not given to under-estimating itself; it would have expected the bulge to hold out at least as well as it did.

Viewed from the Indian side the picture looks the same. It was important for India to eliminate this bulge. But unless its defences were grossly underestimated, it should have been obvious to the Indian military command that they would become a wholetime occupation for the 1st Corps for a couple of weeks at least. In the meantime the balance in the south would be as Pakistan had planned it. This was a bigger price to pay than the bulge was worth. Unless Indian strategists grossly over-estimated the danger of Pakistan striking out of the bulge they would have known that the relative balance further south would be more in favour of Pakistan if Indian commitments suited Pakistan's designs than if they did not, and that Pakistan would gain more in the south than it would lose in the north if India committed a whole corps to the bulge. It turned out that Pakistan could take no advantage of the parity it achieved in the south. But that came later. When the two sides were drawing up their military plans it could not have been foreseen by the Indian side that within three days Pakistan would virtually lose the war.

Much better would it have been for India, as seen from any vantage point before 3 December, to invest less in taking slices of the bulge and more in the thrusts out of Rajasthan either by allotting a larger force to them to begin with or by making diversions to them later. They would have given India something more worthwhile to bite into, some sensitive spot in Pakistan to sit upon during the negotiations which would follow the cease-fire, some situation which would have really hurt Pakistan. Pakistan would have paid much more to move India off its main communication artery than to get back the marginal territories India captured elsewhere. With the given disposition of the opposing main forces, it was to Pakistan's advantage, therefore, to have brought about the kind of engagement map which began to emerge on 6 December.

Opposite Rajasthan, Pakistan lived up to the expectation that with forces borrowed from the Multan sector it would be able to hold its own though it did not have an independent formation corresponding to India's Southern Command. With the 12th Indian Infantry Division thrown off its plans, the 11th now had to carry the whole command objective, and it just did not have the means to do so. Its efforts were strenuous but did not get very far. It tried to cope with the desert terrain by re-building in the immediate wake of its advance an old, abandoned railway from Barmer, its own launching position in southern Rajasthan, to Mirpurkhas in southern Sind and beyond that to Hyderabad. By the time the war ended Indian trains from Barmer could go over 48 kilometres into Pakistan along this track. But the division had neither the sinews nor the logistics for a decisive push, and what it had was scattered over several thrusts across the border into the vacancy of the desert, instead of being concentrated behind a single drive to one objective.

Pakistani resistance became stiffer every day as Indian forces got closer to the first cross-communication position in the line of their advance, Naya Chor, 57 kilometres from the Indian border. Pakistani troops here had been reinforced by two bri-gades of infantry and a regiment of T-59 tanks borrowed from the 33rd Infantry Division, and also had adequate air support. But even if Naya Chor had fallen, Indian troops would have been 70 kilometres away from Mirpurkhas, the first station on a north-south railway, and 150 kilometres from Hyderabad, on the railway to Karachi. There was no early chance that the hope expressed by Southern Command on December 14 would be fulfilled and "Punjab separated from Sind." India could not cut the railway link between the two provinces.

But that was the limit of Pakistan's good fortune. In every other way the position was daily becoming more desperate for it, on both fronts from the first day on, but more particularly in the second week and on the eastern front. India found the going tough in the Shakargarh bulge, and here again there was a little friction between the air force and the army: the army wanted the air force to take on a series of strong and well cam-ouflaged gun emplacements with which the bulge was infested, the air force, after suffering heavy losses to ground fire, replied that objectives like these were better tackled by firepower on the ground. But the disagreement was shortlived. The IAF went in in a big way on interdicting missions behind the bulge, attacking Pakistani reinforcements moving up from the rear. Here the reinforcements were without the benefit of camouflage and, being in motion, were easily identifiable. The army found speedy and reliable ways of dealing with the defences within the bulge. The combined result was an improvement in the rate of Indian advance.

By adopting the tactics of the east on a miniature scale, that is cutting in along strips of high ground and between the beds of nullahs and streams, the 1st Corps managed to push in three prongs, from the east, south and north, and started to carve out triangles of cleared territory. The state of battle inside the bulge was substantially changed in the course of the following week. On December 15 and 16 the battle raged throughout the day and night. By the end of it the three regiments of Pakistani armour which were defending the bulge had lost 45 tanks. Indian losses were 15 tanks. By the time the war ended the First Corps had captured 768 square kilometres of the bulge. It had barely reached the base defence line of this network, which runs north-south from Zaffarwal to Narowal. It was nowhere near posing a threat as yet to either of these towns, or to Sialkot and Pasrur or the railway line between them, objectives which were still further back. But the danger of attacks on India from within the bulge had been greatly reduced for the future.

The air war was going badly for Pakistan. By avoiding air combat Pakistan was able to keep its losses down. Its ground and air defences showed their strength only when the IAF tried to strike at main PAF bases which are well to the rear and where most of its aircraft were parked; IAF losses in these raids were serious enough for it to become more cautious. But this only encouraged the IAF to concentrate on strikes at the battle front, where it took a mounting toll of enemy armour. The Pakistan Army was thus paying heavily for the conservation of Pakistan's air strength. This caused bad blood between the two services. The army accused the air force of cowardice, the latter replied that the army had no plans to support.

By leaving the IAF free to roam the forward air, the PAF all but nullified its own and the Pakistani ground forces' success in holding up the Indians at Naya Chor. The IAF now pounded away at the Karachi-Lahore-Islamabad railway so mercilessly that no large-scale military movement could take place on it. Any traffic which looked like being useful in war, especially oil tankers and oil installations at railway sidings,

suffered very heavy damage; so did the main railway marshalling
yards. During the last couple of days of the fighting,
the PAF was seen to be flying continuous air patrols over the
railway line. It might have been protecting some particularly
sensitive traffic below. But Indian intelligence believes the more
likely explanation to be that by now railway traffic staff were
refusing to run trains without air cover.

The PAF also nullified the Pakistan Army Command's
advantage in bringing about the pattern of main engagements
which it desired. Firstly, it could not prevent the Indian Navy
from delivering and the IAF from supplementing some powerful
blows at Pakistan's oil reserves without which Pakistan could not
have sustained armoured warfare for long. This must have
reinforced—though this is only a conjecture which cannot be
tested until more is authoritatively disclosed about the war from
the Pakistan side—the army's hesitation to commit its armour in
open and wide ranging warfare when the air force was not giving
it the necessary cover; the fate of the tank force sent to Longewala, and what began to happen in the Chhamb sector and the
Shakargarh bulge when the IAF intervened, must have already
magnified the hesitation.

But the IAF's most direct contribution to dissuading Yahya
Khan from committing the 1st Armoured to battle was sustained
air attacks on its rear concentration and forward areas from
almost the day the war began. Even before that, Indian Army
Headquarters, acting on intelligence about the division's movements, had asked for close surveillance of the suspected area of
its deployment. The IAF kept it up, and when it lost four
Mysteres to ground action in photo reconnaissance its suspicions
were confirmed; there was nothing else in the area to explain the
concentration of anti-aircraft defences in such strength. Immediately after this very suggestive enemy reaction, the IAF
began shooting up every suspected target with bombs and rockets,
flying more than 300 strike missions into the area and setting
ablaze large patches of dry grass and scrub. Fires were also
noticed in the forest after some of the attacks. IAF aircraft
taking off from Sirsa and Nal airfields in Haryana attacked an
armour-carrying train near Chistian Mandi, suspected to be one
of the launching positions of the 1st Armoured. Fourteen tanks
were destroyed in this attack. Simultaneously, air raids were

made on the division's other known or suspected forward assembly points, Pak Pattan, Fort Abbas, Haveli, Mandi Sadiqganj and Bahawalnagar.

According to the testimony of some Bengali defectors from the 1st Armoured, enough damage was caused to dislocate any intended offensive by it. They said the IAF destroyed the division's petrol dump at Chistian Mandi, the power house at Bahawalnagar, 27 tanks, five guns, 13 vehicles and, more important for the disruptive effect, 14 bridges of different sizes. Fresh plans were said to have been drawn up for an attack on 10-11 December. But by that time the tide of war had become so discouraging that Pakistan thought the better of it. Even before the war ended in the east, the IAF lifted two brigades from there into the Fazilka area, and with further reinforcements obviously on the way as the war declined in the eastern theatre any offensive by the 1st Armoured was placed out of the question.

By the time the war began to turn in India's favour in the Chhamb salient and the Shakargarh bulge, it had become positively menacing for Pakistan in the eastern theatre, especially the eastern sector, the area of the Indian 4th Corps. Within the first two days, 4 and 5 December, the Corps's advance towards Sylhet in the north, Akhaura in the middle and the Comilla-Maynamati complex in the south had eliminated the danger of any Pakistani attack on the corps's own lifeline, the Agartala road. Now the corps was ready to begin the march on Dacca. It had two approaches to choose from: the longer but probably more lightly held southern approach coming to Dacca up the east bank of the Meghna from the river ports of Chandpur and, smaller but much closer to Dacca, Daudkandi; or the shorter but probably more strongly defended northern approach coming down the railway line from Bhairab Bazar after crossing the Meghna at Ashuganj, a Pakistani divisional headquarters, where the river is much narrower than south of Dacca, at Daudkandi or Chandpur.

The 4th Corps decided on a simultaneous push along both approaches but with greater stress on the southern because the northern was expected to have a strong shield strung out along the Akhaura-Brahmanbaria-Ashuganj line on the eastern bank of the Meghna. The southern approach would also have Comilla-Maynamati and Laksham to contend with, but they could be by-passed. In the event, both approaches prospered.

On the night of 3-4 December, three brigade groups were simultaneously launched on the southern approach: one to by-pass Comilla-Maynamati from the north and to cut off the retreat of the Pakistani forces in this complex; one to by-pass and cut off Laksham from the north-west; and one to capture Laksham itself, to control the only railway going to Chittagong.

On the northern approach, the brigade which had attacked and captured Akhaura, initially a defensive move to make Agartala secure against a Pakistani attack was now asked to move to the next objective along this approach, Brahmanbaria.

Before the evening of 7 December, columns of the 4th Corps had completely disrupted the Pakistani defence pattern on the whole of the eastern sector. Sylhet, itself a brigade headquarter, was isolated with the capture of Maulvi Bazar, another brigade headquarter, and Kalaura and the Shamshernagar airfield. The whole of this sub-sector was also isolated from its companion brigade at Brahmanbaria and its divisional headquarters at Ashuganj. In the central sub-sector Akhaura had been captured and Brahmanbaria contacted. Hopes of easy capture of Brahmanbaria rose when the Pakistani brigade at Maulvi Bazar, threatened with encirclement, withdrew north-east to Sylhet instead of south-west to Brahmanbaria where it would have reinforced the approaches to Dacca. It was at this point that the first airlift of troops was made, helicopters picking up a battalion of the force which had captured Kalaura and putting it down near Sylhet to add to its isolation. In the southern sub-sector, Comilla-Maynamati had been by-passed and cut off from the main river port and divisional headquarters, Chandpur, as well as from Daudkandi; a double wedge had been driven between Comilla and Laksham by the columns by-passing and attacking Laksham; and Laksham had been isolated from Chandpur.

Pakistan collapsed on the whole of the southern sub-sector the same day, December 9: Comilla, Daudkandi, Laksham and Chandpur fell within a few hours of each other to the three-brigade Indian advance. The force in Maynamati held out but the one in Comilla made the first mass surrender of the war. With Laksham and Chandpur gone, both land and river routes between Dacca and Chittagong were simultaneously cut. A double approach from the south-east to Dacca was now open from across the Meghna, one from Chandpur and one from Daudkandi. Three days later the IAF was to make this a more imminent threat to Dacca by helilifting 1,200 troops and almost 39 tonnes of equipment, including artillery, from Daudkandi to Baidya Bazar, directly below Dacca and on the same side of the Meghna. But the corps commander had changed his plans by now: he had shifted the whole emphasis to the northern approach.

This happened between 7 and 9 December, and for two reasons: Pakistan's failure to reinforce the Brahmanbaria garrison with the brigade which was evacuating Maulvi Bazar, and the chance discovery of a short route from Brahmanbaria to Ashuganj along an abandoned former railway embankment. Lieutenant-General Sagat Singh decided that Brahmanbaria was now weak enough to be safely by-passed, and he made a dash for Ashuganj along the new route, leaving Baria invested by a small encircling movement. Ashuganj was contacted on 9 December and the same day Brahmanbaria fell in the rear, the Pakistani brigade, 27th of the 14th Infantry Division, having pulled out to Ashuganj. But the Indian advance could not save the bridge at Ashuganj to Bhairab Bazar across the Meghna above Dacca. The Pakistani retreat was faster than the Indian advance, and the divisional headquarters of the 14th Infantry had withdrawn on the 8th night to Bhairab Bazar, blowing up the bridge as it went. It was in coping with this gap that the IAF improvised the biggest airlift of the war though it was not a part of the plans drawn up to that date in army-air coordination.

The Indian divisional commander in charge of the northern approach first tried sending his amphibious tanks across the Meghna but they let him down: the river was too broad for their breath and the opposite bank too steep to climb. He tried taking them across on country craft but the boats broke up under the weight. The Mukti Bahini told him there was a steel boat further up the river but that would take two or three days to come. The IAF was asked for help. Its response was immediate. Helicopters began an airlift at 4 A.M. on the night of 9-10 December, and by midday had put down two battalions on the opposite bank, making a firm bridge-head about four miles south of Bhairab Bazar while the Pakistani divisional commander there, dismissing the helicopter flights as a feint, patiently waited for a frontal crossing from Ashuganj. In the first 36 hours 12 helicopters flew 110 sorties among them. By 14 December they had put across one brigade headquarter, four battalions, one troop of PT 76 tanks, one mountain regiment, one light battery, four medium guns, two tractors as prime movers for guns and one platoon of engineers. This was in addition to the helilift from Daudkandi to Baidya Bazar in a practically overlapping period.

With the bridgehead visible and growing and a slope built on the river bank, hundreds of local people jumped into the Meghna to push other amphibious tanks across when their engines gave up, and a day or two later the steel boat was also floated down to Ashuganj. By December 14 two brigades had got across and they started a two-pronged advance towards the Lakhia, the last river obstacle before Dacca. The Indian forces now had four approaches to Dacca: two from the north-east, and two from the south-east, from Chandpur and Daudkandi-Baidya Bazar. But in the meantime a fifth had built up to the north-north-west with the help of India's first paradrop operation though it was not initially meant to be built up as an alternative advance upon Dacca.

In joint army-air planning before 3 December, Aurora asked the IAF to provide for three paradrops. But the IAF had its own logistical and operational problems, and it could promise only one as certain. Aurora chose for it a spot south of Jamalpur, an expected enemy strongpoint east of the Jamuna and south of the Brahmaputra. An Indian advance in brigade strength, with a supporting brigade to the left and rear, was to come down on this axis from Tura, but it would only have the resources of a communication zone behind it, not a division, much less a corps. It could possibly make a dash for Dacca, because once it crossed the minor river which goes here by the major name of the Brahmaputra, it would have no great natural obstacle on its way. But the purpose envisaged for it was to create a strong diversion to the north or north-west to make entry into Dacca easier from the south-east and north-east of the capital.

The Mukti Bahini and local guerrilla forces were fitted into the operation before the war began. One of the best organized and aggressive guerrilla groups, under a flamboyant leader, Kader Siddiqui, had been working in the Phulbani forest area, south of Tangail, the spot chosen for the paradrop. In the course of

October or early November the Pakistani forces carried out a sweep through the forest and squeezed the Kaderites, as they were known, into the clear to the north.   Kader asked for help and he was given weapons, communications, a company of the Mukti Bahini trained by the Indian Army and he was sent back into the forest.   Kader was told as soon as the Indian troops, a battalion with its supporting arms, were airborne on 11 December.   The guerrillas joined the paratroops just in time, because soon after landing the para battalion ran into a battalion of the 36th Pakistan Infantry Division's 93rd Brigade at Mymensingh; the brigade was under orders to withdraw to Dacca and the battalion was preceding it along the Mymensingh-Tangail road.   Three hundred Pakistani soldiers were killed in hand to hand combat and the para battalion, shortly to be joined by the Indian brigade coming down from Jamalpur, resumed on the road to Dacca.

A couple of days later, and closer to Dacca, it ran into heavier resistance at Jaydebpur, on 13 December, but by that time a splinter section under the Communication Zone Commander, Major-General Nagra, had chanced upon a by-pass which was not shown on maps.  He accepted the chance gratefully, went down south-east behind Jaydebpur, and on the morning of 16 December, stood at the gates of Dacca. From there he sent his ADC with a note to a former friend, General Abdullah Niazi, Commander of Pakistan's Eastern Command, which read: "My dear Abdullah, I am here.  The game is up.  I suggest you give yourself up to me and I'll look after you."

Inside Dacca in the meantime, civilian authority had already cracked up, under the impact of a more forceful message from the IAF.  On 14 and 15 December, a number of messages sent by Dacca to Islamabad were intercepted by Indian sources which showed the state of demoralization in Dacca.  On 14 December, a message sent at 10 A.M. said:   "We have been living on hope —please confirm something.  Whatever has to happen should happen fast."   A little later another message said:   "We have no missiles.  What are we to fire?  And no air force.  Air raids are worrying us a lot."   At nine minutes after 4 P.M. the same afternoon:   "Let us see how the night passes.  But the situation is critical.  Allah takes mercy.  But it is not known when He will take mercy on us."   At 11.45 in the morning the next day a message from Dacca to Rawalpindi said:   "Only Chittagong is left. All else is gone." Within minutes a message from Dacca to Flying Officer Qureshi in Peshawar said: "It looks as though they will destroy Dacca. Everything is being destroyed. We are lost."

But the most valuable information was in the message the previous day at ten in the morning. After reporting the state of morale it said: "At 12.00 hours we are going to Government House." When the message was received at Air Headquarters in New Delhi three quarters of an hour later, it was immediately interpreted as meaning that a high level meeting was going to take place at Government House in about an hour and a quarter. The Chiefs of Staff Committee met immediately in the Ministry of Defence and decided to attack the venue of the meeting for the demoralizing effect it would have on the enemy. Instructions were sent to Eastern Air Command at Shillong, Assam. There, pilots were shown Government House on a tourist map of the city, instructions were still being given to them when they were air-borne, and 35 minutes after the instructions from Delhi the attack on Government House had started. A rocket fell on the room where the meeting was taking place, the Governor of East Pakis-tan, Mallik, presiding. The Governor ran into an air-raid shel-ter, met a foreign correspondent there, borrowed his ball point pen and wrote out his resignation. He could not take it any longer. Nor could Niazi; he told his Indian captors two days later that air attacks had kept him awake for 12 nights, and he just could not continue any more.

## The Causes

A war is not so quickly lost, nor so decisively, for any single reason; many potent mistakes must go into the making of such a collapse. Yet, if one were to put one's finger on any one cause, or rather one each for what happened in the east and west because there were in fact two different wars, one would say that Pakistan lost in the west because of poor coordination between the army and the air force and in the east because it completely misunderstood Indian intentions and capabilities. These are, of course, rather broad reasons, not specific by any means; many causes went to the making of each and many consequences ensued from each which in their turn became contributory causes. But each stands apart in its totality from the totality of other, and on the whole, less important reasons.

Pakistan had drawn up a good strategy in the west and it had manoeuvred India well into falling in line with its expectations. But the strategy failed because India imposed new conditions upon it which Pakistan could not meet. If India had fought the third war as she had fought the second, Pakistan might have done very well out of it. But India fought an all-services, modern, coordinated war, not the one-service war it had fought six years earlier. Pakistan could have done it too; in fact in ground-air coordination it had a six-year lead over India. It also had the planes to do better in 1971. If it had pushed the Mirages into front line combat it could have denied India control of the forward air even after the failure of its pre-emptive strike; if it had retained the Mirages in Karachi instead of hiding them away (probably in the Sargodha complex, which had the best ground to air defences in the whole of Pakistan) it would have kept the IAF away from the oil installations; it might also have reduced the effectiveness of the strikes at Karachi which the IAF coordinated with the navy, adding to the effectiveness of the naval raid. By withdrawing them the PAF preserved the Mirages but helped Pakistan lose the war. It repeated the error a couple of days later by withdrawing the F104s also, which encouraged the IAF to attack Karachi in daylight with Hunter fighter-bombers, which are slower than the F104s, instead of bombing it mainly at night with Canberras.

Indian military intelligence gives military reasons for the shyness of the PAF: that it had maintenance problems because of the sizeable proportion of East Bengalis in the ground maintenance staff, or that the PAF, long accustomed to having to fly and maintain only one line of aircraft, American, could not easily adjust to flying and maintaining a variety of machines—French, Chinese, Russian, American, a problem which the IAF, for long called the international air force in maintenance hanger ribaldry, had learnt how to handle.

But the real reasons are probably more politico-military. The Pakistan higher command was divided at the start, of which one testimony came from Niazi who said he was not told that war was going to be started in the west and was caught unprepared for its repercussions in the east. There is also quite a lot of well corroborated evidence that Air Marshal Rahim Khan was at variance with Yahya Khan on this policy of war and generally resentful of Yahya Khan's overriding behaviour towards him. Friction between army and air echelons travelled down from the top, because of which much the greater part of the PAF action was very half-hearted, from the pre-emptive onwards. Given such a background, and the example of any number of countries where political power is held by the armed forces and which service holds more of it depends upon whose powder is more dry, it is not surprising that the PAF tried to conserve its power for postwar needs instead of investing it in Yahya Khan's gamble; what happened after the war to Yahya Khan and Rahim Khan, respectively, corroborates the conjecture. It is not contradicted by the active support the PAF gave in Chhamb. The Corps Commander there was Tikka Khan whose equation with Rahim Khan was always better than Yahya Khan's and continued to be so after the war. Yahya Khan's ouster after the war is believed to have been brought about by a critical vote by Rahim Khan in a tie at a meeting of the ruling junta in Islamabad after the war.

Whatever the reasons for the absence of full air support, it tore a hole the size of a bomb crater in whatever Yahya Khan could have hoped to do with the 1st Armoured. But looking now only to the army's acts of omission and commission it is amazing to see the contrast between the audacity with which the war was started, the intelligence with which the initial dispositions were made, and the total lack of a spirit of adventure later on. Yahya Khan showed unrestrained strategic boldness in launching the war on December 3 but an excess of tactical caution in not launching the 1st Armoured when he could have. If he had played the same gamble in the Ganganagar-Fazilka area as in counting on Chinese intervention he might have got somewhere. But he allowed time to slip, possibly waiting for the 1st Indian Armoured to make a move first; but whereas it suited India to wait in the west while the war in the east was brought to a successful end it did not suit Pakistan, and by waiting Yahya Khan suited himself to Indian ends, cancelling his own earlier gains.

Destruction of the oil storage at Karachi contributed some to Yahya Khan's hesitations. On how much it contributed the

Indian Army's estimate ("very little") differs, understandably, from the IAF's and the navy's ("a very great deal"). But the contribution was probably very substantial. The Indian Army estimates it low because of its own experience that a prudent command will dump enough petrol, oil and lubricants in forward positions before the war to last at least two weeks of full operations, and keep in the middle-rear supplies for another month at least. On this calculation, army experts believe the destruction of main reserves in the rear could not have affected operations in a war which lasted only two weeks. But even on that estimate a prudent command will become cautious in judging how far forward it should commit itself, knowing the end of the road is only six weeks away, and upon the Pakistani Army there was a further and very special restraint.

West Pakistan, more particularly its military heartland, West Punjab, and the adjoining districts of NWFP, is a very compact and tightly controlled area, well served with communications and with logistics which are easy to regulate. Secondly, a highly elitist and exclusivist junta exercised absolute power over it for more than a decade, controlling the military, political and state apparatus by the same short rein. This bred in it a highly centralist mentality which, while it succeeded, was very efficient and economical. Not for them dispersed and more or less self-sustaining processes scattered all over the country, but a powerful and decisive control mechanism at the centre, with the longest reach towards the periphery which discipline and the crack of the whip could ensure. This affected—or had till the junta went overboard after the war—their military thinking and operations as well, and as in the disposition of military formations so in logistics they believed in switching quantities back and forth according to a central plan rather than in the "wasteful" alternative, which they could not afford anyhow, of dispersing local sufficiencies everywhere. If among such people there was the belief, and there is evidence there was, that Karachi was safe beyond the enemy's reach, they would not have ensured dispersal of local supplies, and loss of the rear reserves could have affected forward stamina much more than it would in India's case.

In the eastern theatre Pakistan made the more fundamental and formative blunder from which many others followed, of continuing to believe till far too late that India's objective was limited to obtaining "lodgement" areas on the periphery of East Pakistan. Hence the line of well fortified strongpoints just behind the rim. At the time it was made this manoeuvre did not look so foolish as in retrospect, and even in retrospect what makes a folly out of it is not the Pakistani Army's weakness but the enormous advantage which the Indian Army's strategy, brilliant in any case and by any standard, derived from air support and the Mukti Bahini, the former giving it speed and mobility, the latter secrecy and ubiquity. And once this combination came into play, Pakistan was doomed in the eastern wing.

Within at most four or five days of the start of the fighting, and before Indian arms had scored any spectacular successes, it became obvious that Niazi would hang in the noose of his own strategy. As Indian Army columns, now grown to 21, began to push in from all directions, it must have become clear even to Niazi that India was developing a swift and mobile war, rejecting the rigidities of copybook prescriptions to get to the target, Dacca, as fast as possible, leaving points of resistance on the periphery to be assimilated later. This meant that what Pakistan had built up as a shield had in fact become a terrible liability.

The shield exposed Pakistan to three weaknesses simultaneously, each of them fatal by itself. The fixed strongpoints were as immobile as fortresses compared with the swiftly flowing streams of Indian advance; invested or not, they would be cut off from Dacca before the soldiers holding them could even pack their bags to fall back upon the capital. Their defences looked outward, in the direction of the expected frontal assaults. They were helpless when attacked from the flanks or the rear, which is what the Indians were doing to the extent they were attacking these positions at all. Finally, there was no depth in defence behind them; once the Indians flowed through the holes they were punching in the shield at the rim. There was nothing to stop them.

Some time before the war began, probably about the beginning of November as far as Indian intelligence has been able to judge, Yahya Khan realized that Indian intentions were maximum, not minimum; perhaps he was alerted to this by the deployment of India's northern forces all around East Pakistan, to which he tried to draw the attention of the United Nations. From this warning he came to two conclusions, one wrong, one unavailing. He decided India would blockade East Pakistan—correct—and for that would so heavily concentrate its naval power in the eastern waters—partially correct—that it would not have a great deal of punch left in the west—wrong, and expensively wrong because it added to all the other reasons, discussed earlier, for his neglecting the defence of Karachi.

The unavailing conclusion had two parts to it: that instead of investing everything in the defence of the rim, Niazi should also have a contingency plan to fall back upon Dacca, and there should be the means to bring the eastern army home across waters which, as he now realized, would be dominated by the Indian Navy.

As seen in the operations there was indeed a fall-back plan of sorts. The 9th Infantry Division tried to get across the Madhumati and Padma from the west, the 14th Infantry Division from the east, the only brigade of the 36th from Mymensingh. The 39th at Chandpur did not try but there would have been no point in its doing so because it was closer to the sea outlet and a point of embarkation for evacuation at its headquarters, Chandpur, than it would have been at Dacca. The 16th Infantry also did not try. This may have been because it was caught in the crook of the confluence of the Ganges and the Jamuna or, more likely, because it was thought that if the Chinese intervened this northernmost division would be needed where it was; also, documents captured at Jessore—not very many; the retreating Pakistanis managed to destroy most of them—confirm there was a fall-back plan.

But everything that could, went wrong with it. It was neither prepared well—there was no evidence of adequate logistics at important river crossings —nor communicated in time to lower formations, so that we have the picture of the 313th Brigade of the 14th Infantry at Maulvi Bazar retreating north-east to the 202nd Brigade at Sylhet, instead of towards the divisional headquarters at Ashuganj or the 27th Brigade at Brahmanbaria; the 202nd making no move towards the south or south-east when it came under pressure almost simultaneously with Maulvi Bazar; the 93rd at Mymensingh not making a move towards Dacca until almost a week after the war began; the 16th Infantry Division reinforcing Hilli instead of falling back upon Bogra to retain control of the communications going south. Hence it happened that of the total number of prisoners of war taken, only a third were taken in Dacca though the capital had not only the command headquarters but also the headquarters of the 36th Division. The remainder were captured in the three sectors, western, northern and eastern. The 16th Infantry was captured almost in tact in the north; two-thirds of the 39th and 14th were captured in the east, only one-third escaping to the Dacca area; and only the 9th at Jessore managed to get about half its men across the Madhumati towards Dacca, especially the brigade at Khulna.

What remained of the plan after poor preparation and poorer command communication was made nonsense of by the speed of the Indian advance. The withdrawals from the west were blocked by the very fast Indian advances to Magura and Khulna. In the north the paradrop blocked the retreat of the Mymensingh brigade. In the east and south-east the simultaneous fall of Laksham, Comilla, Chandpur and Daudkandi blocked the western retreat to Dacca and southern to the sea for the 14th at Ashuganj and the 39th at Chandpur; a plan the 39th had to dribble into Arakan, about which Indian intelligence learnt through evesdropping, was choked by an amphibious landing— the first ever made by Indian armed forces—at Cox's Bazar with troops borrowed from the western sector after Jessore fell.

Mistakes of planning and strategy are sometimes overcome by resolution and dedication, but the Pakistani soldier in the east showed very little of either. Soldiers summon up these qualities when they are fighting for their homes or for a cause which commands their deepest loyalty. The West Pakistani soldier in East Pakistan was not. East Pakistan was never home to the Punjabi or Baluchi; he never treated it as such. To the Bengali it was; hence the incomparable fortitude and individual heroism displayed by the Mukti Bahini. Nor was the West Pakistani soldier in the east a disciplined animal any longer, whom sheer dogged adherence to command or duty might carry over an obstacle; the unprecedented rapacity in which he indulged for many months had made him a mindless brute without the intelligence to innovate when a set plan was overturned by the enemy.

This failing was displayed as much by officers as by the men. Condemned already to being an unthinking tool of higher authority by the dictatorial regime under which he grew up, and made mentally inflexible by a kind of national temperament of the Punjabi Muslim soldiery, the average Pakistani officer stuck to the copybook rule and outdated doctrine despite the evidence that the enemy was fighting a new kind of war in which the rules learnt at regimental parades were all but useless. Severed from higher command, he could not take the initiative to think on his feet when he found the last order in his pocket overtaken by events. Hence it happened that, as narrated earlier, not only his overall strategy of standing stoutly at the rim but tactics in individual battles as at Jessore, Hilli, Ashuganj and Comilla played straight into waiting Indian hands.

On India's side also there were failings—in the west. Perhaps the reason for them was that in the senior Indian army command there were not many who had any intimate and personal experience of the western theatre. When Sam Manekshaw chaired the Joint Chiefs Committee at sessions taken up with the eastern theatre, he provided a leadership which was richly illuminated by his own detailed knowledge of that entire theatre from the Tibetan border downwards. His theatre commander had the same advantage, although he is a Punjabi Sikh by birth, education and regimental upbringing. But matching knowledge of the west was not part of Manekshaw's intellectual baggage. He was born in the Punjab and did much of his early soldiering there but did not have much command experience in the west. Nor did either of his two commanders in the west, Candeth and Bewoor.

The failings one speaks of are only relative to what could have been done, what was done being remarkable enough. India bit much deeper into West Pakistan than in 1965, showed far greater imagination and military sophistication in the use of the three services, and barring the fluster over Chhamb in the first couple of days, acted according to plan, with a proper distribution of responsibility between higher and local command. But with as much responsiveness to the needs of this war as was shown in the east by higher and local commands alike, India would have been in a stronger position despite the sudden announcement of a unilateral cease-fire by Mrs Gandhi. The menace and importance of the Shakargarh bulge were grossly overrated; a much smaller force than an entire corps, assisted by the river Ravi which stands between the bulge and the more important Indian targets, would have been enough to hold any enemy attack that could have been reasonably expected in this sub-sector. Greater investment elsewhere, especially opposite Rajasthan, would have brought greater gains and more crucial to the success of the political negotiations with Pakistan after the war. Alternatively, by taking on the 1st Pakistan Armoured after effecting a superior assembly against it, instead of simply watching it for any flicker of a movement, far greater losses could have been inflicted on Pakistan where they would tell the most, on the iron backbone of its army, carrying on the process of attrition where Chaudhuri left it off after his very considerable success in it in 1965.

As it happens, Pakistan's military machine has not been seriously hurt by the loss of the eastern wing or the losses suffered there. Even according to Indian claims Pakistan suffered a total loss of 94 aircraft, 246 tanks, two destroyers, two submarines, two minesweepers and 16 gunboats (not a loss which is difficult to make up, considering previous levels of direct American aid till 1965 or after that direct and indirect Chinese, American and Russian aid). The eastern campaign contributed to this 74 tanks, about 20 aircraft, one submarine and all the gunboats. The east did not contribute much ever to the country's war machine; its financial contribution was also diminishing and by the start of the 1970s it was a net consumer of resources, not a net producer; and if Pakistan continues to give the same priority to military spending as it—unwisely—has always done, it will not break under the weight of making up the loss of the four divisions which surrendered in Bangladesh (with a total of 72 tanks). It can replace them in a couple of years, being a country which, even with what is left of it, remains populous.

It was the navy and the air force which brought India the greater success in the war in the west. The navy shone in the careful audacity of the raids on Karachi. Its more solid achievement was the blockade of Pakistan and the protection of merchant shipping which was so credible that there was hardly any fall in traffic in the customary shipping lanes to and from India. But greater skill and daring were required by the raids. In the eastern war luck favoured the navy in the sinking of the *Ghazi* and in the *Vikrant* being available when and where it was needed. But all of its remaining contribution to the winning of the war in the east was the fruit of careful and joint planning to win it. Especially the contribution of the naval air arm.

The IAF showed the keenest understanding of the enemy's mind, which enabled it to anticipate not only the timing and nature of the pre-emptive strike but also the enemy's response in later operations. The tactical refinement of its attack routine, especially of attacks on the railway line to Karachi, led Pakistanis to suspect that India had the aid of a super Russian device to which they gave the nickname "spider." Similarly, the IAF's MiG-21s, they thought, were too good to be the planes they knew by that name and they credited India with a (non-existent) MiG-23. The mythical spider was only a routine IAF plane, possibly with improvements in its electronics, which flew high overhead in a fixed circle when Indian strike planes flew below the radar horizon for the sake of safety; it relayed the return movements of the planes to the ground observation system so that defending aircraft may not take to the air, mistaking the homecomers for enemy planes. The MiG-21s, like the Gnats both in 1965 and 1971, performed very well but that was simply because they were in very good hands; the stepped up training routine in the course of the summer, especially in operations close to the ground, paid very good dividends.

The IAF was at its best in the humility with which it preferred the supporting to a spectacular role. The victory of ground forces remains their victory, no matter how much other services might have contributed to it. A daring raid by the air force on the strategic targets of the enemy is unshared glory for the air force alone. Yet the IAF decided long before the planning of joint operations began that it was more important for it to support the two other services in their wars than to reserve its resources for a separate war in the air. This is the best illustration of the decision taken very early on by the political, civilian and military echelons that while this war would not be fought from New Delhi—as the politicians and generals alike fought the war of 1962 with disastrous consequences—it would be planned as a unified war, with every individual ambition subordinated to the overall aim.

This is what made it so smoothly possible for General Aurora to function as virtually the theatre commander, not as the commander of the ground forces in the eastern theatre. The contribution this made to the evolution of a united strategy for all elements in the entire theatre was probably the most important single cause of India's very quick and total success. Because of the coordination, Indian forces could simultaneously attack in all the three elements, ground, air and water, which meant that they were enveloping the enemy, not simply attacking him, and in this way were accentuating his sense of isolation. With the Indian Army controlling all land frontiers and the navy all the outlets to the sea as well as the sea itself, Pakistan's soldiers in the east could have had no doubt about the physical fact of their isolation. Now they were experiencing it in its military totality. Perhaps the psychological impact of this was as great as the purely military one.

But the maximum psychological contribution was that of the IAF and the Mukti Bahini together. The relentless dominance of the IAF was a serious enough strain by itself on the enemy's nerves, and even before the crisis built up from December 11 onwards, the Air Officer Commanding, Dacca, was heard early in the morning on December 8, telling Air Headquarters in Peshawar: "Dacca runway crated again. Cannot fly. Sending away pilots. Destroying top secrets and keeping demolitions ready...." Coming in a message from a senior officer to his service headquarters this was an indication that a serious state of demoralization was developing because of the non-stop Indian air attacks. Later, Niazi was also to speak about their effect upon his nerves. But it is the extension which the IAF and the Mukti Bahini jointly gave to the army's reach which broke the enemy's back.

The Mukti Bahini's contribution to Indian intelligence was absolutely unique; there are parallels for its audacity in the annals of warfare but none for audacity in this volume. Its men flowed like quicksilver behind the lines of the enemy, giving pin-pointed information about his weaknesses to Indian commanders. On the other hand they surrounded the enemy with such a screen of hostility that he could see and hear little about Indian intentions. According to the *Sunday Times*, London, Niazi told his captors: "You always seemed to come round behind us." The credit for this goes very largely to the Mukti Bahini. Its effect upon the enemy was to destroy such balance and self-confidence as he had left in him on December 3.

Jointly, the IAF and the Mukti Bahini destroyed the logic of Niazi's strategy; on the other hand, for the Indian Army's strategy they created a favourable environment which made it even more creative and variable, opportunistic in the best sense of the word, than it would have been otherwise.

Because of the IAF and the Mukti Bahini, the overall Indian superiority was so much greater than the numerical—seven divisions against four—that even if India had been dissuaded by China from withdrawing a division or two from the northern front it would have only delayed the fall of Dacca a little not prevented it, once Pakistan had committed the blunders it made. Examples confirm this retrospective conjecture. At Comilla, India had only one division opposing one Pakistani division, which was excellently fortified in a network of defences between Comilla and Maynamati. Yet it was the drive westwards from Comilla which sealed the fate of Dacca and pushed much the larger Indian force into it although the first Indian elements to enter Dacca were paratroopers from the north. At Sylhet, another exellent strongpoint as strongpoints go—or went in this war—three Indian battalions of troops, one of mortars and one of guns invested and reduced two enemy brigades, one initially located at Sylhet and another which had withdrawn there from Maulvi Bazar. India's opening attack was with a matching force. But so secure did the Indian divisional commander feel that he withdrew more than a brigade towards Dacca, leaving behind only the two battalions and their weapons. He could do so because, thanks to the IAF, and the opposing commanders knew it, India had a mobility because of which she could concentrate forces at a time and place of her choosing. There was no danger that Pakistani troops in the strongpoints which were being left behind lightly invested would break out into bids to escape, or undertake disruptive raids. This encouraged the Indian commanders to elongate their drives without fear of being caught too thin anywhere. It was thus that they tore up Niazi's control of his war machine so rapidly. His theatre headquarters lost contact with his divisional commands, the divisional commands with the brigade headquarters; before the war ended his troops had become an aimless crowd. Later, Niazi gave this as the most important single reason why he thought it would be irresponsible for him to throw more lives into a war he knew he had lost already.

# Sino-US Reverse

After the war Niazi confirmed what India had suspected since the war began, and with rising anxiety since December 10, that the chances of foreign intervention on the side of Pakistan were far greater than India calculated. But this only turned out to be a blessing in disguise. A man encouraged to hope and then betrayed is more easily broken than one who has never had the cherry knock at his lips. More important than that, India's management of the same crisis which was the cause of high hopes in Pakistan enhanced the significance and magnitude of India's victory. Without it the outcome would have been simply the victory of the side which fought the war with greater military efficiency. With it, India's victory became greater than Pakistan's defeat, a regenerative new experience for India, and for Asia an event which will affect the development of the power balance for some years to come.

On December 12 there was an exchange of several messages between Dacca and Rawalpindi which would have caused a weaker leadership acute anxiety because of circumstances which were known at that time only to a handful of people. At 7.45 in the evening, the Prime Minister of Pakistan, Nurul Amin, was heard saying in Bengali to a subscriber in Dacca "...they have reached the Bay of Bengal. About the north we have reminded them again in the morning and spoken to their representative who was here in the afternoon. *Insha Allah* arrangements are being made in the north." At 8.30 the same evening he was heard telling the Finance Minister of East Pakistan: "Those people have done some operation. They will start some operation either from the north or the south. These arrangements have been made." Probably unsure that he had carried conviction he added in another conversation at 9.25 P.M.: "There are many things which cannot be told now [but] they are coming from the north and the south." New Delhi was unable to dismiss all this as a last minute effort to build up morale in Dacca.

New Delhi had known since the war began that its expectations about the weather in the north had completely misfired. There was a suspicion a few weeks earlier that this might happen. With the monsoon lingering in the eastern region till long past the normal time for its termination, it was realized that snowfall might be less and later than normal. But not as much as it was. Even after December was a few days old there was hardly any snow on most of the passes. Of the 24 passes on the UP-Tibet border, 13 received no fresh snowfall and had no residual snow from the previous winter. Only five had an aggregate snow, new and old combined, exceeding 50 centimetres, only on one it exceeded 100 centimetres. Those without any snow included Joshimath and Mana and five others which are below 3,350 metres in altitude, Ghamsali, Malari, Chhiyalekh, Gunji, and Go. In the eastern, that is the NEFA sector, 14 passes were without any new or residual snow and on six the aggregate was less than 20 centimetres. The former included Nathu La, Jelep La, Niti and Kibithoo; the latter Bum La and Se La.

India's hopes of a quiet northern front were based upon other calculations also apart from the weather. But one calculation was obviously knocked sideways: that military intervention by Peking would be even less likely since a sufficiently wide choice of passes would not be available to the Chinese for coordinated entrance, operations and exit. Therefore, anxiety grew in New Delhi as the war became a few days old without Indian forces recording some conspicuous success. Indian military planners knew how great was the worth of this apparent delay. By not wasting time on conspicuous targets they were dragging Pakistan into a total collapse. But the danger was that the Chinese might see lack of spectacle on the battle front as evidence that the Indian attack had faltered; this could encourage thoughts of at least marginal intervention in their minds, towards which they might have been tempted by the state of the passes.

If the Indian leadership had weakened in its resolution it would have decided to scale down withdrawals from the north, where the bigger enemy could be more dangerous; the scale was decided, after all, when circumstances were expected to be more favourable than they turned out to be, and prudence suggested a reconsideration. But the effect of scaling down would have been more dangerous. It would have prolonged the war in the east, delayed the full northward return of troops which had been borrowed from there and deployed already, given the Chinese a weaker front to deal with if they chose to intervene, and thus brought about for India a prolonged three-front situation which would have been of the greatest disadvantage to her. The same thing would have happened if India had returned some of the borrowed forces to the north before they had finished their work in the eastern war. It was therefore decided to stick to the plan of withdrawals and deployment at the risk of greater loss of territory in the north than would have been probable with snow on the passes. Concentrating on one enemy at a time was still much the wiser thing to do. It was India's good fortune that those responsible for the higher conduct of war showed the nerve to stick to this option.

India had to make a similar but a more daring calculation about the possibilities of an American intervention, which at one stage threatened to be jointly Sino-American. Here again some ominous things were already known in New Delhi when Nurul Amin said on December 12 evening "...they have reached the Bay of Bengal." About a week or ten days before the beginning of the war, the Foreign Office inquired of the American Ambassador in New Delhi what was the significance of reports which had been received by then that the jurisdiction of the US-Seventh Fleet was being extended to the Bay of Bengal. The ambassador dismissed this as a routine shift of command. The Foreign Office decided there was more to it and the move was not unconnected with the developments taking place and impending in East Pakistan. The Indian Ambassador in Washington was asked to make similar inquiries at the State Department. The replies he received were even more bland and unconvincing.

Up to the time when the Indian Foreign Minister arrived in New York, on December 11, for a possible meeting of the Security Council, Indian information was confined to three points—that a powerful task force of the Seventh Fleet had been ordered the previous day to proceed to the Bay of Bengal, that its operational mandate was very wide, and that some of the governments along the route had been told about the intended movement of the force, the impression given them being that its mission was to back up plans for the evacuation "by other means" of a small number of Americans who were still in Dacca. The first two points were confirmed two days later when a US spokesman said in Saigon: "We have all kinds of contingency plans for many situations," but no one in New Delhi took the planted reports about the fleet's alleged mission very seriously.

The Government of India had already placed two alternatives before all countries, including the USA (and the UN) whose nationals were still held up in Dacca: that either the Government of India on its own responsibility would fly their nationals out of Dacca provided the Pakistani authorities (still in control of the city) handed them over at the airport, or the IAF and the army would stop their attacks on Dacca for a specified duration to be agreed upon in advance to enable use of the airport by the governments concerned to arrange the evacuation of their nationals by any aircraft of their choice provided that on their way out the aircraft touched down at Calcutta for India to make sure that no Pakistani officers were being allowed to escape. Most governments, and the UN, had accepted the offer, none had threatened to send its air force or navy to force an evacuation without Indian authorization, and the only government, the British, which had thought of sending naval units (purely for bringing out British nationals) gave up the idea when India represented that this would be misunderstood as a show of force in a situation of conflict. It was therefore considered most unlikely that the United States would send a powerful armada, including missile ships and the nuclear powered aircraft carrier, *Enterprise*, for the purpose merely of evacuating, and that without any prior consultation with India, some 20-odd Americans who were still in Dacca.

The natural deduction was made that the purpose must be commensurate with the size of the force and it must be one which brooked no prior consultation with the Government of India. "Gunboat diplomacy" was a purpose which naturally sprang to mind at once; colour was lent it by the fact that leaks had been planted along the route of the force so that India might know well in advance what a powerful threat was going to be hung over her head and she might be induced to mend her ways before too late. In other words the intention was to cow down India as a minor Sheikhdom on the Arabian Sea might be.

This explanation did not hold the floor very long, but while it did, for the best part of a day, the decision was taken to make a calculated display of defiance so that whatever psychological time-bomb was going to be planted by Nixon might be declared a dud in advance. Immediate diplomatic journeys between New Delhi and Moscow were chosen as one response to make the

Indo-Soviet Treaty a visible and credible presence: D. P. Dhar, Chairman of the Foreign Policy Planning Committee and more responsible for the treaty than any other single person on the Indian side after the Prime Minister, left for Moscow on December 11, and the same day V. V. Kuznetsov, Soviet First Deputy Foreign Minister, left for New Delhi. It was hoped these moves would be read by everyone in the light of the Soviet warning to all governments on December 4 to keep out of the Indo-Pakistan conflict, and the earlier declaration by the Soviet Foreign Minister, Gromyko, that no country could now make its policy towards India or the Soviet Union without taking into account the Indo-Soviet Treaty.

India's second response took one's breath away for sheer audacity. For public demonstration of defiance of what was interpreted to be a public act of intimidation, it was decided that the Prime Minister should make a forceful speech at a public meeting; no private demarche delivered in the secrecy of diplomatic channels would do. Throughout December 11, All India Radio announced in its news bulletins that the Prime Minister would address a public meeting in New Delhi the next day. In other words, in the capital city of a country at war, at a place and time announced in advance, a couple of hundred thousand people would assemble in the open to hear a speech of national assertion by the Prime Minister. The IAF was asked to be on the alert, and Delhi saw more sorties flown over it that day than at any time during the war. But it is impossible for any air force to give a fool proof cover for the length of time that this enormous congregation would offer a target the size of three or four football fields. But it was decided that only such an act would measure up to the intention to intimidate India. Mrs Gandhi's speech, full of scathing phrases and anger, certainly measured up to the size of the meeting, which was large even for her meetings. She did not refer to the USA directly but her meaning was clear; she did not refer to the fleet but her references to the arrogance of certain powers, clear to those who knew the facts already, became clear to everyone when reports of the movement of the *Enterprise* appeared in the press on December 14.

In the meantime, word was received from New York which changed the picture but only made the steps already taken more necessary in retrospect and called for some more. The Foreign

Secretary, Kaul, received information in New York from Washington, which he relayed to Delhi, that the US task force intended to establish a beach-head on the Bangladesh coast; it would not confine itself to an off-shore demonstration of force.  This was immediately after the "huddles" in Washington on December 10 at which, as Jack Anderson disclosed a little later, the decision was taken to order the move by the fleet.  But it was before the first message of Nurul Amin that "...they have reached the Bay of Bengal."  The fact that Nurul Amin said so two days before the ships entered the Bay, and before their departure for the Bay became public knowledge, shows Pakistan had the benefit of prior information and probably prior consultation as well.  Here was a contingency which India had taken into account even less than the new situation on the northern passes in the calculations which preceded the war, and yet it had to be sized up and countered within a matter of days and in the midst of all the other tensions of war.

Kaul's message fitted in with a number of other indications. First, there were reports on December 8 that the USA was trying to fly military equipment to West Pakistan, and Manekshaw remonstrated about this with the American Ambassador.  There were also reports, confirmed later by Anderson but suspected by Indian sources much earlier, of attempted release of US arms to Pakistan through Libya and Jordan during the war and earlier through Turkey.  Therefore India had enough reason to suspect that the US President would try to do something for Pakistan if he could.

Secondly, the plan of Pakistani withdrawals in Bangladesh had now begun to fall into the pattern of an intended, or at least a hope for, evacuation though the Indian advance appeared to have forestalled it.  Thirdly, as was known already, General Farman Ali had sent a message to the UN Secretary-General on December 10 appealing for his good offices in ensuring the peaceful evacuation of Pakistani troops to West Pakistan across seas which, as he knew by then, were controlled by the Indian Navy. But most clearly Kaul's message tied in with information sent only hours earlier by the naval wing of the Mukti Bahini, that Niazi had got five merchant ships and two coasters ready at different ports to carry his troops to West Pakistan.

With all these indications in hand it was decided to take the

US Navy's intentions more seriously. They began to be considered as three different or simultaneous possibilities of menace.
(A fourth and the most menacing possibility was to dawn upon
India a little later.) It was thought that the minimum aim of the
task force would be to compel the Indian Navy at least, if not the
IAF as well, to divert its attention, especially the air activity of
the *Vikrant,* from the land war in the eastern theatre to the defence of the Indian coast on the Bay of Bengal, and if for no other
purpose than at least to keep a watch on the movements of the
task force. This part, the Indian military leadership decided,
would best be answered by ignoring the task force altogether;
in so far as its intentions impinged upon the eastern war, they
could best be countered by concentrating upon the war unswer-
vingly.

The next level of its aim also had to be played the same way:
that the force might try to engage in actual hostilities to prevent
the Indian Navy from attacking or isolating East Pakistan. The
Indian Navy simply did not have the strength to cope with such
an assailant and must go on with its allotted task until prevented.
Whether the task force would in fact prevent it would not depend
upon how much resistance it thought the Indian Navy could
offer but whether Nixon felt politically free to undertake a direct
conflict with Indian forces. The political leadership was told
that this was more a matter of political than military assessment.
A parallel political appraisal began at once but Indian naval
intelligence was asked to assess the countervailing effectiveness
of such Soviet naval power as was already in or near the Indian
Ocean or could be brought there within a couple of days. India
could rest on the assurance, and after the exchanges with Moscow
on the night of December 11 she certainly did, that any direct
involvement of the US Navy would provoke the involvement of
the Soviet Navy on the Indian side. But the value of this
assurance in the immediate context depended upon whether such
Soviet naval power as could be assembled quickly in the Indian
Ocean would be credible enough to deter US naval power, or
effective enough if combat ensued.

It was at the third level that US intentions called for assessment,
planning and counter-action in greater detail, against the possibility that the task force might try to make a limited intervention
on Pakistan's behalf in different ways or combination of ways

which would not amount to an act of war against India and would not result in a serious clash unless India retaliated with an act of war, in which case the onus for the consequences would be upon her. As in the case of the possibility of local level intrusions by the Chinese in the north, Indian preference was not to invoke the Indo-Soviet Treaty against a lower level and local collision with US naval power. Yet it was realized that even by local and limited intervention the US Navy could create an unpleasant situation unless it was forestalled, and the Indian Navy was asked to give its appreciation of the possibilities open to the task force and what could be done to foreclose them.

The navy estimated that the force had a limited capacity for sustained action on land; the composition of the force suggested that its marine component would not much exceed 5,000 men. With that it would hardly wish to engage an Indian force consisting of seven divisions. There was, of course, Niazi's army, but the problem for the marines would be how to link up with it, with sizeable intervening areas under Indian control. It had not been able to link up its various sections scattered north of the Khulna-Dacca-Chandpur line despite the advantage of numbers it had there; once the Indian Army cut them up they stayed cut up. How could it link up with American beach-heads further south, where its strength was small even in numbers? The only sizeable force below this line was at Chittagong, where ten thousand Pakistani troops were to surrender in the following week. But that would not offer a link up further north, because of the distance between Chittagong and the nearest sizeable garrison up country, and the especially strong Indian force interposed between them on the Comilla-Laksham-Chandpur and the Comilla-Daudkandi axes.

Could the beach-heads be moved right up to the Khulna-Dacca-Chandpur line? Here, it was estimated, the task force would be under a double limitation. Most of its ships were too large to move up the estuary, which is a grand mother's crochet piece of soft land interlaced with waterways. It had a number of smaller craft with very great firepower. But their capacity to transport manpower for building and holding beach-heads was estimated to be very limited. With the Indians able to concentrate quickly, and with the scarcity of points for landing men from sophisticated boats, it was not considered likely that an impregnable beach-head could be built before the Indian forces isolated it. The Mukti Bahini in particular could simply choke the beach-head and the approaches to it without being the first to fire a shot.

Only two ways remained by which the Americans could attempt to evacuate Pakistanis without attacking the Indians in strength. Firstly, by using their quite considerable heli lift capability, which would be enough to evacuate the officer corps at least. Secondly, by taking under their naval umbrella any Pakistanis who managed to reach the high seas under their own power. If the Indians tried to prevent either operation, it would be they who would be attacking the Americans without the latter undertaking any warlike action.

The Indian Navy, jointly with the air force, therefore undertook intensified preventive action in the period which it knew would intervene before the task force could approach the coast of Bangladesh. It kept all the southern airfields under a much heavier attack than hitherto—the air force doing the same with the airfields further to the north—to make it impossible even for helicopters to use them in safety. More importantly, it began direct attacks upon Pakistani ships in harbour, which it had avoided so far in the hope of capturing them whole. Attacks on Barisal were especially heavy. From intercepted messages it was gathered that Pakistani troops would try to slip down to this port by smaller craft and then board a fleet of eight ships of eight thousand to ten thousand tonnes which had been assembled at and below Barisal under fictitious international colours. Air attacks made all of them unfit for use even in the shallow inland and territorial waters. About 50 smaller vessels were also sunk between December 11 and 14, some suspected to have fleeing Pakistanis on board. At the same time the naval Mukti Bahini stepped up its surveillance and in New Delhi the hard decision was taken, which had been considered several times but always shirked hitherto, that any ship with fleeing troops on board which managed to weigh anchor, either at Barisal or any other port, should be sunk before it reached the open sea. So successful was this combination of counter-measures that three days after it began India was able to reject out of hand a Pakistani offer of total abandonment of Bangladesh if only India would let Pakistani troops withdraw to the west in peace and order. India knew now she could prevent the evacuation and was determined to do so.   And this she did with singular success.

Only two possibilities remained after the Indian counter-action began; but the military leadership ruled out one, the political leadership the other.   The first was that the task force might run the Indian blockade of Karachi and escort Pakistani reinforcements to the eastern wing; the second that the combined naval and air power of the task force might be used, despite the risk of a direct attack on Indian forces, in an all-out assault to link up with the Pakistanis at any of their main concentrations in Bangladesh.   The Prime Minister and her seniormost advisers ruled out the second possibility on the basis that a lame duck President would not dare risk a mainland war with India on an issue on which he carried an even smaller proportion of visible domestic opinion than he did on Viet Nam.   The former possibility was ruled out by the Joint Chiefs Committee on the basis of two firm assessments to which it committed itself: first, that the situation on the western front would be such within the next few days that Yahya Khan would dare not spare any troops for the eastern front—to reinforce the assurance the army and the IAF hurriedly put together a 2,400 kilometre shuttle, and before December 11 ended they started lifting troops to the west, taking two full brigades across in under two days—and second that within less time than it would take for reinforcements to come from the western wing the war in the east would be successfully concluded.   The political leadership proved as right as the military, and the biggest naval force ever assembled in the Indian Ocean was thus left roaming the sea without any purpose to which it could address itself.

All this happened within the first 36 hours of Kaul's message from New York, a speed made possible by the closely knit conduct of higher command.   Not only higher command by the Joint Chiefs Committee, which was excellent, but below and around it, and especially at the very apex where the cream of political, civilian and military talent was gathered in a single and constantly functioning coalescence.   There was a precedent for it in the 1965 war, but now it acquired the dimensions and the authoritative efficiency which was required for meeting the much bigger crisis of the 1971 war.

To cover up the embarrassment of a conspicuous failure, US sources in New Delhi began to put out the explanation immediately after the war, first in private conversations and then more publicly, that the fleet's mission concerned the war in the west. They had it from Indian sources; they said, that India intended to conquer or dismember West Pakistan after occupying the East. They had privately conveyed a serious warning to Russia that it must persuade India to desist, otherwise Nixon's visit to Moscow would be called off. The fleet was dispatched only to back up the warning and to convince Russia that the USA was serious. This was the theme of American conversation at every gathering in New Delhi before the line came down publicly from Washington. The logic of this argument is so seriously flawed that it must be termed either ridiculous or dishonest.

First consider the route taken by the USA before coming to this position, at each stage contradicting the preceding position. First reports, admittedly unofficial, said the fleet was a back up force for the evacuation of some Americans "by other means." That there was some plan for evacuating someone is clear. It is clear from these reports and it is clear from the statement by the US Defence Secretary on December 14 in Washington that "we do have certain contingency plans to cover evacuation." It is also clear from what became known a little later, the statement by the Assistant Secretary of State, Sisco, at the WSAG meeting on December 6, disclosed by Anderson, that "the Dacca evacuations have been aborted." Whether the reference in all of this was to the evacuation of a score of Americans as Washington once wanted everyone to believe or a hundred thousand Pakistanis as India suspected then and does till today, there is no reference here to any Indian or American objectives in the West.

Next it was put about that the American fleet moved in because the Russian had already; the Seventh Fleet was only imposing a check on the Russians. This is also the explanation in the Anderson papers. But whether there was any Russian movement or not, and whether it was in response to or the cause of the Seventh Fleet's, the decision to send the task force was taken somewhat late on December 10, by which time it was early December 11 in India. The ground situation in Bangladesh was such by then, and had been so since the Ashuganj crossings 24 hours earlier, in fact since the earlier fall of a string of towns in the Comilla sector, that there was neither any need nor any role for Russian

naval assistance to India.   Indian forces were fully in command
and needed only a few days more to finish the job.   It is inconceivable that either India asked for or was offered Russian naval
assistance at this stage of the game.   There is no evidence of
it in the Indian record at all.   Assuming there were any Russian
ships in the Bay at the time, they could only be there for contin-
gencies completely independent of what was happening within
the eastern theatre.   The Russians knew the Indian appreciation
of the state of operations in Bangladesh and knew their help
would be superfluous.

With these very poor antecedents came the third and last
American explanation.   It was the poorest of the lot.   Militarily
it made no sense whatever.   The Indo-Pakistan land war in the
west was neither so accessible from the sea nor so amenable to
naval air power as the war in Viet Nam which the Seventh Fleet
fought while standing off-shore.   Standing off Karachi, the
task force would have been a few hundred kilometres from the
battle front in Sind, about 1,100 to 1,300 kilometres from the
battle front in central Punjab, and almost 1,600 kilometres from
the war in or immediately south of Kashmir, where the greater
part of the Indian force was assembled.   It is impossible to see
what naval air power could have done with it—unless it went
nuclear.

Politically, it made less sense, if that is possible.   At the very
outset of the fighting it was made clear to the State Department
by the Indian Ambassador in Washington and by the American
in New Delhi that India had no territorial objective in West
Pakistan.   This is not contradicted by Alsop's claim in his column
of January 14 that on December 14 the Indian Ambassador,
Jha, declined to give Kissinger the assurance he asked for that
"India did not mean to follow up the conquest of East Pakistan
by a major offensive in West Pakistan."   He could not give it because India certainly had military objectives in the west though
it did not have any territorial ones.   India intended, as stated
earlier, to secure a more durable frontier in the west, especially
in the cease-fire line area of Kashmir.   This objective required
an offensive in the west of some magnitude, both to seek attrition
of the Pakistani war machine and capture of territory which
would be bargained against a durable settlement.   But this is
not the same thing as conquest or dismemberment of West

Pakistan. But that the US Government would not understand. Alsop quotes no evidence for the territorial appetite he attributes to Mrs Gandhi (nor did Keating when the Indian Foreign Office asked him after the war on what basis Nixon had accused India of wishing to dismember West Pakistan). But Anderson cites a CIA report. In it the CIA quotes two sets of sources. One told it that Mrs Gandhi "would accept a cease-fire and international mediation as soon as East Bengal had been liberated." The other said: "India now intends not only to liberate East Bengal but also to straighten its borders in Kashmir and to destroy West Pakistan's air and armoured forces." Thus, even the minatory set only accentuated the known Indian objective; it did not attribute to India the objective of conquering or dismembering West Pakistan.

At the meeting of the Washington Special Action Group held just before the decision was taken to send the naval task force to the Indian Ocean, senior American officials tried to convince Kissinger that India did not have the ambition attributed to her. According to Anderson, Sisco "doubted the Indians had this objective" and the air force chief, Rayan, said the Indians appeared to be content with "holding action" in the west. In India's own words the position was amply stated in the Security Council on December 13 by the Foreign Minister, Swaran Singh, when he answered the demand by the US Ambassador, Bush, that India state its aims in the west. Swaran Singh outlined three Indian conditions for the termination of hostilities. All of them related only to Bangladesh, and only added up to a demand that Pakistan must accept the verdict delivered by the people of East Pakistan in the elections held in December, 1970. He then added unambiguously: "If these three essential ingredients are accepted as an integrated whole then we are confident the cease-fire can be brought about without any further delay and withdrawals of the armed forces of Pakistan from Bangladesh as well as the armed forces of India from there and mutual withdrawals of both India and Pakistan from each other's territory through appropriate consultations."

The Russians never doubted that this was in fact the exact Indian position—with one important difference. Swaran Singh spoke about the withdrawal of the Pakistan Army from Bangladesh. New Delhi did not uphold him on that, the divergence reflecting the pace at which events were moving. Mrs Gandhi had clearly seen the chance of a total surrender of a hundred thousand men of the Pakistan armed forces, and she was not prepared to let go of it. But as far as Indian "aims" in the west were concerned, the Soviet appreciation right up to the end continued to be that India did not aim to dismember Pakistan. It recognized that India might try to take over Azad Kashmir but it also conceded the legitimacy of this aim and distinguished it from the conquest of Pakistan. Therefore, there was no question of Russia joining hands with America to force India off a policy which it knew India did not have. Thus in the west also the US naval task force did not have a role which was either required politically or feasible militarily.

Then why was it sent? Not in a fit of absent-mindedness; an action which could have led to a collision with India and escalated into a collision with Russia could not have been taken lightly.

One possible explanation is that this was a simple case of miscalculation, and given the familiar stereo in the American mind of a weak-kneed and muddle headed India, the miscalculation is understandable. When, on December 7 according to Anderson, the despatch of the task force began to be considered, and even when it was decided finally to send it, on December 10, the White House believed that the war in Bangladesh would still be something of an open affair, open enough for the fleet to set up a beach-head at the invitation of an ally on soil which would still be under the control of the ally. If such a thing had happened the situation indeed would have been tricky for India. She would have been faced with an open ended war, and could not have forced the issue without attacking what Radio Pakistan reported on December 15 would be "an American base in East Pakistan."

By December 10, the real position was altogether different, but there were experts at WSAG meetings who said it was not, General Westmoreland said on December 6 that Niazi's army could hold out "for as much as three weeks." The man under whose orders the fleet was to despatch the task force, Admiral Zumwalt, said on December 4 that Pakistan forces could "hold their line," which at that time could only mean the Pakistan defence line along the border, "for approximately one or two weeks before the logistics problem became overriding."

Oiling the acceptance of such estimates and actions based upon them was Nixon's pique, Kissinger's forcefulness, and the overpowering desire on the part of both not to "let down an ally." According to these estimates and biases, then, with the wish fathering the thought, there would be enough left to salvage about the middle of December.

The explanation is plausible but not convincing. Granting the divorce from reality which marked Nixon's attitude towards Bangladesh and Pakistan throughout the crisis, it is still not conceivable that in a situation of actual war, and one impinging so heavily on what had become his overriding concern, the Washington-Peking-Moscow equation, he would have acted so superficially and thoughtlessly. It is far more likely that deep calculation went into the decision and that Nixon's bias only reinforced the counsel of shrewd judgment.

Nixon knew what the ground situation was on December 10. He also knew that at the December 8 meeting the CIA Chief had said that Pakistan could not hold out on the eastern front for more than three days. But Nixon's decision was based upon criteria and strategies unrelated to the local scene of battle. Post-war evidence confirms this; and this is certainly the view held in New Delhi, a view which is bound to make the outcome of this war a major influence on Indian foreign policy, and perhaps not Indian alone, for the next decade at least.

As Anderson disclosed in January, at the same WSAG meeting where the decision was taken to despatch the task force, the Defence Intelligence Agency read out a report according to which China might be planning "actions regarding the Indo-Pakistan conflict" and the agency reported Yahya Khan as believing that "within 72 hours the Chinese Army will move towards the border." According to what Niazi said after the war, Yahya Khan had conveyed the same assurance to him. So also to Nurul Amin, Yahya Khan's Prime Minister at that time and later Vice-President of Pakistan. Corroborating his messages to Dacca during the war, Amin said on January 5 at a public meeting in Karachi: "Even a day before admitting the loss of East Pakistan, Yahya Khan assured me that our forces were in control and were expecting a Chinese intervention and the American Seventh Fleet any moment."

But it was an obvious essential prerequisite for China that the purpose of frustrating India and saving Pakistan should be met without the intervention in the north having to be of massive proportions. Since Niazi had nearly collapsed by December 10, the question for Nixon was only the limited one whether the presence of the naval task force off the coast of East Bengal would give China the encouragement which the Pakistan Army had failed to provide.

As the minutes of WSAG meetings show, it was known in Washington that China was taking daily readings of the weather on the passes, and it is a reasonable conjecture that Washington realized Peking would be encouraged and New Delhi dismayed by the absence of snow on the passes. Could the expectation of a supporting role by the Seventh Fleet tilt the balance of Chinese judgment? To Nixon and Kissinger it must have seemed it would, given their strong desire that it should. The fleet would not need to intervene but only to reassure China and warn Russia that the USA was serious about supporting Pakistan. With the passes open, China would only need marginal assurances of support, in case of need, to make an intervention which would be effective without being massive.

In this reading of the situation, despatching the task force would make equally good sense whether the Russians were headed for the coast of Bangladesh or not. If they were, they would be deterred. If they were not, the Chinese would be doubly reassured. For neither purpose would it be necessary for the Americans to have a foothold on land in Bangladesh or to commit any overt act of war against India—that would be left to the Chinese. But at the same time the task force would be present in such strength that it could repel anyone who might have been tempted by a smaller force to make a counter intervention. The task force was given the strength as well as the extensive mandate required for meeting any situation that might arise. This would be a case of maximum political advantage at minimum military investment for the United States as well as China, satisfying their obligations and saving Pakistan.

The United States and China faced a more or less identical dilemma. Kissinger focussed it sharply when at the WSAG meeting on December 8 he put the rhetorical question: "Can we allow a US ally to go down completely while we participate in a blockade?" The reality of Pakistan's alliances with the United

States and China was too great to be obfuscated by the techni-
calities of treaty protocol. The dilemma was not eased for Peking
by the absence of a treaty with Pakistan, or for Washington
by the official American statement in December—of questionable
validity in view of the background discussed on earlier pages—
that the United States had no bilateral agreement with Pakistan
under CENTO and SEATO. By China's own repeated declarations the world saw it as an ally of Pakistan. That is how
the world saw the USA too, especially when Nixon and Kissinger,
a more egotistical combination than has adorned the White
House for a long time, were showing a strong partiality for
Pakistan. Kissinger's famous statement: "We do not want to be
even handed—the President does not want to be even handed,"
and Nixon's confession that he wanted to "tilt" in Pakistan's
favour did not become public knowledge in these precise terms
until the Anderson disclosures in January. But Washington's
bias in favour of Pakistan and against India was one of the better
known facts of life for the subcontinent. The United States
had no option—nor had China—but to live up to this fact or face
the ignominy implicit in Kissinger's statement.

Here was the cutting edge of the obligations of big power status—the price you pay if you lose credibility. By losing it at one
place you lose it also in another, by a variation of the domino
theory. Sulzberger only exaggerated the variation—he did not
invent it—when he reported in the *New York Times* in April
1972, that Washington felt in December "if an unchecked India,
armed and backed by Russia, went unchallenged it might change
Moscow's assessment of the United States, encourage Egypt to
initiate another round of fighting against Israel…and lead Peking
to fear that the Russian-backed Indian victory was but a dress
rehearsal for a later Russian attack on China itself." A bit far
fetched but not untrue version of the reasons why the fleet was
sent.

The American calculus of power was correct. It was Nixon's
judgment of India and China that went wrong. Of China
because it was not realized how reluctant the leadership
in Peking would be to put a foot into a dissolving situation.
Of India because no account was taken of the changes which
had overtaken the Indian leadership since the United
States last attempted to understand it. It is more than

likely that the Chinese, being much closer to the Indian scene and a shrewder judge of it than the present leadership in Washington, more readily appreciated that no amount of offshore encouragement would serve any purpose without Pakistan holding the battle on land. Sino-American relations, although good enough for Washington to expect favourable responses to its own initiatives, were not good enough for plans to be concerted between them in advance.

Hence it came about that although China was written up as the main actor in the plot constructed by WSAG on December 10, it was Washington, the supporting actor, which was left holding the stage in a most embarrassing fashion. Every hour which the task force spent in the Indian Ocean, without any role which the force or anyone else could see for it, mocked at American power. China, on the other hand, became an amused member of the audience, while India turned her back upon the entire drama as a matter which was no longer of any consequence to her.

India made a final display of cool self-assurance in making a unilateral declaration of cease-fire, with the Indian Army ready to spring forward in the west if given the signal to do so. As soon as Niazi signed an unconditional surrender at 4.30 P.M. on December 16, India's war aims in the eastern theatre were fully met; Bangladesh, recognized by India on December 6, was now a total reality. The aims in the west had not been met so far. For a while Mrs Gandhi considered whether the war should continue until they were. The political advantages of an immediate and unilateral cease-fire, partly conceived in terms of prestige, were weighed against the military advantages of inflicting further attrition on the enemy and capturing some crucial territorial point. Within a few hours Mrs Gandhi consulted senior cabinet colleagues, the three Chiefs of Staff, and leaders of the main Opposition parties in Parliament. Swaran Singh, who was still in New York, was consulted over the telephone. In varying degrees nearly all of them preferred the political advantage, Swaran Singh most of all because, he said, such a gesture would put India's critics in the wrong and the effect of the adverse vote in the UN would be greatly diluted. The Soviet Union had the same preference. Even according to CIA reports read at WSAG meetings, the Soviet Union was reconciled to India continuing the war for a bit to complete the eviction of the Pakistani forces from Kashmir. But its preference was for an immediate cease-fire because of the isolation in which it was placed at the UN by the vote in the General Assembly. This, however, is all the trace there was of Soviet "pressure."

After considering these different opinions, Mrs Gandhi came to the conclusion, at about 7.30 P.M., within three hours of the surrender in Dacca, that since the objective was in the final analysis political—that Pakistan should not venture to make war upon India again either in a misconceived estimation of its own strength or on the encouragement of other countries—the political gains of a unilateral cease-fire were more important than the military gains of continuing the war for a few days more. The decision was eminently right. Its gains would have been greater if the Indian armed forces had performed better on the western front in the 13 days since the pre-emptive air strike by Pakistan. But Mrs Gandhi, guided once again by her highly developed sense of timing, decided that the victory won in the east would be further embellished by a unilateral declaration. She waited to hear Yahya Khan's broadcast which came at 7.45 P.M. but before it was over she made her announcement, writing into history a fine counterpoint to 1962.

# V The Second Liberation

# A New Strategic Balance

In helping Bangladesh towards its liberation India has fortified her own independence. But the fortification is not yet complete, and for this India will need to muster every resource she can in the allied fields of diplomatic skill and military strength. The time remaining for doing so is not much more than the next few years, perhaps no more than the next three or four. Events are moving so fast in Asia that unless India consolidates her gains very quickly she may discover that they have slipped out of her fingers. Only six years passed between Lin Piao defining the doctrine of a seige of the cities by the countryside and the visit by Nixon, mayor of Lin Piao's archetypal city, to the seat of the power of the "countryside," Peking.

The power structure in the Asian countryside may take only half as many years to assume a definite trend, especially in South-East Asia where new tendencies will develop particularly fast when the Viet Nam war comes to an end. Within that time India has to ensure that it does not take a trend hostile to her interests. The first among her interests which she will have to safeguard is, of course, her security and she will need to safeguard it both against local and larger forces.

India's experience has been that local causes of conflict are often used by big powers for their own purposes. This tendency may be less conspicuous in future. There is a growing belief that as relations between them become more relaxed big powers will not try so hard as in the past to use the smaller powers as pawns in their own games; tensions between the smaller powers will be allowed to work their own way out without the big powers stoking or using them for aggrandizement against each other. But only those smaller powers and local conflicts will benefit from this abstention which do not seriously impinge upon the balance between the big powers. Those which do will inevitably enter the power calculus of the senior league; each big power will seek to exploit, promote or prevent them as may suit its purpose in relation to the other big powers. Therefore, if a local or regional power, on account of its size, location, or control of some essential raw material or some other cause of its greater significance, is in a position to tilt the balance between one big power and another it is bound to attract the attention, favourable or hostile, of all the big powers.

India happens to be in that position, which may be only a mixed blessing. Her quarrel with China, combined with her significant geographic position in relation to the Sino-Soviet conflict, inevitably makes her, as discussed earlier, one of the important figures in China's and Russia's and therefore also the USA's calculations in their mutual conflicts. Any serious local conflict in which India is or can be involved will continue to be the playground of big power politics. For protecting her interests in this game India may need more diplomatic skill than military strength. But, and here again India's own experience is a reliable witness, successful diplomacy presupposes credible evidence of military strength. A country which is or is believed to be vulnerable to present military threats cannot be very successful in diplomacy either.

Even before the liberation of Bangladesh reduced Pakistan to half its size, India had taken care of that source of threat. Whether Pakistan was convinced or not, India was—and the fact was—that in spite of American military aid Pakistan could not take a successful offensive against India either on the ground or in the air unless China actively aided it by mounting a serious and simultaneous threat. After the 1965 war, India also acquired the beginnings of a reassuring belief that it was much more difficult for China to stage an effective intervention in support of Pakistan than India had feared since 1962. In 1971 this reassurance was confirmed and enlarged, while at the same time a war on three fronts disappeared as a foreseeable possibility.

Now India is assured against three levels of danger on her land frontiers. First, any kind of attack, however wholehearted, which Pakistan can mount by itself. Second, a combination of a wholehearted attack by Pakistan and a partial attack by China, that is an attack mounted by China only with the normal force levels maintained by it on the Indian frontier. Third, an all-out attack by China so long as India does not have to face a simultaneous war on the western front. With India now politically able to trade territory for time and strategic advantage, any land attack by China will quickly expose the invading forces to the enormous logistical disadvantages of China's geopolitical spread.

It is possible that one day India will lose the advantage of political stamina and repeat the blunders she made in 1962; it is also possible that the centres of Chinese military power on land will significantly shift to the east and south, thus reducing China's logistical disadvantages on the Indian marches. But both possibilities are rather remote. Whether or not India remains, as I think she will, as consolidated politically as she is today, the lessons she has learnt in military strategy, from her contrasting experiences in 1962, 1965 and 1971, will remain with her. She will not repeat the blunder of fighting on grounds of China's choosing. China's centre of politico-military gravity may shift south-westwards in response to the Russian threat. But in terms of offensive military capability the shift is unlikely to be significant enough because there are three simultaneous constraints upon it: China cannot shift too much of its strength away from the seaboard, which is exposed to a traditional enemy; China will be more tempted to shift such offensive strength as it can towards the north-west and north-east where it would confront areas of relatively less consolidated Russian power, not towards the west or south-west where the whole Soviet system is much stronger and China's primary role must be defensive; and an excess of Chinese offensive capability in Sinkiang or western Tibet, which will in any case take many years to build up, will only provoke a coordinated build up of Russian and Indian strength in the areas opposite, a development which China cannot consider with equanimity. India cannot do very much in these areas, but two can play the game China played in 1962, with a reversed Aksai-Chin standing in for NEFA; this can have a diversionary effect upon the balance between Sino-Soviet land forces.

India is also reasonably safe against Pakistan's air power. Also against China's so long as it remains non-nuclear. For reasons discussed earlier, China's air capability against India faces physical limitations which are not easy to overcome; even a Chinese equivalent of the "spider" may not be of very great use when the task is not the very limited one of guiding back home-coming aircraft but the longer duration task of guiding a whole

combat operation across the radar shadow of the Himalayas.
In any case, conventional strikes, whether Chinese or Pakistani
(or Indian in retaliation), have little military weight unless
coordinated with serious action by land armies, or unless they are
staged, as by the Americans in Viet Nam, with such uncontestable
mastery in the air as the Indian Air Force is most unlikely to
concede even to a combined Pakistani and Chinese opposition.

China and Pakistan, each by itself or the two together, face as
serious limitations at sea as in the air in any offensive intent
against India.  China has a much bigger navy than India;
it is Asia's biggest.  But not all of it can operate in the Indian
Ocean for any length of time; India can more quickly assemble a
bigger naval force at any point in the Indian Ocean area and can
keep it there for longer than China can unless it gets land based
facilities in the Indian Ocean.  Therefore, unless the disparity
greatly increases in future or unless India neglects the precautionary expansion of her navy which will be discussed later, China
cannot by itself make the waters of the Indian Ocean dangerous
for India beyond acceptable limits.  Nor can it in conjunction
with Pakistan, which would have to face heavy retaliation across
land frontiers because no naval action can pose any serious
threat unless it crosses the line which divides hostility from
belligerency; when it makes the crossing it opens the door to
total action by either side.  Only a country which shares no land
frontiers with India can help China against India with forces or
fac lities without running any great risk of Indian retaliation.

Therefore, to sum up the security situation in the limited Asian
triangle—China-India-Pakistan—India is in a much better
position on land, in the air and at sea than ever before against
a joint or separate threats by China and Pakistan.

Within the means already available to her India can also
develop another dimension of safety:  against a *partial* nuclear
threat by China, whether China deploys it for purposes of blackmail or actual assault.  Until a few years ago Indian thinking on
this subject was inhibited by two factors.  The first is geographical.  Significant Indian targets are within easy reach of Chinese
launching positions in Tibet while significant Chinese targets
are 3,000 kilometres away from the nearest points of Indian
territory.  This is an advantage for China which is further
enlarged by the fact that Chinese positions can be safely hidden

away in the wasteland of Tibet, far from centres of population, while Indian positions cannot be. The second inhibition India suffered was financial. To the burdensome cost of developing a nuclear warhead she had to add in her calculations the crippling cost of delivery vehicles which would have the range to reach significant targets in China. But both inhibitions are now less severe because of the possibilities of waterborne use of retaliatory means.

While the possibility was known to scientific theory for a long time, perhaps to scientific theory in India too, lately it has been more clearly realized than it used to be that even countries at India's level of technology can utilize the possibility without breaking under its financial burden. The crowded shipping lanes along China's coast, only a few miles off critical Chinese targets, offer a variety of options. These range from such an unsophisticated and yet perfectly feasible option as mounting the retaliatory weapon on a merchant ship and hiding it away in this heavy traffic, to a more sophisticated one of launching it from a submarine which surfaces only for this purpose, to the more distant but not unattainable sophistication of launching it from a submerged position. The range required of the delivery vehicle would be so small in each of the three cases that cost and technology would no longer be insurmountable barriers to limited retaliation against limited attack or threat of attack. The waterborne vehicle would be an added cost. But it would also contribute to naval expansion, which is now a high priority must for India whether she takes the nuclear option or not.

If China decided to use the last ounce of her nuclear muscle it would still be much superior to India; superior enough that is, to use the threat as a compelling argument in many situations. Therefore India has no available or potential answer yet to the blackmailing effect of such a threat. But to a limited attack and therefore to its limited blackmailing effect India has a potential answer, which can be made actual without too much difficulty. It can no longer be argued, as it could be and was when the cost effectiveness of land based nuclear retaliation was compared with the cost effectiveness of the land forces required for a possible three front war, that the next 100 crores of rupees available for defence would buy greater security if invested in conventional land forces. A limited nuclear strategy meets the test of cost effectiveness of a nuclear force very well.

There are, of course, diplomatic implications. But they appear to be serious only because they have not been tackled as yet with the necessary resolution. India hung back from the nuclear option because it would annoy both the super powers to whom she would have to and could turn if China became actively hostile again. Therefore she did not squarely confront them with the natural corollary to their urgings upon her that she should not go nuclear to any extent whatever. Now it has become easier for her to do so. Because of Nixon's new China policy, India's anxiety about China no longer evokes Washington's concern in the sense in which it did before Washington decided that India had become a proxy power of Russia. Now, in fact, it would be happy to see an effective Chinese restraint upon India if for no other reason than at least as a check upon Russian influence in southern Asia. The Soviet Union on the other hand has acquired and demonstrated a stake in ensuring that China does not succeed in harming or weakening India either through a direct confrontation or indirectly via Pakistan. Therefore, in respect of both powers, India can better afford now to take a stand which would help to counter one of the remaining dimensions of a Chinese threat, the partial nuclear threat. The stand need not be that India must go nuclear immediately or regardless of whatever other safeguards might be offered to her. It need only be that if no other course avails her in obtaining for her a credible deterrent to what is already a credible danger, then she will have to develop on her own such deterrence as she can. Diplomatic resolution and skill are the first requirement for such a course; before deciding to develop her own nuclear weapon she has to discover whether there is a diplomatic alternative.

So far India has taken only one diplomatic initiative in the nuclear field. Soon after he became Prime Minister, Shastri floated the idea of a protective umbrella to be held by the nuclear super powers over the non-nuclear. But the idea was so thoroughly riddled with holes that it would only have deprived India of a nuclear option of her own without substituting in its place a reliable even if alien guarantee. The only kind of guarantee which the Indian initiative appeared likely to generate would have had so many e capes in it for the guarantor as regards the circumstances in which, and the extent to which, it could be

invoked that it would have had lit le deterrence value in the eyes
of the aggressor.  The only form in which it was spelt out at all
left the guarantor plenty of room to judge as to who was the
aggressor and what was the balance of merit in the cause of the
war.  Applied, for example, in the 1971 war, it would have left
Nixon as the guarantor completely free to decide whether or by
whom the guarantee could be invoked.  Possibly, issues such as
these would have been clarified if any serious discussion had
followed the Indian initiative at the official level.  But there was
hardly any, and partly for the reason that the claims India made
about her nuclear capability were not taken seriously by the
potential guarantors.

What India needs to do now is to take a better initiative with
better preparation.  She must more seriously pursue the suggestion, which has been halfheartedly considered for the past few
years and has been in the air once more since the liberation of
Bangladesh, that she should stage a nuclear explosion for peaceful purposes to carry conviction about her capability with other
countries.  Secondly, with or without such a demonstrative bang,
India must launch a sustained diplomatic drive for a foolproof
protective guarantee by the nuclear to the non-nuclear countries,
and she should do so in coordination with other countries, of
which there are perhaps half a dozen around the globe, which
have potential nuclear capability and like India are being urged
not to convert it into actuality.  The anchor of the guarantee
must be that the guarantors will massively retaliate, by nuclear
means, against any country which makes a nuclear attack of
any magnitude against any non-nuclear country and that they will
do so regardless of the real or alleged cause of war or merits of the
case so that the deterrent effect of the guarantee may not be
dissipated.  In other words, they must themselves accept and
force others too that no dispute or cause of war can justify the use
of nuclear weapons.

In one way it would now be easier and in another way more
difficult to formulate such a guarantee than when Shastri initiated
the idea.  More difficult because in a world made by the Nixon-
Kissinger diplomacy the USA might decline to join the Soviet
Union in giving India a guarantee which China would see as
directed against itself.  This would oblige India to choose
between no guarantee and one which comes only from Russia

(assuming Russia is willing to give one  single-handed) which would mean putting too many Indian eggs in the Russian basket. It would be easier because at least while the Sino-Soviet rivalry lasts, a solo Russian guarantee would be more credible in Chinese eyes than one complicated by a joint American component. The USA would probably still require, as it did in the early 1960s, that India make up with Pakistan before she could qualify for full American assistance against China.  This would open the floodgates of disputed interpretation.

The US component would also run into problems of logistics, darkly political in colouration, which India discovered in 1964, soon after China exploded its first nuclear bomb.  At that time President Johnson said: "Nations that do not seek national nuclear weapons can be sure that, if they need our strong support against some threat of blackmail, they will have it."  The idea was explored  in unofficial Indo-American exchanges, some conducted in the context of Shastri's idea of a joint guarantee and some in that of Johnson's more or less solo version.  But in all of them it was pointed out by the US side that for operational and  psychological  reasons  it  would  be  necessary  to  station American nuclear retaliatory capability on Indian soil.  Otherwise the USA would have to operate from a distance and therefore, for equal success in containing the Chinese threat, would have to maintain a more powerful posture and deny itself the chance to use intermediate pressures in graduated escalation. The Soviet Union would not have any of these problems, whether as joint or solo guarantor.  Being China's next door neighbour along an enormous frontier, it would be able to apply pre-calculated pressure at a number of points on a graduated scale, and before doing so it would not question India on her relations with Pakistan in the new situation.

On the whole it would be probably better for India and other non-nuclear powers if the protective guarantee came, jointly or severally, from more than one power.  India would not object if China gave it too.  Multilaterality is better in this case.  But that is a matter of tactics and details.  The more important matter of principle is that any guarantee India gets must be proof against  questions  of  interpretation  about  the  circumstances in which it may be invoked.  Only upon such a commitment can the non-nuclear lean.  If India gets one, she can afford to forego the nuclear option. If she does not she will have no alternative but to bear the financial burden, which in terms of cost effectiveness would be fully justified, of developing her own capability to the point of off-setting the blackmailing effect of a partial nuclear threat by China.

This is one of those situations in which halfmeasures are better than none: developing the capability to meet a partial threat makes eminent good sense if it is not possible to meet a full scale threat. China's lead over India in developed capability is so great already that it cannot be closed except at such great cost in scarce resources that it may more seriously weaken other aspects of security than it strengthens the nuclear aspect. Therefore, that is a dimension of danger which India can meet only by non-military means. But a partial answer is not, for that reason, irrelevant. In fact it harmonizes with a major diplomatic aspect of India's recent defence policy: that she must counter limited threats with her own means, as in the case of China's threat on the northern front last December, and invoke the support of other countries only when the threat exceeds her own capability.

As far as China and Pakistan are concerned, then, India lacks the actual or potential means as yet for only two dangers: a nuclear attack by China to the maximum limit of its capability, and a conventional attack by both China and Pakistan to the maximum limit of their combined capability. To this one should add a third danger, which is of lower intensity but higher probability: that seeing India as the proxy power of the Soviet Union, or as an independent future power in an area of the world which is of increasing importance to the big powers, countries which are worried by the rise of Soviet influence or countries which have their own hegemonistic claims to protect or project in this area may wish to keep India under the restraint of some counterbalance. They would attempt, and "they" here essentially means China and the USA, to revive the diplomatic techniques and objectives of the 1950s by which the USA prevented the emergence on the subcontinent of what Galbraith, quoted earlier, has described as "the North American formula." This, at any rate, is the Indian expectation and fear, and Mrs Gandhi gave very clear expression to it when she said in Dacca on March 19: "Those people who have consistently opposed Bangladesh's liberation are now very much interested in seeing that they are proved right and not we. I think they will try to weaken the subcontinent because this was their policy all along, not just on the question of Bangladesh .... That was the purpose of encouraging confrontation with India [by Pakistan]."

These are, however, three aspects of the same problem, the problem of the balance between the aggregate of the forces favourable to India and those hostile to her, and the answer to it has to be found in diplomacy, not in military strength except in so far as some military strength is a prerequisite for effective diplomacy. Neither a nuclear attack by China on India nor a combined conventional attack by China and Pakistan can remain a matter to be sorted out within the confines of the relations between these three countries. It would immediately attract the imperatives of the big global triangle, Russia-China-USA. Its outcome, whichever way it went, would affect drastically the balance of the big triangle, and neither the USA nor the Soviet Union could afford to keep aloof from it; whichever stayed out would lose out to a very significant degree. Therefore, what began within the confines of the smaller triangle would, willy nilly, spread out into the larger one. Apart from other reasons, China's involvement in both triangles would make that inevitable.

This would also be the case with low combustion diplomatic attrition aimed only at denying India the place conferred upon her always by her geographical position in southern Asia and now magnified by the liberation of Bangladesh. Whether China practised the attrition or the USA, their motives and weapons would relate to the big triangle. The United States has said more than once since the war in December that while it is willing to accept India's new position as the dominant power of the subcontinent, it will do so only on condition that India does not become (or does not appear to the USA to have become), a proxy power of the Soviet Union. Or rather, that it does not remain a proxy power in *American* eyes because in the whole drama of the liberation the USA had already regarded India as a Soviet proxy; in the Indian victory last December the *New York Times* editorially saw "a Soviet victory and a major increase in the Soviet influence in the subcontinent." In saying so the USA implies that if India's association with the Soviet Union remained within the limits of American tolerance there would be little reason for

Washington to practise diplomatic attrition against India, but that if it exceeded these limits the game of attrition would be resumed. Upon being resumed it would be probably played in conjunction with China's diplomatic leverage in the areas and countries of special importance to India such as Burma, Nepal, Ceylon and Pakistan and, further afield, South-East Asia and the third world as a whole.

In other words, the American intention would appear to be to accept Indian primacy on the subcontinent, regardless of what that might do to the India-Pakistan-China triangle, provided India's proximity to the Soviet Union did not impinge adversely upon American interests in the big triangle. But that is a contradiction in geopolitical terms. India's primacy on the subcontinent is bound to diminish China's advantage in the little triangle and as a consequence also in the big triangle. On the other hand it will help to improve the Soviet Union's position and not only on the subcontinent but globally because of the difference it would make on the southern flank of the Soviet confrontation with China. The United States can no more isolate than the Soviet Union or China can the position India now occupies in one triangle from the changing balance in the other triangle. Conversely, if India can favourably influence the balance in the bigger triangle she can make her position more secure in the smaller triangle.

The overlap between the two triangles is equally firm when seen from Peking. China may wish to continue to invest in what was from its point of view in the second half of the 1960s a low-risk and low-cost confrontation between India and Pakistan. But neither the cost nor risk are going to be low any more. The cost of belligerency towards India has always been heavy for Pakistan and for those who have tried to subsidize it. But only a small share of the cost had so far fallen upon China, and for that share China was able to carry off a disproportionate dividend in terms of influence in Pakistan. It is not very likely that this disproportion will continue in the 1970s. China will have to invest heavily in Pakistan, taking over much of the burden which the US arsenal and treasury bore until 1965, if it wishes to use Pakistan as a strong enough pawn on the South Asian chess-board. And it may turn out to be an unwise investment, infructuous at best and at worst dangerous. It may be infructuous because no matter how much assistance China gives Pakistan it will not be able to coerce India into courses desired by China unless China reinforces the coercion by risking its own direct involvement. It may be dangerous because Pakistan will certainly incur Indian retaliation if it revives belligerency, and in a future conflict between India and Pakistan China will have to face the question more quickly and squarely than ever before whether to wage war against India or to suffer the humiliation again of seeing an ally dismembered without doing or being able to do anything about it. The only country which can ease the predicament for China is the USA; it can share the burden of the belligerency first and then of war should there be one. But the moment that happens the small triangle game will move into the arena of the big triangle.

Therefore the answer to each of the three dangers which India still faces lies in the global balance of forces, not the purely local or subcontinental, and the essence of the answer is to ensure that in areas of critical importance to India a higher aggregate of world forces is favourable to her than is unfavourable and, as a second strike, her own diplomatic and military weight is such, and is used in such a way, that each side is reluctant to push India into the arms of the other for fear that this would tilt the balance against it. It will not be easy to pursue both objectives at once. The first assumes a system of alliances, by whatever name they may be called, and India's active involvement in them, however informal. The second assumes non-alignment of an even purer variety than heretofore. But it is not impossible to reconcile them if India uses more resolutely her old and indestructible asset, now more valuable than ever before, the geopolitical significance of her size and location.

A policy which would bridge the gap between the two objectives is to build further upon the existing friendship with Russia where India's or Russia's crucial interests are better served that way against any imminent danger, and in other respects to develop a more vigorously independent role. India in distress cannot count upon Russian help unless she reciprocates in Russian distress. In any case the obligations of assistance are meaningless or demeaning if they are not mutual. But India does not have to dilute for that reason either the fact or appearance of her independence, whether exercised in areas of proximity to Russia or further afield. The restrictive implications of the obligations will further diminish as India develops more her own defensive capability, which would make her even less dependent upon external assistance than she is at present; and the less "allied" to either side she appears to be the more interested each side will be to see that she does not have to become the other's ally to ensure her own safety.

With the simultaneous rise in her own strength and in the perception thereof in other countries, India will be called upon less often to defend herself with the force of arms and, should the need arise, will be better able to do so without invoking treaties or understandings with other countries. Therefore she will have better resources than in the 1950s to carve out a role of independence, using non-alignment as a security resource and security as a resource for non-alignment. In fact, she can now lift Nehru's non-alignment to a plane which was not attainable for him. But at the same time she can also prove herself more worthy of help when she needs it by proving that now she is better able to give help when others need it. In other words, she can simultaneously practise the diplomacy of detachment and of obligations. Fortunately for her, the two areas in which she most needs assistance, her land frontiers in the north and the Indian Ocean, are also the areas in which she can most effectively render help to others. The same is true of the diplomatic arena which is of particular concern to her, namely southern and south-eastern Asia. This makes it easier to accept and practise both military and diplomatic obligations in areas where these are most relevant. Much of the rest of the world is free for the practice of detachment from the big powers.

The obligations are a product of the tensions between the Soviet Union, the United States, China and India; this was so in the past decade and will remain so in the next. With American counterpressure threatening to create a nuclear stand off, the Soviet Union faces China's enormous land army on the plane of conventional warfare only. This gives China a relative advantage which it would not have if both sides resorted without restriction to all weapons. But the advantage is diluted by China's continued confrontation with India, in which comparable resources in manpower meet along a front which has many diversionary possibilities. Similarly, Russia stands in a powerful diversionary position on the left flank of India's confrontation with China, offering India the same protection against China as Pakistan expected China would offer it against India in the eastern theatre last December.

This creates a complementarity between Russian and Indian policies in an important area, a phenomenon which prompted *Al Ahram* of Cairo to say that Russia was shifting its interest from West Asia to the Indian subcontinent "as the focus of a decisive test of power" with America. The shift will endure so long as the mainspring of global diplomacy continues to be the Sino-Soviet conflict and the old rivalry between the two super powers. As the USA and China draw together in their mutual opposition to the Soviet Union, so do Russia and India in their mutual opposition to the power of China, thus recreating at least in this sense and to this extent conditions of bi-polarity in international diplomacy. This new bi-polarity recreates in a more accentuated form the environment of the 1950s, which was so conducive for the practice of non-alignment. That this may also recreate competition between the two sides for the allegiance of India was acknowledged by Sulzberger in the *New York Times* in the middle of February. A few days after Mrs Gandhi told him in New Delhi that probably the US policy towards India changed for the worse when it changed for the better towards China, he wrote: "The United States and China should help to disengage India from the Soviet Union."

In the complex world of South-East Asia the bi-polarity is seen in a diplomatic divide, on one side of which stand the Soviet Union and India, and on the other side China and the USA. Neither pair is a monolith. The Soviet Union would prefer to see its own influence grow there instead of India's, and the USA would any day play off Russia against China to strengthen its own position, in Viet Nam particularly but elsewhere also if it can do that without adding to its military commitments. But as circumstances force the USA to withdraw from the Asian mainland, including South-East Asia, it will prefer to withdraw in China's favour than either India's or the Soviet Union's. The Soviet Union would rather see Indian influence grow here than Chinese or American. It is therefore significant that every indication of closer relations between Hanoi and New Delhi is welcomed in Moscow but frowned upon in Peking. The contrast came through very clearly when Hanoi differentiated its position on Bangladesh from Peking's, approximating it to Moscow's, and India responded by raising diplomatic relations with Hanoi to the ambassadorial level, causing intense annoyance in Washington. It is also significant that it was during bitter denunciations of India by China over the liberation of Bangladesh that Hanoi pressed India for exchange of ambassadors, and that an added reason why India agreed so readily after the liberation was to prove to Washington by this further token that US diplomacy had failed to intimidate India.

Indian and Soviet diplomacies are not moving on identical axes in South-East Asia but the lines are parallel and very close. One evidence of their proximity is the similarity between the ideas of collective security of this region which Mrs Gandhi and Brezhnev have been expounding for the past few years. It is more than likely that they will further supplement each other when South-East Asia moves towards new and more native shapes in the wake of American withdrawal from Viet Nam. In both diplomacies the primary effort will be that some indigenous association of the sub-region, in which Hanoi takes its due place of honour, should be the main stabilizer, its neutrality respected by all major powers and its internal frontiers made safe by them if it so desires. The views of North Viet Nam and the ASEAN countries on these aspects came encouragingly close in the summer of 1972 following an ASEAN resolution favouring neutralization of South-East Asia with guarantees by the major powers. But there will be a subsidiary effort in both Russian and Indian diplomacies that the USA should not retain and China should not develop an influence in this sub-region which would be hostile either to Russian or Indian interests. For ensuring this, both are likely to invest more in Hanoi than in any other capital in this neighbourhood.

Russian ideas are well advanced on this and, as seen in New Delhi, include a scheme for an international council the boundaries of which would be flexible enough to extend up to Japan and ideological composition sufficiently heterogeneous to include both North and South Viet Nam and North and South Korea. Russia and India would be included as Asian powers (in one version of this idea the compositon differs little from that of ECAFE with the USA coming in as a Pacific power) but

abstention would be forced upon China by including Taiwan on
the same basis as both Koreas and both Viet Nams, that each divided country would have representation for each of its parts until
its people resolved the problem of reunification.

There is as much similarity between Soviet and Indian diplomacies in the South Asian sub-region as in the south-eastern.
Both the Soviet Union and India see an area of hydrographic and
other economic linkages, and historical and cultural affinities, in
the greater part of the region which covers Afghanistan, Pakistan,
India, Nepal, Bhutan, Bangladesh, Burma and Ceylon, that is
countries which are separated from West Asia on the one hand
and South-East Asia on the other and are joined together by their
common drainage into the Indian Ocean. This overview reinforces such specifics as Soviet efforts from the mid-1960s to carry
India and Pakistan together, from the late 1960s to bring India,
Pakistan, Afghanistan and Nepal together into a trade and transit
plan which would also be an outlet for southern Russia, and from
the end of 1971 to have close relations with Bangladesh as well.
A matching set of specifics which the overview reinforces are a
by-product of India's vision of herself. They include Indian
efforts ever since independence to cultivate special relations
with Bhutan and Nepal, from the late 1950s with Ceylon and
Burma, from the middle of 1971 with the future Bangladesh, and
since the liberation with Pakistan also in so far as that is
possible. This vision of India which is fully shared by Russia
extends beyond the belated US recognition of India's place in
a "North American formula" for the Indian subcontinent.

Indian and Soviet objectives here coincide up to a point. Both
wish to see developing here not only a local stabilizer (much
bigger in area than South-East Asia, West Asia or the EEC)
but also a barrier to the expansion of any adverse Chinese influence to the south and west. Thereafter, a divergence can
ensue between Russian and Indian interests if India desires the
stabilizer to be more independent of all outside influences than
Russia desires it to be independent of the Russian. But it is
highly unlikely that the divergence will degenerate into a conflict so long as Sino-Soviet hostility and US-Russian rivalry
persist. In one dimension of this area, the Indian Ocean,
there is already a peaceful coexistence between Indo-Soviet
convergence and divergence. Perception of shared danger has

promoted the convergence; beyond that lie the perspectives of divergence.

In this oceanic dimension of the potential stabilizer there is a dangerous combination of the high strategic purpose of the two super powers and the acute friability of local political and economic structures. The USA finds here the most profitable access to sensitive areas of the Soviet heartland, and about the only possibility of cutting one of the main economic arteries of the continent-wide Soviet land mass whose internal lines of communication are otherwise immune against any American threat unless it crosses the nuclear threshold. Once the technique was developed for launching nuclear missiles from nuclear submarines prowling under the surface, it was inevitable that the Indian Ocean would become their favourite hunting ground and hideout. It offers proximity to Soviet central and southern Asia, reported to be the Soviet arsenal of the future, and it combines this proximity with the depth and expanse of waters which large submarines require for their deployment and escape tactics. To make the environment just about ideal, it also offers through much of the year a sufficient cloud cover to baffle thermal detection through satellite surveillance. Consequently the Indian Ocean excites much interest within the Super Powers.

The Indian Ocean is also one of the more vulnerable stretches for the enormous maritime traffic between East European and Far Eastern Russia. According to a testimony by William Bundy, former US Assistant Secretary of State for East Asian and Pacific Affairs, before the House of Representatives on 20 July 1971: "The Soviet Union more and more depends upon the southern sea routes to link up its Pacific provinces with the rest of the USSR." He quoted reports according to which this movement might be "of hundreds of ships a month." Giving a vital comparison, he added: "The southern sea route has become a Soviet lifeline, almost as much as for Japan."

The high military value of the Indian Ocean is accompanied by its vulnerability to economic, political and diplomatic pressure. On both shores there are long stretches which are populous enough to give "influence" an entry. The eastern littoral, from Akyab to Singapore, is strewn with endemic economic and political unrest or ethnic, tribal and religious conflict or irridenticism. On much of the western littoral there are these causes of instability plus a more vigorous conflict between neighbouring governments. In the north-western corner great riches parcelled out in small Sheikhdoms make ideal pieces for international chess. Numerous permutations are possible here. Whether some of them would be inimical to Indian interests, or how inimical, depends upon many imponderables. To mention only three: How far will China succeed in its diplomatic thrust on the East African coast? Will Pakistan become more integrated or less with Iran and Turkey?—a grouping in which at least one member, Iran, has the declared intention of building up a strong navy. And will Pakistan remain internally integrated or break up into an independent maritime Sind, which would be caught between India and Iran, and an independent NWFP which would be sandwiched between Afghanistan and India with the Pakistani areas of Kashmir forming a bone of three-sided confrontation between India, Afghanistan and NWFP? But these imponderables also confirm, as do more concrete and measurable factors, that India will have to choose a wary path in shaping its policy for the Indian Ocean area. Her ability to discover the right mix between the diplomacies of obligations and of detachment will be put to a very difficult test.

Hitherto India has practised the diplomacy of detachment more than of obligations, thus bringing to the fore a point of divergence with the Soviet Union. In the first place India has firmly discouraged any Soviet expectation of getting a naval base on Indian shores. Even a Soviet proposal for a merchant shipping base was declined in 1970 on the ground that the facilities asked for were rather extensive. This was done in spite of the risk, which the Soviet Union cleverly left unconcealed from Indian eyes, that Pakistan might be willing to offer facilities at Gwadur in return for a stepping up of Soviet favours. India continued to offer this discouragement after the liberation of Bangladesh, though now she had to think of the added possibility that Bangladesh might offer a lodgement to the Soviet Navy. The threat created by the US Seventh Fleet did not shift India from this approach.

To this negative aspect of the Indo-Soviet divergence India has also added a more positive aspect: she has actively pushed a proposition, hitherto favoured by other countries also which are washed by the Indian Ocean, particularly Ceylon, that foreign navies and certainly foreign naval bases should be withdrawn from the Indian Ocean, leaving behind only a neutral zone. Despite Soviet opposition, India supported in the 1971 session of the UN General Assembly a Ceylonese resolution demanding neutralization of the Indian Ocean. Before that and with greater diplomatic boldness, Mrs Gandhi pressed the same proposition upon the Soviet troika when she met its members in Moscow in September 1971. Although faced already with Soviet resistance to the liberation of Bangladesh with Indian arms, Mrs Gandhi did not hesitate to push another issue also on which there could be a marked divergence and the wording of the joint statement issued at the end of her visit confirms there was. But once again Mrs Gandhi stuck to her position and won at least partial recognition to it. "The Prime Minister of India re-affirmed" says the joint statement, "that the Indian Ocean area should be made a zone of peace. The Soviet side expressed its readiness to study the question and to solve it together with other powers on an equal basis." The expression of readiness was a paraphrase of an earlier Soviet position, of which India got some details at meetings between the two Foreign Ministers in the course of June, that if the United States responded, the Soviet Union would agree to equal and simultaneous American and Soviet naval reductions. But Mrs Gandhi pressed the Russian leaders to go much further and agree to total neutralization.

But neither the negative nor positive aspect of the Indo-Soviet divergence makes for a viable naval policy for India. Take the positive first. It is not at all certain in the first place that all the Indian Ocean countries are necessarily keen on its neutralization; in fact, Singapore was at one time reported to be willing, out of its mistrust of China's naval intentions, to give shore facilities to the Soviet Navy upon the departure of the British. Nor is it certain that those who were keen on neutralization before the end of last year continue to be. Hesitations may have appeared among them, perhaps even in Ceylon, following the demonstration of its offensive power by the Indian Navy, especially its power to impose an effective blockade both in the Arabian Sea and the Bay of Bengal. But what is more important, it is not at all certain that neutralization can be attained through a diplomatic initiative, even a unanimous one, of the countries which border on the Indian Ocean. The stakes are so high for both the Super Powers in this ocean that they cannot bow out

of it simply because the littoral countries desire neutralization. They may possibly do so when an overall and general
*detente* between them progresses to the point that they can lower
their guards by mutual agreement. But they cannot do so in
the Indian Ocean in isolation from the rivalry between them in
the rest of the world.

Quite possibly it will be more difficult for them to disengage
completely in the Indian Ocean than elsewhere. Here more
than in any other waters they not only have to take each other
into account but also China, and the Chinese have no interest
in promoting a disengagement between the two major rivals.
Even the possibility of a Chinese naval presence will impede a
US-Russian withdrawal in each other's favour. There have
been reports since the liberation of Bangladesh that the Chinese
Navy may acquire a toe-hold on the coast of Ceylon. For much
longer there have been reports of increasing Chinese influence
on the coast of Tanzania. Should the Chinese Navy materialize
in either of these countries the Soviet Union would have two
reasons, not one, to ensure its own secure presence. As it is,
according to one American opinion—William Bundy in the
National Security Sub-Committee of the US House Foreign
Affairs Committee on 21 July 1971—"the desire to oppose China
in the Indian Ocean area is the stronger motive of Russians in the
area than the desire to compete with the western powers."
Bundy's reasons are of particular interest to India. "The re-
awakened Chinese," he said, "would like to establish a strong
position in the Arabian Sea and the Bay of Bengal, both for
themselves and as way stations to Africa.... The Chinese
interest is not maritime, as the Soviet interest is in large part, but
rather the simple extension of Chinese influence, and whenever
possible hegemony or even domination."

This exposes the vulnerability of the negative aspect also of the
Indian divergence from the Soviet position. The Americans
have a base at Diego Garcia which they can use without the
approval of any littoral country. If the Chinese also acquire
facilities, the Russians will be comparatively at a disadvantage,
and this is not a situation which can be of any advantage for
India. India will therefore have to calculate where the balance
of advantage lies for her between, on the one hand, the virtue of
pressing uncompromisingly for neutralization, and denying shore

facilities to the Russian Navy, and on the other hand the risk of the Russian Navy finding itself handicapped against the Chinese and American, being without any local anchorage. Genuine neutralization, which would apply to all navies, including the Chinese, which are not indigenous to this ocean, could be beneficial for the Soviet Union as well as for India. It would eliminate the US naval threat to Soviet central and southern Asia and to Soviet domestic traffic which commutes through these waters. It would also eliminate the tensions of an unnecessarily high level of competition and the risk of accidental conflagration which goes with it. But if it is not possible to eliminate the competition, then only that naval policy is safe for India which would keep the balance of naval power in favour of India in an ocean which is of vital importance to her.

But whatever the off-shore environment may be, India has no option now but to expand her naval capability. This is required as much for the diplomacy of obligations as for the diplomacy of detachment, and as much for a state of high competition as for low or no competition. The need for expansion had always existed ever since the British departure in 1947. But India remained oblivious of it for the reason (if lack of foresight may be called reason) that she had little experience of naval responsibility. While the defence of India by land was mainly based upon Indian manpower even in the days of British rule, naval defence was ensured by British naval power anchored at strategic positions in the Indian Ocean, like Aden, the Cape, Trincomalee and Singapore. Even its manpower, let alone control, was almost entirely British. India was only required to furnish victualling, repair and some financial resources. Therefore India found herself completely unprepared, and as much mentally as in terms of resources, for the naval consequence of the British departure. This partly accounts for the failure of Indian military thinking to respond to naval possibilities in the 1965 conflict. The passivity appeared to be so permanent that an Indian Ocean expert like T.B. Miller assumed in *Indian and Pacific Oceans* (Adelphi Paper No. 57, May 1969) that the Indian Navy would not be able to do anything more than "to exercise a watch on its own and Pakistani ports and patrol selected ports of the area." It was only in 1971 that the navy crossed the threshold by responding to Ceylon's appeal for naval assistance in conditions of potential combat. Having once thrown off the inherited mental inhibition, it grew up with amazing speed and in the liberation of Bangladesh befittingly carried out a multifarious role. Now it cannot slide back into insignificance except to the grave detriment of Indian security.

India cannot compete with either of the two super naval powers. But it cannot be indifferent to the competition between them in nearby waters. The least it must have in relation to them is a greatly expanded capability of surveillance, which is at present astonishingly meagre for a country which has to look after two seaboards and a coastline of more than 3,000 kilometres. But that is only the beginning. Surveillance has to have a strategic purpose. It is no use for India to spend large sums of money in order to discover what is going on around her unless she then wishes to do something about it, and the least she must—and can —do calls for a much bigger navy than she has at present.

In a situation of close off-shore competition, India can be one of the factors which influences the balance. Her contribution towards it can be at least as important as that of other countries which are relevant to the Indian Ocean such as Iran in one corner, South Africa in another, Australia in a third and, more distantly, China. All of them, except for the time being Iran, can deploy greater off-shore power than India has at present. But India can substantially make up for that by the enormous spread of her proximity both in regard to the Arabian Sea and the Bay of Bengal. If properly developed, her shore-based naval-air power and close-shore power afloat can make a critical difference in a conventional battle if it is not taking place too far off-shore, and as shown by the success of the raid on Karachi, the cost of acquiring some medium range capability is neither devastating nor disproportionate to obtainable results.

But even if the big power competition declines the need for expanding the Indian Navy will not. In fact, in that situation the need will grow further because there is no likelihood of a Chinese abstention and there will be no Russian Navy to counterbalance the Chinese. Secondly, the withdrawal of Super Power navies will not mean the withdrawal of Super Power politics as well. On the contrary, the political game will be played with greater vigour when it is played through proxies because there will be less risk of a direct confrontation by accident. The Indian

Ocean is particularly rich in opportunities for distant brinkman-
ship. There are any number of *causus belli* which can be made
the carriers of physically remote ambition. In the situation
which has developed since December last year, remote motives
may be even keener than before to manipulate the proximate: India has demonstrated her naval possibilities but not
achieved them yet; that is, she has entered the zone where the
desire to nip her in the bud out of fear or envy or a passionless
global calculation is spurred by the thought that this will become
more difficult with the passage of time.

The first and the last main events on the Indian Ocean calendar
in 1971 show what kind of calls may be made upon India's naval
capability. They also show how short she is of ability to meet them
and what needs to be done to keep the ability abreast of the likely
demands upon it. At the request of Ceylon, the Indian Navy
put a loose ring around the island to detect and prevent smug-
gling of arms to an insurgency in central Ceylon. This can be the
forerunner of other similar situations. On both outer shores of
the Indian Ocean, internal tensions and the manipulation thereof
by hostile outside forces may compel the victim government to
turn to sources of friendly external assistance. One of these may
well be India, and with increasing frequency as three very
probable trends d.velop: as it is realized more than it is now that
confident of her internal consolidation and able to match up to
external threats, India is increasingly able and willing to render
assistance; second, non-Asian countries become increasingly unwilling to involve themselves in Asian troubles so long as these
do not threaten their own essential interests; and that external
manipulation comes from countries, Asian or other, which are
also hostile to India. It may well be prudent for India to stand
aloof from local tensions, especially when they arise from genuine
and long neglected social, economic and other popular discontents. Even then, however, India's own strategic interests or
the plight of an especially friendly government may require that
India should go to its aid against an externally instigated attack
upon it if it is wholly unmerited. This is not a case of projecting
Indian power to the far confines of the Indian Ocean; nor is
it swagger or pompous altruism. It is only prudent statecraft
and enlightened self-interest.

But as it is the navy is not an adequate vehicle of self-interest.

Even for effective in-shore defence against an enemy who may use his navy more daringly than Pakistan did, the Indian Navy has to expand substantially its detection, interception and counter-attack capability especially for anti-submarine warfare. It is still more inadequate for carrying effective assistance to a distant friend in distress because its air cover is weak and fire-power outdated except for the newly acquired fast missile boats. To meet the deficiency in anti-submarine warfare it needs to take two immediate steps: to acquire at least a few long range shore-based surveillance aircraft which are also equipped to make a kill so that a killer submarine does not escape even after detection, as the killer of the *Khukri* did; and to expand its frigate-mounted anti-submarine helicopter fleet, both for detection and counter-attack. To expand fire-power it needs, apart from rapid expansion of its missile boat fleet, such extensive conversion from gun firing to missile systems that it would be worth India's while to set up its own electronics and fuel capacity to design and manufacture missiles. For improved distant air cover the tested answer would have been another aircraft carrier. But the enormous costs apart, a carrier of the size suited to India's needs is not available in the market. Therefore India has to make do for the time being with the *Vikrant* which has many years of good life in it yet but needs replacement of its outdated and slow aircraft. But over the long range also a more flexible, efficient and cost-effective answer according to the navy's new thinking would be increased air power but dispersed over a number of smaller warships, not concentrated on another flat top. For this expanded floating capability the navy will need more launching positions, closer to the likely areas of needs, in order to make better use of the important asset it has in the enormous reach of its long shore line. The Kathiawar coast, which is closest to the most sensitive part of the Arabian Sea linking Pakistan, Iran and the politically unsettled Trucial coast, is completely undeveloped for naval or any other purposes.

## New Nonalignment

But in spite of every conceivable expansion of its own capability on shore or at sea, the navy will still not be able to face on its own a major hostile power, as it vividly realized when the US task force came into the Bay, the last item on the naval calendar last year. The only military answer to such a threat, once it arises, can be the matching power of a friend whether borrowed or hosted. But it may be possible diplomatically to forestall the threat by sufficiently raising the political cost of alienating India. This can be done with the same technique as Nehru discovered in the early 1950s: make India a leading member of an important club, and every major country will think twice before alienating her for fear of alienating the club as a whole. But now the technique can be made more potent and nonalignment played at a much higher level than Nehru was able to play it. In Nehru's days nearly all countries of any military or economic importance were allied to one power block or the other. He was therefore left with only the undeveloped world as the raw material of nonalignment. This was a severe limitation upon the influence of the nonaligned, and of India as one of the leading countries among them, upon international diplomacy, and even such influence as they had till then suffered two serious setbacks in the quinquennium preceding 1962. The first was the twist China gave nonalignment in the name of Afro-Asianism. It internally split the nonaligned into two groups, one associated with Nehru, Tito and Nasser, the other with Chou En-lai, Soekarno and Nkrumah. The latter group became such an aggressively and vociferously anti-American and anti-Western camp that it remained nonaligned only in the sense that it was anti-imperialist. The second setback came when China and India first fell into an estrangement and then into conflict. In its old form nonalignment withered away from 1962 onwards.

But now the picture is very different, and more than ever favourable to the old and true purposes of nonalignment both as statecraft and philosophy. China has lost its grip on the Afro-Asians. On a number of issues it could not have its way with them, for example, in the period from the middle to the late 1960s, on the admission of Malaysia and representation for the Russians; on the army repression in East Pakistan before Bangladesh won its liberation; and on the admission of Bangladesh after liberation. Its crusade against western imperialism has lost some of its magnetism following the summit meeting with

Nixon. The summit has put China into the big power league, but at the expense of what was its greatest attraction to important elements in the developing world, its image of revolutionary fervour; the decline in its political stock among the young radicals is not confined to India and Bangladesh.

The larger picture is also more favourable. The two icebergs of the cold war days have disintegrated, releasing new quantities into the stream of international diplomacy which are large, important and more or less unattached in fact, whatever the position might be in protocol. Japan, France, West Germany, Britain and the entire Scandinavian complex, followed at some distance by Canada and Australia, and as regional associations the Common Market and, potentially, ASEAN or some other form of the same idea—all these new quantities are both the causes and consequences of the thaw in the cold war, and they will be followed by others when the lines dividing eastern and western Europe begin to melt. It is with and among them that India should now play the diplomacy of nonalignment while still keeping together as many as she can of the old converts to nonalignment in the developing world. These new and larger quantities are at least as anxious and twice as able as was the earlier generation of nonaligned countries to set sail on their own independent courses conceived by them in their own judgments. The occasional hesitation, for example, in Japan and in West Germany about further dilution of the American alliance, are no reflection upon their desire to assume the full rights of independence. They are only unsure whether they have all the means as yet to afford their full rights and the security responsibility which goes with them while some of the antagonisms of the cold war persist. But the more they concert their diplomatic efforts, as the older generation of the nonaligned did in the second half of the 1950s, the more they can help to dissipate what remains of the cold war, while at the same time assisting each other as a new diplomatic grouping in shouldering their full rights and responsibilities.

In the whole of western, southern and south-eastern Asia, they can find only one matching member for this grouping. Much of what India lacks at present in economic development—and that is a question mark over India's future which has not even begun to disappear as yet—she makes up by the enhanced geopolitical importance of her new situation. Therefore what she contributes to this group's overall resources, political and economic being taken together, can match the contribution of many members of the group. She will not have the pre-eminence which in the old group Nehru shared only with Nasser and Tito. But the group being more important than the old nonaligned were, she will be better able to serve her essential interests in association with it. The most essential interest, though in a more complex version, will continue to be the old one of ensuring that each Super Power, and now China as well, should continue to realize that even if it cannot win India over to its side it should not push her to the side of a Super Power opponent because that would make an intolerable difference to the balance of forces in an important area. This would be the security rationale of the diplomacy of detachment in all areas of the world which, unlike the Himalayan frontiers and the Indian Ocean, do not directly impinge upon India's security. It would supplement from a distance the security aspect of the diplomacy of obligations which India needs to practise along her immediate frontiers on land and water.

Whether obligations or detachment will be the dominant theme in her foreign policy at any given point will depend very much upon two variables—her appreciation of any immediate threat to her security and her estimate of her ability to meet it without anyone's help. If the two are in balance, detachment will have the greater salience; otherwise obligations. The greater the gap between the estimated threat and the estimated ability to meet it the more India will feel obliged to call available aid, which will probably be Russian. The size of the gap and therefore the salience of obligations will thus be a function of US and Chinese diplomacy in southern Asia. For reasons given earlier, no single country and few combinations of countries in southern Asia can now generate a level of hostility which India cannot counter within her own resources. Only external forces can, and that means only China and the USA, which alone among the major countries today have a recent record of hostility towards India. Or rather only the USA can because unencouraged by the USA even China is not likely to put that much force behind its hostility that India cannot cope with it herself.

To a lesser extent the size of the gap will also depend upon factors indigenous to southern Asia, and their core is India's relations with Bangladesh and Pakistan. Even if Russia helps India foreclose a military threat, hostile diplomacy can keep India constrained and off balance by working upon the less consolidated Indian frontiers or some of the more sensitive domestic sutures. It can operate in many complex and subtle ways which can be effective and yet remain short of that level of provocation which may force India to take drastic counter-measures and break out of the ring. But it can only operate through the agency of India's immediate or very proximate neighbours. Among them the most important in this respect are Pakistan and Afghanistan in the west, Nepal in the north, Bangladesh in the east and in the south, Ceylon. So long as India's relations with these countries are sound enough to keep them from becoming willing pawns of clearly anti-Indian diplomacy, India cannot be exposed to any serious anxiety. The core of this problem, to peel the onion a bit further, is the littlest triangle of Indian diplomacy, the relations between India, Bangladesh and Pakistan. If this triangle holds firm, then the other four neighbours, Nepal, Ceylon, Afghanistan and Burma will find it easier to arrange themselves in harmony around it. The attraction of the core will prove stronger for each of these four than any counter attraction from the opposite side.

Just as it was a very weak India, or one believed to be weak, which encouraged Pakistan in its hostility towards India and also encouraged others to exploit and sharpen Pakistan's hostility, it will be a weak and unstable inner triangle or one which appears to be so which will encourage hostile ambitions along its periphery. The triangle may then break along a familiar cleavage. Bangladesh, more akin to Malaysian than West Pakistani Islam, may drift towards a South-East Asian configuration, either by vaulting over the barrier of Burma's isolation or by wearing it down, and Pakistan may drift into a West Asian grouping, whether in one piece or many being only a matter of further detail. But the converse may be at least equally true, that just as India's demonstrated resurgence has for the first time created an opportunity for consolidating the subcontinental triangle, the consolidation of the subcontinent will pull others towards it from the countries on the next concentric ring. There-after the cultivation of the most suitable forms of bilateral, multilateral or regional relations will be more a matter of discovering the most agreeable tactics, not of defining the most acceptable aims, which will slowly evolve within a frame of natural similarities. Therefore the most formative and basic influence to watch will be the equation between India, Pakistan and Bangladesh. Or more precisely between India and Bangladesh on the one hand, and India and Pakistan on the other because Bangladesh and Pakistan have far less in common with each other than each has with the neighbouring area of India. India cannot pull the same weight in international affairs or narrow her security gap so effectively if her relations are good with neither or only one of the two neighbours as she can if she carries both of them with her. The subcontinent as a whole will certainly mean much less in world affairs if it speaks in three discordant voices.

Relations between India and Bangladesh can be more friction-ridden than those between India and Pakistan because both in Bangladesh and India, there are people who expect a closer relationship than should or can exist between two independent countries; so little is expected of relations between India and Pakistan on the other hand that whatever little is achieved comes to both as a pleasant surprise. India and Bangladesh thus ran into a cloud of suspicion and recrimination—the more dangerous for being half-muttered and whispered around—on the very morrow of the liberation. Newspapers in both countries, especially India, were full of veiled expressions of disappointment in each country with the other for the first six months of 1972. But what was happening under the surface was very different: the inner drives of Bangladesh's domestic politics were setting the direction of its foreign relations in a manner favourable to India. They made it more obvious than it was till then that the forces and combinations which were bound to be dominant in Bangladesh for many years to come had far more in common than at variance with India in their outlook on foreign affairs and diplomatic priorities. These are Sheikh Mujib's own Awami League, the Communist Party of Bangladesh and, hardly distinguishable from the CPBD, the better organized, more durable, vocal and larger Muzaffar Ahmad wing of the National Awami Party; it became clear that between them they would hold the stage at least until the end of the 1970s. Their annoyance with Peking and Washington is as great as India's, their gratitude to Russia is equally firm, but as strong is their desire as Mrs Gandhi's that India and Bangladesh in close cooperation should keep the subcontinent as free of external influences as they possibly can, including possible Russian influence unless China and the USA make that impossible.

An incipient combination of the more radical left and traditional religious conservatism which is inclined to be pro-Chinese for diverse and sometimes conflicting reasons is likely to remain a pressure group on the fringe—troublesome, vigorously agitational, but never decisive as a force in the democratic process. At the same time the non-ideological, non-political and technocratic economic planners in both countries have been learning even more from their practical experience than from their economic theories that India and Bangladesh cannot cooperate with any third country more profitably than with each other. Therefore, as the first anniversary of its liberation approaches, Bangladesh is more convinced than ever before, and so is India, of the value of close foreign policy and economic cooperation between the two countries.

There is some divergence in their estimates of China. While India desires close relations with China and in rare moments of optimism even hopes to have them, her more settled expectation is unfair weather. Bangladesh expects to be better off. The liberation movement was as bitterly disappointed as India was when Mao Tse-Tung and Chou En-lai came out in support of Yahya Khan and opposed a democratic freedom movement. But since May this year Bangladesh has been more impressed than India by China's decision not to intervene militarily on the side of Pakistan. Dacca attributes the decision more to a choice by China as a future investment in Bangladesh while India attributes it more to the force of military circumstances which China could not ignore. As for Yahya Khan's belief that China would help, Dacca says it was an illusion created either in Yahya Khan's mind by Bhutto for Bhutto's own dubious reasons or in Bhutto's mind by China for China's own still more dubious reasons. This belief in Dacca has been wrought by Kaiser. This seniormost Bengali diplomat in the Pakistan foreign service was Pakistan's Ambassador in Peking and uniquely had the confidence of Chou En-lai, Yahya Khan, and the Provisional Government of Bangladesh when it was still housed in India. The provisional government began to put its trust in him when he privately conveyed to it that, like many other Bengali diplomats who had done so in other parts of the world, he too was willing to defect to it. The provisional government asked him to stay at his post, where it thought he would be more useful both as a concealed spokesman who could put across the Bangladesh point of view the more effectively for apparently still speaking in the name of Yahya Khan, and as a tap on Sino-Pakistan exchanges. It is not certain that he retained Yahya Khan's and Chou En-lai's trust up to the end. When Bhutto went to Peking before the war broke out, Kaiser was kept out of some of Bhutto's meetings with Chou En-lai. But in September, when no doubt could be cast on his standing in Peking, Kaiser conveyed it to the provisional government that he d d not think China would intervene on the side of the military regime. Dacca believes that this was in fact China's real position. New Delhi sees in this a slight opening which the Chinese might try to exploit later; the effort would certainly fit into the larger picture of Indian suspicions about separate or joint Chinese and American diplomacy on the subcontinent. But the opening is not likely to matter very much; nor will improvement in Sino-Bangladesh relations, which even Kaiser foresees as only marginal because there are some very real psychological and material constraints upon the equation between them. The war of liberation has set a powerful mould for all of Dacca's policies, domestic and foreign, and the most dominating of its features is that while India assisted the liberation, China opposed it at least in political and diplomatic manoeuvres whatever its reasons for not intervening militarily. The resulting bitterness against China is stoked by domestic politics in which forces favouring closer relations with India and Russia are far stronger. Any gestures Mujib might make towards China will be only gestures of convenience though he may make them more readily than Mrs Gandhi. Towards the USA also there will be more gestures than from New Delhi because of the more pressing need for economic assistance from all possible sources. But apart from these also being gestures of convenience, in no way able to obliterate the searing memory of what happened in December, no amount of assistance can outweigh the fact that for every kind of reason, including economic, Bangladesh's relations have to be the closest with its closest neighbour, and that good relations with Russia also have an insurance value which cannot be overestimated. With these assets in hand, Indian diplomacy would have to be crassly stupid or Bangladesh's would have to be imbued with a death wish for relations between the two countries not to be set in a durable mould of goodwill.

On the other hand, there is far greater potential for friction than goodwill in the relations between India and Pakistan. There is the dispute about jurisdiction over the prisoners of war, and beyond that the three-cornered issue of substance of their release. India's plea that she does not have the authority to hand them over without the consent of Bangladesh because the prisoners surrendered to a joint command of the two countries does not convince Pakistan. It considers the plea to be more a matter of legal fiction than fact. Passage of time has made this a matter of substance, not only procedure. India and more particularly Bangladesh are loath to let the prisoners go until Pakistan recognizes Bangladesh and settles all the other bilateral disputes with its former half. With more time the problem will only become still more complicated: if Bangladesh puts senior captured Pakistani officers on trial as war criminals, as it is determined to do, and if they are awarded serious sentences as they will be, Dacca will come under public pressure to execute the sentences which, once carried out, will embitter all future discussion of this or any other problem. Very early recognition of Bangladesh by Pakistan, not unlikely at the moment of writing, may yet forestall these complications. India will then be able to use its considerable good offices for ensuring the release of all prisoners and clemency for those who may be sentenced. But not if the issue drags on for long.

Pakistan's domestic frictions can also contaminate relations with India. At the least they can compel Bhutto to agitate for Kashmir in the United Nations once more. Not that Pakistan can hope to get more out of the UN than it did in the past 25 years. But Bhutto is under pressure to show that the issue has not been put into the deep freeze. India would regard any further reference to UN as a violation of the accord signed by Bhutto and Mrs Gandhi in Simla in July 1972, and the agreement as a whole may thus be placed in peril. Bhutto and the Simla accord will face this test not too far hence. India has clearly taken the stand that the United Nations, and therefore the group of UN observers who patrol the cease-fire line in Kashmir, do not have a role to play any longer. The UN will have to come to grips with this Indian position before very long, if for none other than at least budgetary reasons, and that will not only put the Indian position to the test but also the extent of Bhutto's acceptance of it.

Worse is possible. Public opinion in Pakistan is less inflamed about India than it used to be. That is why Khan Wali Khan, leader of the Opposition in the Pakistan National Assembly, is able to speak openly in favour of a confederation with India, as he has frequently done in press interviews and public speeches. Bhutto does not go nearly that far, but in a rhetorical manner has often asked the audiences at his mass meetings: "You tell me, is peace with India better or confrontation?" But domestic politics is very unstable yet, and fissures are active along the provincial, linguistic and cultural boundaries. This not only makes it difficult for the more constructive politician to consolidate the new mood about relations with India but can at any time give it a very sudden set back. The classic remedy for a country falling apart is to proclaim the imminence of external danger, and the most plausible one for Pakistan continues to be "Indian expansionism." It is also a law of politics that in a country swinging from a moderate to an impassioned mood the moderate politician is either swept aside or sucked into an extremist position. Wali Khan's moderation will have little relevance if an intensified political confrontation with India became the condition for the survival of Pakistan or what remains of it.

There is, finally, what remains of the old international diplomacy of keeping Indo-Pakistan relations as unsettled as possible. The new limitations it faces have been discussed already. Here it only need be mentioned that it will not forego any chance it may get of re-entering the subcontinent, and it may see a chance in the survival of Pakistan's war making potential and in the many intemperate speeches which Bhutto makes for every one that is moderate.

But in spite of these very adverse possibilities, there is a better chance now than there has ever been in the past 25 years that neither Kashmir nor any other dispute will encourage Pakistan to wage war upon India. That is because of India's dual advantage:

the new military balance on the subcontinent and in southern Asia, which Mrs Gandhi has often referred to as "the new realities," and the legitimacy conferred upon it by the agreement President Bhutto and Mrs Gandhi signed in Simla in July 1972. That means India not only has the military sinews for discouraging Pakistan from starting up another armed conflict but also a firm international agreement in the name of which she can enforce the peace. Or to put it another way, the subcontinent is not only bound to a peace treaty now, but there are the means available within the subcontinent for enforcing the treaty by making its violation extremely expensive. This is a position which India had sought for the best part of two decades; now, at last, she has been able to get it, and more or less on her own terms.

Ever since the very early 1950s, there has been one constant in India's efforts to prevent the recurrence of a Kashmir war. She has tried to get Pakistan committed to a "no war pact." Not in the generalized and formal sense in which every signatory to the UN Charter commits itself to the renunciation of force, but in a more specific and obligatory sense. To this India added another constant in the early 1960s, that Kashmir should be partitioned more or less permanently, and more or less along the cease-fire line which came into being after the 1948 war although India was willing to modify it in Pakistan's favour in bringing it into line with local geography. If India had succeeded in either effort there would have been little danger of another war over Kashmir. An agreed partition would have extinguished the only serious internal cause of war; a "no war pact" would have shut out external incitement, without which Pakistan would never have allowed belligerency to rise to the level of war.

But it was not to be expected that Pakistan would voluntarily agree to either approach. Even a modified cease-fire line would leave the more worthwhile part of Kashmir in Indian hands although Pakistan would get a larger area. That is why when Pakistan was invited to suggest modifications in the line in the spring of 1963 it proposed a line which India was bound to reject; it had to claim so much to make the partition worthwhile from its viewpoint that it left India no option but to withdraw this approach. Similarly, Pakistan could not be expected to renounce use of force without making sure that it could get Kashmir by peaceful means. Therefore Pakistan made a counter offer:

that it would agree to a "no war pact" if India agreed to arbitration in case mediation and negotiation failed to produce a Kashmir settlement. This was contrary to the declared Indian position that there could be no arbitration on a matter which involved not determination of facts but issues of sovereignty. Both Indian initiatives thus came to an end before Nehru's death. Later on there was a halfhearted third offer which was doomed to failure anyhow: that in addition to renouncing the use of force, both parties would reject the intervention of third parties, committing themselves to a bilateral settlement of all mutual issues. The addition could not make the old "no war pact" any more acceptable to Pakistan.

Under the Simla accord, Pakistan has accepted all the three ideas. The agreement substitutes the new cease-fire line, brought about by the 1971 war, in place of the old 1948 line. In prescribing the arrangements for mutual withdrawal following the cease-fire the agreement specifically refers to "the line of actual control" brought about by the hostilities in December; it makes no reference to the old line at all. To put the meaning of this omission beyond a shadow of doubt, Mrs Gandhi repeatedly declared before and after the summit meeting in Simla that the old cease-fire line had ceased to exist. The new line gives India some additional territory, but what is more important is that the agreement gives India what is virtually an international frontier instead of a cease-fire line. This is the effect of the provision relating to "the line of control resulting from the cease-fire of December 17" and the next provision that "neither side shall seek to alter it unilaterally, irrespective of mutual differences and legal interpretations. Both sides further undertake to refrain from the threat or the use of force in violation of this line." The line therefore becomes a permanent frontier which can be altered only by mutual agreement.

This also concedes to India the old constant of her Pakistan policy, a "no war pact." Kashmir was the only dispute with Pakistan which created the ever present risk of war. By specifically foreswearing the use of force to alter the cease-fire line Pakistan accepts a pact where it matters most. More comprehensively also the agreement enjoins renunciation of force. While in the Tashkent Declaration the two countries only reaffirmed "their obligation under the UN Charter not to have recourse to force and to settle their disputes through peaceful means," the Simla accord goes much further. It says: "The two countries are resolved to settle their differences by peaceful means through bilateral negotiations or by any other peaceful means mutually agreed upon between them. Pending the final settlement of any of the problems between the two countries, neither side shall unilaterally alter the situation and both shall prevent the organization, assistance or encouragement of any acts detrimental to the maintenance of peaceful and harmonious relations." More concretely than any previous agreement, the Simla accord gives each side the power to rule out the intervention of third parties in any bilateral dispute. If bilateral negotiations do not succeed, choice of any other peaceful means will depend upon mutual agreement. Not only in relation to Kashmir but all problems, bilateralism is thus enjoined upon both countries.

There are some weaknesses in the accord. For example, it does not specifically say in the name of bilateralism that the ongoing intervention of third parties in mutual disputes is also to be excluded in future. Bhutto has already used this ambiguity for claiming that he can still activate the Kashmir issue in the United Nations. Secondly, the accord does not foreclose claims by either side on the part of Kashmir held by the other; thereby it weakens the character of an international frontier which the cease-fire line implicitly acquires under other clauses. India had to accept these weaknesses because she was not in a position to impose upon Pakistan an agreement wholly satisfactory from her point of view. She would have been, if Indian troops had been sitting astride the railway line to Karachi while Bhutto was negotiating in Simla.

Pakistan's lifeline would have been in India's grip, and rather than suffer asphyxiation for a day longer than he could help it, Bhutto would have accepted an agreement which had no weakness from India's point of view. As it was, he could haggle and cajole and throw tantrums—for which he has a fine sense of timing—until he succeeded in diluting India's terms. Both sides knew that India did not have any trump card to play.

For a couple of months after the cease-fire, India had a strong bargaining counter in the fact that she held 93,000 prisoners of war. Their collective fate was not her exclusive jurisdiction. She needed the consent of Bangladesh for continuing to hold or for releasing them because they had surrendered to a joint Indo-Bangladesh command. But obviously she had the more decisive voice. Or at any rate, and that is more important here, Pakistan was convinced she had. Therefore, so long as Bhutto was under strong domestic political pressure to get the prisoners back, as he was for a time, India could hope to manipulate him on the negotiating table. But long before he left for Simla, he had succeeded in deflating the issue by making good use of the argument in party polemics at home that it would be an insult to the patriotism of the soldiers to sell the country's interests for their release. Thus, the prisoners became a wasting asset for India because Bhutto could wait while India tired of looking after them. That is why India failed at the summit to get Bhutto's consent for the one condition which Sheikh Mujib had placed upon the prisoners' release: that Pakistan must recognize Bangladesh. That is also the reason why India had to accept an imperfect agreement.

But whatever the agreement concedes clearly is fortified by the new circumstances created by the war. Thanks to the outcome of the war, but thanks also to the many frank admissions in public by Bhutto after he became the President, Pakistan is far more aware now than after the 1965 war that it is no match for India in any single combat. It also knows, as a consequence, that India has the means to enforce the agreement—unless its violation is underwritten by a third country. Therefore, so long as other powers do not militarily intervene, Pakistan cannot use the imperfections of the agreement for doing much more than to raise debates in the United Nations or make unenforceable claims on the Indian portion of Kashmir. If other powers intervene it will only be for their own reasons, not Pakistan's, or only if their own purposes justify a serious investment in Pakistan. If India takes good care of their reasons and purposes, which must now become a major aim of Indian diplomacy, the lacunae in the agreement or the risk of Pakistan exploiting them in bad faith need not worry her too much. If India mans the outer ramparts of her diplomacy well, she can consolidate the inner fortress without any serious threat from any immediate neighbour. Conversely, as the inner fortress becomes impregnable, those inclined to be hostile from a distance will lose interest in making breaches in the outer defences; they will realize that the end result is not worth the effort that they put in.

Some awareness of the changes in India's environment is already reflected in the altered mood of India's diplomacy towards her small neighbours and towards the intermediate powers which have been breaking lose from the Super Powers. Towards both, Indian diplomacy now shows a quiet and unpretentious self-assurance which it has never displayed before. In her relations with the ring of small neighbours around her, upon which the strength of the inner fortress depends, India now shows neither the petulance nor the unnecessary aggressiveness which used to be the cause of perpetual friction some years ago. Her posture is generally low all around, there is a soft-pedalling of disagreements and underplaying of even the more obvious causes of tension. The emphasis now is upon setting at rest any misapprehensions that might have been aroused among neighbours by India's unexpected display of efficient power.

This, not the intrinsic weakness of her position, is the greater reason why India did not try at Simla even as much as she could have to impose upon Pakistan an agreement with sharper edges to it. Mrs Gandhi showed noticeable interest in ensuring that Bhutto did not return to Pakistan an embittered man because that would make the future task of Indian diplomacy that much more difficult. After the agreement was signed, Mrs Gandhi scrupulously refrained from claiming any success for Indian diplomacy, although it had now achieved some long desired goals. She also refrained from contradicting some exaggerated claims made by Bhutto, because she was more interested in Bhutto succeeding in selling the agreement to his country than in contradicting him. When faced with domestic criticism, mostly from Hindu orthodoxy, that she had let down the Indian side, Mrs Gandhi did not extoll what India achieved in Simla because that would have jarred on Pakistani ears; she only described the agreement as an honest effort by both sides to make a new beginning in their relationships.

The restraint has been even more marked in India's relations with Bangladesh. In the first few months after the end of the war, Indian troops and civilians in Bangladesh made mistakes of behaviour towards the people of the new nation. The mistakes were few, but in the state of heightened sensitivity which existed then, they obliterated the memory of the exemplary conduct of the Indian armed forces during the campaign, which had evoked enthusiastic acclaim throughout Bangladesh and in the world's press. The reaction made it difficult for India to set her policy direction, especially in economic relations, the most important aspect in the post-war period. It was foreseen that unregulated aid and trade would lead to a maze of unofficial practices, many of them corrupt and disruptive of the economy of Bangladesh and of many of India's own border districts. But regulation was resented as an Indian imposition, and the resentment was exploited alike by those who would personally profit from informal transactions and by those in search of a stick to beat India with. But the makers and executors of Indian policy recovered their poise very quickly, benefiting in this from India's own experience in receiving aid. With sympathy but without overwhelming enthusiasm, they began to wait for Bangladesh authorities to discover themselves where they needed aid and to ask for it before they were given it. When aid was given it was mostly left to be handled by local authorities until Indian assistance was asked for. When Indians went in at all, in most cases only as technical advisers, they remained as inobtrusive as their duties would let them. This restored relations to their true perspective. Controversy subsided not only at the minor points of irritation but also around the two major developments in Indo-Bangladesh relations—an elaborate treaty of trade and a treaty of friendship which is on almost the same lines as the Indo-Soviet Treaty.

Since then India has maintained an attitude which is warmly helpful but not obtrusive; it allows India not to leave unstated what she expects in return but does not allow her to expect too much or to be too demanding even in that which she does expect. Even in the matter of the release of Pakistani prisoners, which would greatly help India in smoothening out her relations with Pakistan, she has scrupulously respected Mujib's insistence that Pakistan must first recognize Bangladesh. The result has been wholly beneficial for both countries, and seeing its profits India has, since the Bangladesh war, adopted the same attitude towards the other smaller countries around her whenever potentially disruptive issues have arisen in her relations with them.

The best example is Nepal. This small but strategic Himalayan kingdom has always been a good point of vantage for observing India's diplomatic climate. In the past it was nearly always true that whenever India felt that she had an important place in global diplomacy she tended to take Nepal for granted. Alternatively, whenever India felt weak and insecure she stepped up her courtship of Nepal and became petulantly jealous of Nepal's relations with Pakistan and China. Insecurity made her demands unreasonable, and Nepal's understandable resentment thereof only increased India's sense of insecurity. It is in the aftermath of Bangladesh that India has been neither demanding nor indifferent. Although now facing much less danger than in the past from either China or Pakistan, India has tried consistently but with courtesy and dignity to ensure that Kathmandu understands and supports her position on the subcontinent.

India's efforts towards Ceylon have been the same. The development of Ceylon's own diplomacy has been so complex lately that the Indian thread in it is difficult to trace. But it is a notable fact that although Ceylon paid back in doubtful currency for the help the Indian Navy gave it in the spring of 1971—throughout the rest of that year Ceylon gave the right of transit to Pakistani planes flying between East and West Pakistan although India greatly desired after the summer that the facility should be denied them—India has not allowed either that or any earlier disputes with Ceylon to raise their heads in Indo-Ceylon relations. Previously, these were never absent for long.

India's relations with Burma and Afghanistan have always been good and have continued to be. Only, they have been strengthened a bit further: with Burma because of the help received in keeping a watch on the security situation in northern Burma, with Afghanistan because of the heightened affinity of interests between the relations of both countries with Pakistan.

In her relations with the middle powers of Europe, India shows even greater awareness of what her new diplomatic requirements are. Setting the pace for all other agencies of India's relations with other countries, Mrs Gandhi has especially invested her charm and skill on improving relations with four countries: Britain, France, West Germany and Sweden. These are the building blocks of the new nonalignment. They are also the most important components of the new Europe which is emerging as the middle area between the Super Powers. India's efforts to cultivate them show a farsighted self-interest, and it is a matter of great encouragement for her that their response has been very good indeed. As a result, India's relations with Britain are regaining some of the mutual respect they showed during the first few years of India's independence. Feelings of personal regard between Mrs Gandhi on the one hand, and the leaders of the governments in Bonn, Stockholm and Paris on the other, partly make up for the fact that India's national interests have had less in common historically with Germany, Sweden and France than with Britain.

But there is one serious lacuna on India's diplomatic ramparts: her relations with the United States. In one sense it is wrong to describe these relations as a gap in India's defences. An enemy cannot be assimilated into one's defence system; it is against him that the system is built in the first place, and in India's recent experience the United States has acted like an enemy. But it is an unattempted task of Indian diplomacy yet to assess whether the enmity is irreducible, or whether it can be mitigated in order to reduce the strain on her defences and thus enable them to defend her the better should an assault come from any quarter whatever. It is the purpose of defences to hold the enemy out, not to perpetuate an enmity longer than is necessary.

The United States severely disappointed India before the Bangladesh war, and it was natural that India should voice her disappointment. During the war the United States attempted to browbeat India, and it was not only natural but necessary that India should defy the attempt in the clearest and loudest terms she could. After the war it was inevitable that the mood of defiance should persist for a time. India's resentment was too great either to disappear quickly or to be denied expression. But it is neither natural nor necessary that the resentment should have continued so long or be given such frequent and vehement expression; yet Mrs Gandhi has rarely missed an opportunity of berating the USA, and other Indian leaders have taken their cue from her.

For some time there has been a strong contrast between India's attitudes towards the United States and China; events of the Bangladesh war have accentuated the contrast. India has assiduously looked for every opportunity of floating signals of friendship in the general direction of China. Although

China has only responded with rebuffs India has continued the effort. There is nothing wrong with the effort. Hope of renewed friendship with China touches a deep chord in the Indian ethos; it would also be an important gain in the more mundane terms of power equations. India's perseverance is therefore to be commended as long as it does not hurt the Indo-Soviet equation more than it benefits the Sino-Indian, and there is no evidence that the Soviet Union would be unhappy if Sino-Indian relations became normal.

But the effort does make the persistence of India's hostility towards the USA still more incomprehensible, especially now that there is no reason for hoping that an anti-American attitude would win China's approval. China's sins against India, whether in the remote or more recent past, were not less grievous than the USA's. The USA has done nothing comparable with the Chinese attack on India in 1962. Within the limits of its own capability China has aided and abetted Pakistan with as much eagerness as the USA has. During the Bangladesh war China did not make overt military moves against India while the USA did. But as explained on earlier pages, this does not indicate greater hostility but greater foolishness on the part of Washington. China understood while the USA did not that by the time the Seventh Fleet moved into the Bay of Bengal the Indian advance into Bangladesh had become irreversible. Since the end of the war the US Administration has been much less unfriendly towards India in its utterances and actions than China has been; it was not the USA but China which vetoed the admission of Bangladesh to the United Nations.

But more important than all this: normal relations between India and the USA, at least as consistent with Indo-Soviet relations as normal Sino-Indian relations would be, are known to be ardently desired by the majority of the people of the USA whereas normalization of relations with India is not known to have any constituency anywhere in China. Perhaps no aspect of the Nixon-Kissinger diplomacy is less popular in America than the attitude of the administration towards India, Pakistan and Bangladesh throughout 1971 and since the war. This is a well known fact. On the other hand, there is no evidence whatever that any significant element in China would prefer a more friendly policy towards India than the leadership in Peking has pursued so far. This is something which has to be borne in mind.

Therefore it is a strange defiance of facts, not of Nixon, that authoritative Indian utterances should continue to be as belligerent towards the USA as they have been. The USA may not have held out the olive branch—although it has more than India has and certainly much more than China has towards India, but it is not in India's interests to continue to hold out a nailed club long after the need for doing so disappeared. The interests of national honour were adequately met by Mrs Gandhi's defiance of Nixon in the course of the war; now it is necessary to serve the interests of prudence.

Prudence comes because neither in war nor in peace is it wise to close more of one's options than is absolutely necessary. And it is far from necessary that India should close her options with the USA so firmly without any visible compensating gain in her relations with anyone else. Not only is the USA more permanent than Nixon; it may also conceivably be more permanent than the present picture of India's diplomatic advantage. It is not inconceivable that in certain situations American support for certain Indian positions would enhance India's advantage or soften a disadvantage. This can be accepted even on the most optimistic view of the permanence of Indo-Soviet relations.

But there is more in it than bargaining possibilities. What is involved is the fundamentals of the practice of nonalignment. Nehru finally understood this as he shaped the philosophy of his diplomacy, and especially as he practised it at the Belgrade conference. He knew that nonalignment would be at its best so long as the nonaligned countries kept their lines open to both the Super Powers. Otherwise they would not only be out of court with one or the other but also would fail to carry those countries which, although semi-aligned to one side or the other, would like to detach themselves at least on specific issues and thus add to the total weight of nonalignment. Some of the countries which have lately been loosening their alignments, for example Britain and West Germany at one end and Japan at the other, will be in this position of semialignment with the USA for some years to come. India's ability to carry them with her on specific issues where she differs with the USA will depend upon whether they see the difference to be the product of India's gut reaction to America or the product of the merits of the case. Therefore, new nonalignment requires as much as the old did that India should not slam the door in the face of America. Normal relations with the USA are not of less advantage to her than normal relations with China. They should not be less welcome.

But in spite of this lacuna, and that too will not last beyond Nixon's term in office if indeed it lasts that long, India faces more favourable diplomatic prospects now than she has ever done before. A more far flung course of effective diplomacy is spread out before her than when Nehru's nonalignment was at the height of its popularity. More important, it is a more systematic course, consisting of phases which have a clear sequence as well as complementarity. Completion of each stage can strengthen the assault on the next while at the same time providing a plateau from which the accomplishment to date may be estimated.

The first stage is to consolidate the Dacca-New Delhi-Islamabad triangle (or, to repeat the distinction made on earlier pages, the Dacca-New Delhi and New Delhi-Islamabad axes) so that the subcontinent may once more function as a single economic and geo-physical entity even if divided between three sovereignties. The second: to develop around the subcontinent a South Asian association which would at least have a distinct economic personality if not also a diplomatic and political one. The third: from this sub-regional position to participate in the development of a neutralized South-East Asia, an idea which is now almost equally favoured, although for different reasons and with different motivations, by North Viet Nam and the formerly western oriented South-East Asian countries. The fourth: to spread and consolidate this neutralization over the whole of the Indian Ocean region from the African coast to the eastern limits.

And, finally, to pull together into a larger picture all the separate threads, including India's relations with the Soviet Union, Europe, Japan, China and the USA (this is the probable order of their importance for India) which will naturally develop as the earlier stages are accomplished and without which this accomplishment would face many avoidable difficulties. A considerable part of this accomplishment can be expected in the 1970s.

# Index

# Index

Padma, 120-121; Dhalleshwari, 121; Madhumati, 120, 121, 169
*Round Table*, 10
Russian Navy Chief, visit to India, 168

Sagat Singh, Lt.-Gen., 180
Sartaj Singh, Lt.-Gen., 136
Se La pass, importance of, 108, 196
Security Council, Swaran Singh's reply to Bush, 207
*Shahjahan*, 167
Shakargarh bulge, 44, 129, 130, 134, 135, 147, Pakistani infantry division in, 132; attack at, 172-175
Shastri, Lal Bahadur, 29, 44, 48; floated the idea of a protective umbrella, 222; visit to Tashkent, 30
Sialkot sector, Pakistan infantry divisions in, 130-131; attack at, 44-46
Siddiqui, Kader, 181, 182
Siliguri corridor, 35, 118, 120
Simla Summit, 248-254
Singh, Lt.-Gen. K. K., 136
Sinkiang, 20, 21, 35
Sino-Indian border dispute, 107-109; Capture of Thagla Ridge, 25-26; defensive positions at Se La, 25; causes of, 18-27; Maxwell views on, 22-26; McMahon Line, 23, 24, 26; negotiations, 23-24; Soviet stand, 32
Sino-Soviet conflict, 28, 51, 52, 218, 224; clashes on Ussuri, 50; Indian neutrality on, 31
Sisco, Joseph, 205, 207
Six-Point Programme, 73
South-East Asia, ASEAN resolution favouring neutralization, 23; Indian and Soviet diplomatic relations with, 231, 232; US Senate Foreign Relations Committee mission to, 27

SEATO, 89, 211
*The State of Pakistan* by Rushbrook Williams, 21
Stimson, Henry L., 100
Suhrawardy, H. S., arrested, 63; Bhashani's criticism against, 65
Sulzberger, 211
Swaran Singh, 78; visit to New York 197; statement in the Security Council in relation to India's aim in the west, 207
Sylhet Pakistan infantry concentration on 119, 122, 150

Tashkent Conference, 29, 30
Tashkent Declaration, 30, 75, 251
Thakurgaon, capture of, 165
Thapan, M. L., 120
Tibet crisis, 18-19; India's role, 18
*Times*, 106, 158
Tito, Marshal, visit to India, 68
Toledano, Ralph, 13
Tura, communication zone area, 149

UN Charter, 250, 251
US Defence Intelligence Agency, report on China's planning Indo-Pak conflict, 209
US Library of Congress, report on India's international role, 49
US Seventh Fleet, 88, 116, 197; mission, 205

Viet Nam, US troops in, 28
*Vikrant*, 120, 142, 143, 148, 163, 169, 209, 240

Wali Khan, 248
Walong, 126
Washington Special Action Group meeting, minutes of, 167, 205, 207-208, 210, 212; CIA report on, 212